BECOMING SOLUTION-FOCUSED IN BRIEF THERAPY

BECOMING
SOLUTION-FOCUSED
IN BRIEF THERAPY

John L. Walter
Jane E. Peller

BRUNNER/MAZEL *Publishers* • NEW YORK

Library of Congress Cataloging-in-Publication Data
Walter, John L.
  Becoming solution-focused in brief therapy / John L. Walter, Jane
E. Peller.
     p. cm.
  Includes bibliographical references and index.
  ISBN 0-87630-653-9 :
  1. Solution-focused therapy.   2. Brief psychotherapy.   I. Peller,
Jane E.   II. Title.
  [DNLM: 1. Problem Solving.   2. Psychotherapy.   WM 420 W233b]
RC489.S65W35   1992
616.89'14—dc20
DNLM/DLC
for Library of Congress   91-43491
                                                                      CIP

Published by
BRUNNER/MAZEL, INC.
19 Union Square West
New York, New York 10003

Manufactured in the United States of America

10   9   8

To the memory of John's mother, Afra Walter, and to our parents, William Walter, Jonesy Wagner, Bert Peller, Victor Wagner, and Suzanne Peller, who in their own ways continually keep us optimistic and on track.

Contents

vii

Contents

     A Final Word 259

     References 260
     Name Index 263
     Subject Index 265

Acknowledgments

A book is never written by the authors alone. It is always a team effort and the authors just get to have their names on the cover. We want to thank family, friends, trainees, clients, and workshop participants, all of whom have contributed in their own unique ways.

We want to say a special thanks to Insoo Kim Berg and Steve de Shazer. Through our association and friendship with each of them, we have grown tremendously. We feel honored to be the spokespersons for many of their contributions to the development of Brief Therapy that they shared with us.

John wants to thank Insoo for first asking him, "Why do you want to be a Brief Therapist? It could be a very upsetting change." Jane wants to thank Steve for reminding her to be "simpleminded."

We also want to offer a special thank you to Eve Lipchik, who was the first to suggest that we write a manual. Her support was gentle in each reminder of "You can do it."

We want to thank our friends, Jill Freedman and Gene Combs, who having struggled through the writing and publication of their own book, were a constant source of encouragement and helpful hints.

John wants to thank Michael Banks. Through Michael's outsider's curiosity and provoking questions, John sharpened and developed his own thinking about what we do. Michael's enthusiasm for our project was always there.

Jane wants to thank her chairperson at Northeastern Illinois University, Wanda Bracy, for giving her the release time to work on the book. She also wants to thank Wanda for enhancing Jane's confidence in being able to take on any project by their mutual suffering through the self-study of their department.

Becoming Solution-Focused in Brief Therapy

We want to thank all the individuals who read some of the manuscript and offered us much appreciated feedback. We want to thank Bert Peller, who went over the manuscript many times and always managed to sneak in a compliment before making a suggestion. We also want to thank Victor Wagner, Mary Jo Barrett, and Goldie Lansky for offering not only their suggestions, but also their confusion as we struggled to give words to our ideas.

We want to thank du Ree Bryant, Kate Kowalski, and Kevin O'Connor whose excitement continued to give us energy. We want to thank Jim Weiss who not only kept us in a frame of humor, but also kept our sometimes "resistant" computer up and running.

Of course, there is everyone else who simply asked "How is it going?" and then had the patience to listen.

Our final thanks goes to our editors, Natalie Gilman and Suzi Tucker, whose steady voices on the phone kept us focused during anxious moments.

Introduction

This is a handbook for becoming solution-focused and for constructing solutions in brief therapy. Throughout the past several years, we have provided training for professionals who want to work "briefly." They want to work in a positive way with people, and do not believe that pathologizing is useful. Workshop participants have consistently told us they wanted something more than just a workshop, something more than only an introduction, something useful they could look at between sessions, something they could use to practice with, something that would keep their learning going. The message was clear. This manual, *Becoming Solution-Focused in Brief Therapy* is our answer to all those requests.

In this manual, we describe how we came to a solution orientation. We describe the positive assumptions that inform our work, and then, in step-by-step fashion, provide a sequence of skill-building chapters.

Chapter One reviews the historical progression of assumptions that have informed therapy models for the past hundred years. By examining the presuppositions within the major questions that led to model development, we describe several trends. This leads to the presuppositions of the founding question of a solution-focused approach, "How do we construct solutions?"

Chapter Two lists and explains the 12 assumptions that guide the authors' thoughts and actions. In sum, the assumptions reflect the authors' positive and future-oriented approach.

Chapter Three describes how the therapist can begin to converse with a client on a positive basis by assuming rapport and using presuppositions within questions. The theme—that what we presuppose, even by asking a question, already influences the direction of response and the further direction of the therapeutic conversation—is carried throughout the book.

Chapter Four describes our operating metaphor, that of movie-making, with our clients being both the directors and the principal actresses or actors. We assume that our expertise is not in evaluating normality or pathology but in facilitating movie-making processes. We assume that a well-defined goal is critical in order for movie-making to take place and for the therapy conversation to open up differences and possibilities. This chapter makes explicit the six criteria for a well-defined goal and how to make it easy for clients to create their goal within these guidelines.

Chapter Five provides an overview of the pathways of constructing solutions. The all-important distinction of wishes and complaints versus goals and problems is made first. Then the overview is laid out in terms of frames and the accompanying questions:

1. The goal frame's question is, "What is your goal in coming here?"
2. The exception frame's question is, "When is it happening somewhat already?" or "When doesn't the problem happen?"
3. The hypothetical solution frame's question is, "If the problem were solved, what would you be doing differently?"

Chapter Six is designed to assist the reader to develop skills in how to use the hypothetical solution questions while Chapter Seven helps the reader develop skills in the use of the exceptions questions.

Chapter Eight operationalizes even further our positive orientation by detailing how to offer positive feedback and solution-developing tasks.

Chapter Nine describes how to keep change going and how to make sure the therapy is brief. Suggestions are given for subsequent sessions, spacing sessions, and concluding therapy.

Chapter Ten focuses on those situations where the client initially thinks the problem and the solution are out of his or her control. The chapter explains techniques in how to create with clients control and responsibility over their solutions in both the therapy conversation and the tasks we suggest.

Chapter Eleven concentrates on those situations where solutions take place between people, such as marital problems, family problems, or any problems when more than one person is involved. Chapter

Twelve's focus dovetails with this chapter by discussing the situation where the client wants someone else to change or expects the solution to be a change in someone else.

Chapter Thirteen, Cooperating, is devoted to the metaphor of dance. The therapy conversation is a dance; as therapists, we need a variety of conversational skills in order to be flexible with the different dance styles of our clients. This chapter lists six ways of conversing differently with clients when the conversation appears positive, nearly hopeless, impossible, or "yes, but."

Chapter Fourteen is designed to help the reader integrate skills into a total package. While all the previous chapters have included parts of case examples or sample conversations, this chapter is devoted exclusively to examples of complete cases from start to finish.

Chapters Fifteen and Sixteen focus on the importance of the distinction of voluntary and involuntary client, along with facilitating the involuntary client's identifying a goal for therapy.

The concluding chapter lists some ways to recheck yourself when you think you are stuck. We then offer some final suggestions.

The book is organized so that successive chapters are sequential and skill-building. Each chapter lists an assumption of the approach that is pertinent to learning the skills of that chapter. Each chapter provides explanations and demonstrations of a particular skill and is followed by the questions most frequently asked at our workshops.

As a manual, this book also provides exercises and worksheet pages accompanying appropriate chapters. The exercises are targeted to the skill development and the worksheet pages of that chapter. You may find it helpful to copy and take the material, especially the worksheets, into your sessions or practice seminars.

We add one qualification before you start. We use the word "therapy" throughout the manual although we would rather have used some other word. We do not like the connotations of "treatment," pathology, and expertness of the therapist that "therapy" implies. We would rather stay true to the belief that there is nothing wrong with people, that they have all they need—and that if they are having difficulty, we could just as easily explain such difficulty as due to bad luck as opposed to pathology.

We thought of using the word "counseling" as opposed to therapy, but too many people think of counseling as inferior to therapy. We thought of the word "consulting," but concluded that people most often think of that in regard to non-personal problems. We thought of "conversational facilitator." However, without an in depth and exhaustive explanation of the reasons for that choice, we feared most people would be confused or think the choice cumbersome.

We regret that there is no commonly accepted term within the field that carries a wellness orientation and fits with our beliefs about our roles and process. We have elected to use the word "therapy" and hope the reader will see beyond the traditional use of the word and redefine "therapy" from a new perspective of a positive approach.

We titled this book *Becoming Solution-Focused* because we believe that all is becoming, and learning is never complete. We trust that this approach is not a finished product and that it never will be, that ways of helping people will continue to evolve. In that light we trust that your work is continuing to evolve and we hope that this manual contributes to your own "Becoming Solution-Focused."

BECOMING
SOLUTION-FOCUSED
IN BRIEF THERAPY

1

Becoming Solution-Focused

It Starts with a Question

We begin by giving you the background that leads up to this new approach—a brief history of the development of the ideas and the assumptions forming the basis for therapy models.

We like to think that therapists develop therapy models out of some initial struggle or question. The question may arise from the therapist's particular experiences with a certain population of clients or with certain types of problems—for example, Freud's questions about the repressed sexuality of his Victorian clients. The questions may arise from some beliefs about people. For example, Michael White has articulated the belief that people are separate from their problems and are oppressed by their problems (White & Epston, 1990). This belief is different from traditional beliefs that identify the person as the problem. We believe that their questions form the beginning of the therapy models that are developed. These therapy models begin to take shape as the developers speculate and then articulate answers to their initial questions about their clients or their clients' problems. Thus, Freud's early model development of the repression barrier and the unconscious can be seen as answers to his questions about sexual repression.

The questions that developers of therapy models ask contain presuppositions within them. Therefore, by their very asking the questions, developers pre-select directions toward particular answers or classes of answers. The evolution of the ideas and trends of therapy models can thus be traced through the assumptions within the original questions of the therapy modelers. For example:

1

WHAT IS THE CAUSE OF THE PROBLEM?

In the early part of this century, science was shaped by the objectivism of the traditional scientific method. The chief question modelers usually asked was: What is the cause of the problem?

This question is still frequently being raised. Asking, "What is the cause of the problem?" has presuppositions which are consistent within that time frame of the traditional scientific method. The question presupposes that there *is* a definite problem and that there *is* a specific cause to that problem. The question further presupposes that one can, in fact, find the cause of the problem and describe that cause. Finally, asking, "What is the cause of the problem?" intimates that there is a relationship between finding the cause and solving the problem. This process is consistent with western science's idea—along with traditional descriptions inherent in the scientific method—that the way to solve a problem is to find out what the cause is so that one can then effect change by eliminating the cause. Asking, "What is the cause of the problem?" is also consistent with our own everyday common sense that the way to solve any problem is to find out what is wrong and then fix it. Thus, we seem to relate all problems to the laws of mechanics—when the power lawn mower breaks down, we look for the cause of the breakdown.

Over the past decades, several approaches have been developed to identify direct alternatives in response to the question, "What is the cause of the problem?"

Within the psychoanalytic tradition, for example, the cause of the problem has been described in a number of ways that may include: developmental arrest, failure to pass a stage of life, personality disorder, poor object relations, poor self image, unresolved conflicts, sexual repression, and so on. Usually, the problems are described as symptoms of a particular underlying pathology or sometimes as defenses within a personality disorder.

Within the psychiatric tradition, furthermore, the cause may be described as a chemical imbalance, an organic predisposition, or a disease which has various psychological or behavioral manifestations.

Within either the psychoanalytic or psychiatric traditions, each causal explanation dictates a type of intervention. If the cause is diagnosed as developmental arrest, then a corrective emotional experience may be prescribed. If unresolved conflicts are diagnosed as the cause, then supportive therapy may be prescribed to bring out the conflicts and interpret them in such a way that they can be resolved. If a chemical imbalance is diagnosed, then a course of medication may be prescribed.

Within the psychoanalytic and psychiatric traditions, distinctions between primary and secondary causes may also be used. For example, someone may be diagnosed with schizophrenia as the primary diagnosis, along with a secondary diagnosis of reactive depression to the recent loss of family member. For the primary cause, schizophrenia, the patient may be given medication. For the secondary cause, the loss of a family member, the patient may be given supportive therapy.

Within the behavioral tradition, the problem may be described as being caused by a reinforcement, usually within the family, that progressively created a learned behavior. This learned behavior is subject to being continually reinforced until it assumes a life of its own and becomes self-perpetuating.

Alternative answers have thus been developed for "What is the cause of the problem?" dependent on the assumptions about the nature of "man" within the school of philosophy to which the modeler subscribed. If humans were seen as basically torn by their sexual urges, one looked for explanations within sexual development. If humans were seen as having problems because of having to repress or sublimate their individual desires and ambitions to the restrictions created by society for the greater good, then one looked for explanations within the social and political environment and for signs of stilted creativity caused by that environment.

All of these traditions and schools of thought are consistent with the presuppositions of the original question—that problems are *caused* and that we *can* find the cause. All of these traditions looked for the cause of the problem, but each came up with different answers.

During the 1950s, after the birth of cybernetics, therapy modelers began to ask a different question, leading to different answers. An entirely new direction began to be defined as modelers changed the primary question, "What is the cause of the problem?" to . . .

WHAT MAINTAINS THE PROBLEM

This question presupposes that a problem is being maintained and stresses its maintenance rather than its cause. As with "What causes the problem?" the therapy modeler accepts that there is a problem, but presupposes that the problem is being *maintained* and that there is a relationship that can be found and described between the maintenance and the problem. Most of the answers to "What maintains the problem?" explain the maintenance as taking place within interactional patterns that can be mapped in different ways.

One therapy model describes problems as maintained within certain organizational contexts and sees problems as continuing because they serve a system-conserving function for the family (Haley, 1980; Madanes, 1981). In this Strategic Therapy Model, problems have a system-maintaining purpose, and family members' actions are organized around the problem.

Another therapy model describes problems as being maintained by certain family structures and coalitions (Minuchin, 1978). In this Structural Model, the problems are seen as being embedded in and maintained by dysfunctional family structures. A third therapy model, the Milan Model, says that problems are governed by "the fundamental rule of the family" (Selvini-Palazzoli, Boscolo, Cecchin, & Prata, 1978). Still another—the Brief Therapy Model—describes problems as maintained by the attempted solution (Weakland, Fisch, Watzlawick, & Bodin, 1974).

Each of these therapy models prescribes a course of action consistent with its answer to "What maintains the problem?" The Strategic Model of Haley and Madanes attempts to change the organizational context by changing the present incongruence of power. If a child has more power because of the problem than the parents, then interventions are designed to empower the parents and establish a congruent hierarchy.

The Structural Model of Minuchin would attempt to change the organization of the family, the overt or covert coalitions across generations. The Milan Model would attempt to break up through a counterparadox the endless paradoxical pattern embedded in the family rule. Finally, the Brief Therapy Model attempts to break up the escalating cycle of the attempted solution.

These models are coherent and are consistent with their answer to the question, "What maintains the problem?" Each model describes both the patterns of behavior and the thinking around the problem, with meaning consistent with the metaphor about problem-maintenance. Then it intervenes in a way consistent with the assessment.

HOW DO WE CONSTRUCT SOLUTIONS?

Within recent years, there is another, different, and new question being asked: How do we construct solutions? The presuppositions within this question are:

1. that there are solutions,
2. that there is more than one solution,
3. that they are constructable,
4. that *we* (therapist and client) can do the constructing,
5. that we *construct* and/or *invent* solutions rather than discover them, and
6. that this process or processes can be articulated and modelled.

We think that the answer to "How do we construct solutions?" constitutes a solution-focused brief therapy model that can be summarized in the following story.

A few years back, during that rare year when the Chicago Cubs succeeded in winning their division championship, there was a time when one of the leading hitters was in a slump. Jim Frey, the manager of the team, spotted this hitter in the clubhouse one day. The hitter, with hopes of improving his performance, was watching films of himself up at bat. Now, you can probably guess what films he chose to watch. Right! He chose films of the times when he was in the slump, when he was striking out and generally doing everything but what he wanted. He, of course, was trying to find out what he was doing wrong so he could correct his mistake. He probably subscribed to the "What is the cause of the problem?" question. However, you can imagine what he was learning by watching films of slump batting; he was learning in greater and greater detail how to be a slump batter.

So we like to think that Jim Frey must have been a "closet" solution-focused brief therapist. He joined his hitter, complimented him on his dedication to the game and on attempting to improve himself. Jim then made one suggestion to the hitter—that he go back to the film room, find films from when he was really hitting the ball, and then watch *those* films instead.

We think this story aptly summarizes the thrust of a solution-focused approach: "How do we construct solutions?" Very simply: *One*, define what the client wants rather than what he or she does not; *two*, look for what is working and do more of it; *three*, if what the client is doing is not working, then have him or her do something different.

Step one, find out what the client wants, may seem obvious and possibly even too simplistic. However, think about it for a moment. The vast majority of our clients come in telling us what they *do not* want. It is as if they have become so focused on their frustration and pain that they have not really thought of what they *do* want. At times, we have to use all our skills and support to help clients define what they *do* want.

Step two, look for what is working and do more of that, may also seem obvious. However, we know that in traditional training (even in those procedures that stress looking for client strengths), the important emphasis of diagnosis has been to look intensely at what is wrong and not working for the client.

Step three, do something different, may seem painstakingly obvious. However, how often have you heard the old proverb, "If at first you don't succeed, try, try again"? Our culture has reinforced the notion of persistence in spite of procedures not working.

Solution-focused brief therapy is one answer to this question, "How do we construct solutions?" It is a total model: it encompasses a way of thinking, a way of conversing with clients, and a way of constructing solutions interactively. Solution-focused brief therapy is not a collection of techniques or an elaboration of a technique; rather, it reflects fundamental notions about change, about interaction, and about reaching goals.

You will notice in the progression of our questions—"What causes the problem?" "What maintains the problem?" "How do we construct solutions?"—that we moved successively from cause to problem-maintenance to solutions. We have also changed focus from the past, where we usually look for causes, to the present, where we map patterns of problem maintenance. Finally, with the last question, we look at the present and the future. As we shift our presuppositions away from the traditional linear notions of causality, we move toward a relativistic and "constructivist" view, as well as toward a future orientation.

With the insertion of the pronoun "we" into the question, "How do *we* construct solutions?" we also shift from the notion of an objective reality, or even observed reality, to an interactional construction. On a practical basis, this means that all views are equally valid; therapy becomes an interactional or joint experience, with problems and goals constructed or negotiated between client and therapist.

The most radical implication of this question, "How do we construct solutions?" is that problem information is no longer necessary and, in fact, can be limiting in many cases.

When initially we were involved first as trainees and later as trainers and research associates of the Brief Family Therapy Center of Milwaukee from 1981 to 1984, our task as therapists was to identify the problem patterns in terms of attempted solutions and then attempt to interrupt the patterns. This was consistent with the focused problem-resolution model of the Mental Research Institute of Weakland, Fisch, Watzlawick, and Bodin (1974).

During this time, an attempt was initiated by Steve de Shazer, Marilyn La Court, and Elam Nunnally to help families become more specific in their descriptions of their complaints and goals, and to become more present and future oriented. In order to help the clients who presented rather vague complaints to be able to present their goal more specifically, the therapy team gave the clients this task:

> Between now and next time we meet, we (I) would like you to observe, so that you can describe to us (me) next time, what happens in your (pick one: family, life, marriage, relationship) that you want to continue to have happen." (de Shazer & Molnar, 1984, p. 298)

The focus of this task was to allow clients who had as yet only vague descriptions of their complaints or goals to notice when the goal actually happened and to report back. The idea was that with a fresher memory they might be able to report in a more specific fashion. Also, the task would shift their attention to the present and future, thus implicitly promoting expectations of change.

The results of the clients' pursuing the task—searching for and selecting those signs of their goal that they wanted to continue—went far beyond the original intent. While many clients with vague descriptions came back with more specific descriptions, they also came back describing changes that had occurred, that they wanted, and that they had not previously noted. Very often, the changes were in the goal/solution area.

This task then became routinely used as the "formula first session task," and was used regardless of the complaint (de Shazer, 1985). The complaint may have been about a child-related problem, about a marital difficulty, about a substance abuse problem, or about anything else. In some cases, we hardly knew much at all about the complaint. Yet, regardless of the complaint or of how little we knew about it, clients came back reporting change.

The far-reaching implication of clients' reporting change regardless of whether or not we identified anything about the problem was that *problem information was not necessary* (de Shazer, 1988). Previously, we had thought we needed to know about the sequences or patterns in which the problem was embedded and felt that the solution had to match the problem patterns. The results of the first session task divorced the connection in our thinking between problem and solution. *We realized that only solution or goal talk was necessary, that solution construction was independent of problem processes.*

The interviewing process changed radically. The research team pushed this solution-focused thinking further (de Shazer, Gingerich, & Weiner-Davis, 1985). Instead of having to wait for the second session to ask about changes or positives, they began the first session by asking about recent changes or "exceptions" to the problem (Weiner-Davis, de Shazer, & Gingerich, 1987).

Since that time, we in Chicago have continued to push the limits of the assumption that all we need is solution talk. As you will see in the succeeding chapters, the goal now is to have every aspect of therapy focused on *solution construction.*

In addition to this assumption that all we need is solution-oriented conversation, a solution focus is informed by a number of additional assumptions which will be described in the next chapter.

DISCUSSION

QUESTION:
By focusing on the presuppositions within the questions used in the past hundred years by researchers and modellers, you seem to be suggesting certain trends in thinking about therapy and change. Is that so?

Very definitely, we are suggesting there are several trends. There is the trend mentioned in this chapter away from notions of causality and a focus on the past to notions of meaning-making in the present and about a future. There also is a trend away from pathology and the objectifying of people to a more positive approach where people are viewed within community and as capable of creating what they want (O'Hanlon & Weiner-Davis, 1989).

EXERCISES

1. In order to identify your own working assumptions, write down the three questions that you think are most important to your therapy or the three that you use most commonly. After writing out the questions, examine them for the presuppositions within them. These presuppositions will probably reflect your personal working beliefs about people and therapy. For example, if one of the questions you commonly use is, "How does that make you feel?" then your presuppositions are: (1) the client feels, (2) that the situation is a cause, (3) that there is a linear, causal relationship between the situation and the resulting feeling, (4) that the client can articulate his or her feeling, and (5) that the articulation or identification of the feeling would somehow be useful.

2. After identifying some of your working presuppositions, ask yourself if these are indeed what you believe. If your presuppositions do not in fact reflect your beliefs, what are your beliefs about people and change and how can you change your questions to reflect these beliefs.

2

Assumptions of a Solution-Focused Approach

We think of a solution-focused brief therapy as a total model; a way of thinking about how people change and reach their goals, a way of conversing with clients, and a way of constructing solutions interactively. For us, this way of thinking, conversing, and interacting forms a cohesive and consistent package.

At the same time in order to learn any model of therapy and not just a technique, one has to understand the assumptions from which the model operates. The following 12 assumptions of a solution-focused approach are interrelated and guide one's thinking through solution construction.

Some of the articulation of these assumptions has been previously described by de Shazer, Berg, et al., 1986; de Shazer, 1988; O'Hanlon & Weiner-Davis, 1989; Peller & Walter, 1989. These are our current working assumptions and definitions.

These assumptions have a pragmatic value in that they guide our thinking and acting. Without these 12 assumptions, our actions would be only a collection of techniques, and we could become mere robots in spitting out tasks and suggestions. We could easily become stuck, with nothing to fall back on. The 12 assumptions provide us the freedom to roam and to be creative, with the assurance that we are being guided in our actions. Whenever we become stuck in our work, we can use these assumptions to think through construction of solutions to get back on track.

1. Advantages of a Positive Focus

Assumption: Focusing on the positive, on the solution, and on the future facilitates change in the desired direction. Therefore, focus on solution-oriented talk rather than on problem-oriented talk.

The thrust of this assumption became clear to us in watching the Winter Olympics a couple of years ago. In the bobsled event, we noticed the East German women as they were preparing for their run down the hill. As they were sitting in the sled waiting their turn, their eyes were closed. We thought this was rather strange. Then we noticed that with their eyes still closed, they were making strange weaving motions forward, backward, and side to side. We thought this really strange—until the commentator explained that these women were going through a mental preparation of the run. With their eyes closed, they were visualizing going through the run; their body movements were their body responses as they imagined banking off of turns and experiencing the acceleration of the run.

This self-hypnotic technique of sports psychology enabled the East German women to experience the entire bobsled run and to experience themselves handling the turns and the maneuvers in the way they wanted to. By the time they physically went through the actual run, they had rehearsed it in their minds and bodies.

This technique, used by sports psychologists and teachers, is described in *The Inner Game of Tennis* (Gallwey, 1974) and *Peak Performance* (Garfield, 1984). Very simply, the athlete forms a picture of himself or herself hitting the ball the way he or she wants and then steps into this picture to get the feel and experience of what it is like.

As we converse with clients in solution-focused brief therapy, the same process takes place. As we engage in conversation with clients about what they are doing that is working or about what they will be doing, the clients form mental representations of themselves solving the problem. Changes in the mood of their verbs—from subjunctive to indicative—tells us as therapists that clients may be starting to speak within their representations of solving the problem. In effect, they are beginning (if they have not already) to put themselves into the images they have created and are already experiencing the process they are describing. They are achieving through conversation what the bobsledders were doing as a hypnotic technique.

Another advantage of focusing on the positive and on solutions is that the focus facilitates rapport.

When I, John, was just out of social work school, I conducted interviews with families by focusing on the problem. I remember interviewing families and focusing on the question, "What is the problem?" The parents in one case told me all their complaints about their 12-year-old son (who was also in the room). They told me how frustrated they both were that their son was not doing his homework, was not cleaning his room, was getting Cs and Ds at school, and had a bad attitude. After 15 minutes of this report, I noticed that their son had retreated into his chair and into the corner of the room. He obviously was feeling ashamed and was not likely at this point to want to engage in any conversation with me.

Now, however, I experience this same boy, through other families I now interview, responding in an entirely different way. By focusing, as quickly as rapport will allow, on the times when the problem does not happen (exceptions to the problem) and on how he will be acting when the family is solving the problem, the family describes the boy's successes, or at least what he will be doing. That same boy who used to shrink in his chair as his parents reported the list of problems now sits up and is more likely to be participating as we talk about those occasional times when he does do his homework, has brought home a decent grade, or has done something about his room. He is more likely to describe what is different about those times of success (or at least, not failure). He will describe how he decides to do these things and what his parents may be doing differently at those times.

The other advantage to focusing on solution-based results is that clients often spontaneously associate to other times of success or to other times when they felt more resourceful. A couple may describe a making-up time as one of those times when they do not fight. In describing the making-up time, they may associate to other times when one or the other listens in that same, more successful way. A positive focus is a great advantage.

2. Exceptions Suggest Solutions

Assumption: Exceptions to *every* problem can be created by therapist and client, which can be used to build solutions.

At first, this assumption may seem to defy common sense. After all, if someone has been doing everything they can think of to solve a problem and nothing seems to work, how is it fair or logical, to assume that there are times when the problem does not happen. "The Problem," if you will, is that people sometimes get stuck into only one set of expectations of what the solution will look like. Other times may be diminished as inconsequential because, to their way of thinking, the "exceptional" times do not represent "real" solutions or because the "exceptional" times are not consistent.

An example of clients' initially missing the potential of "exceptional" times (Peller & Walter, 1989) is the case of a couple who came to see us because of recurring fights. During the early 1970s, when it was not uncommon for people to experiment with relationships (as was the norm in the counterculture), each of them had pursued relationships outside of their marriage. Now, during the 80s, however, they had decided they wanted to improve their relationship and to be monogamous. However, each carried memories and resentments left over about the affairs the other had had during this earlier time. The way they were trying to solve this problem was to resolve these feelings of resentment, doubt, and lack of trust by talking them out. Each time, however, they ended up quarrelling over whose fault it really had been. They had attempted this form of resolution so many times now that each could hardly bear to look at each other, much less talk.

In the course of the interview, we asked about times when they were not fighting. They mentioned that on the previous Sunday, they had gone out for a bike ride. We asked how that happened, especially since they had been feeling bad. They responded that it had been such a nice day that they decided to bike along the lake.

To each of them, this experience did not seem significant to their problem. Each considered the experience to be incidental to the "real" solution of talking and trying to resolve the past. We asked how they talked with each other on the ride and how their talk was different from the problem times. We wondered out loud whether the bike ride was a more trustful time for them. "Trust" was what they had stated as the eventual goal underlying all the previous attempts at problem-solving. The couple agreed that this way of being with each other was better. As we talked about how they had created this different time with each other, we asked: "Do you think that if you had more times like your bike ride the past might become less of a problem or you would have better luck at resolving things?" Their answer was, "Maybe."

For them, this bike ride was not significant or exceptional, but to us it was. They had been looking for a "real" solution that might result from talking about the past. For us, the "nonfighting" time was significant and loaded with potential toward building a solution. It was as if they thought that the problem leads to the solution, as if talking about the past was a necessary condition to their reaching their target of being with each other in some trustful way. We saw it differently. We thought the more experiences they could create like the bike rides, the greater the likelihood that they would increase trust, that they might talk differently about the past, or that the past might even become a moot problem. Our work then centered on how they could have more times together similar to those of the bike rides.

Eliciting and constructing "exceptions" is a joint process between the client and the therapist. By eliciting the exceptions to the problem and working on encouraging the exceptions to occur more often, the therapist helps the client develop a sense of control over what had seemed to be an insurmountable problem.

A man who had AIDS had been receiving medical treatment in his home by a visiting nurse and stated that his physical and mental state was okay. The problem that he wanted help with was that he was having difficulty in distinguishing between the times he was physically not well and, therefore, needed to stay in bed, and those times where he was depressed or procrastinating about doing his work. For him, it was acceptable to stay in bed for health reasons, but it was not acceptable to stay in bed because of procrastination or depression. Also, he knew he felt better when he was productive with his work and often by getting out of bed he felt better about feeling or being ill.

His goal was to be making the choice of "Is this a bed morning or a work morning?" It became clear to me, Jane, through the conversation that when he tried to make this decision while literally lying in the bed he was not objective about it. There were times, however, when he would decide to get up and go to the corner for the paper *first*, before deciding what kind of a day it was going to be. He described that in order to get the paper he had to get up, put on warm-ups, walk about 75 feet to the corner, and walk back. Upon returning to his apartment, he would make a choice of reading the paper at the table or in the bed. His answer would then tell him what kind of day it was going to be.

Deciding to go out to buy a paper is much simpler and more active than trying to decide what kind of day it is going to be. Once he was literally doing something, there usually developed a difference in feeling about his day. Clearly, he did not initially see the potential of the exception—to get up and out as opposed to lying in bed. However, by conversing about the times when he bought the paper first, we were able to highlight the significance of the exception and develop the reality of powerful times for the client where he could make a choice about what he wanted to do.

3. Nothing Is Always the Same

Assumption: Change is occurring all the time.

Many of us have had survey classes in the history of Western philosophy. One of the early philosophers, Heraclitus, is generally quoted as having said that you cannot step into the same river twice. In other words, nothing stays the same; things and events are changing all the time. It was our experience that after the 15 minutes it took in class to discuss how things are changing all the time, change was rarely talked about again in the same way in any philosophy class.

From that point on, we then talked about how things stay the same. We talked about the essences of things, we talked about the immutable nature of man and how in the objective world of science there were laws that govern the unchangeable.

However, we never talked about change again. It was as if stability and unchangeableness became a given for all the succeeding philosophies on up until recent times. Part of the problem with this continued assumption of unchangeableness may have been that the assumption was perpetuated by the structure of our language. We became limited by the verb "to be." With this verb, we can say something "is" something, as if it is now and forever. If we say, "I *am* American," we could mean that there are no times when I am not an American. We would probably have no trouble with that statement. Most people would accept the meaning that "I *am* an American" *all* the time.

We have problems on the other hand when we say that this *is* an "enmeshed family." Does this mean that there are no times when they are not enmeshed, when they are not doing something else? (For further discussion of this use of "to be," see de Shazer, 1988).

We would guess that most would probably say, "No, there are times when they must be acting some other way." However, our use of the verb "to be" directs our attention away from those other times.

It seems that as therapists we create problems for ourselves by talking as if things "are" in some immutable way. As soon as we say a family

is "enmeshed," we not only have the problem with self-fulling proph-
ecy, but we also then have to create some explanations for how the
"enmeshed" family then becomes something else.

I, John, remember on an oral exam in a philosophy class I was asked
to explain philosophically how an apple becomes a rotten apple or no
longer an apple. I was being asked to explain change from one state
of appleness to something different and then to nonexistence. We as
therapists are creating a similar situation. We first say the family is
enmeshed and then we have to create explanations for how they
become something else.

In the 70s, when "homeostasis" was the predominant concept of family therapy and was used to describe how systems maintain stability,
Speer (1970) was one of the first to question how relevant a central concept for sameness could be to a profession whose business was change.

Our position is that it is not useful to first talk about stability, sameness, and problem-maintenance and then try to create explanations for
how families change from one state to another. Rather, we think it is
more useful to assume change is happening all the time and eliminate
the need for explaining transitions from one state to another. Our task
then is much simpler. Our task is to help the client select and identify
those meanings, those changes, or those ways of becoming that they
like and would like to see continue.

For example, we are often asked about those "very difficult" cases—
the "multiproblemed" cases. In solution-focused thinking, cases are not
multiproblemed even if the client reports several problems. For example, a case referred to us by an HMO was reported as "very difficult."
A woman being released from the hospital after a suicide attempt had
been diagnosed as suicidal, manic-depressive, and self-destructive. The
referral source was worried about this client and wanted her to be seen
immediately after her release from the hospital. She called and made
an appointment for four days later. In the initial interview, she identified several goals: learn ways to release her anger productively; learn
to change obsessive thinking patterns; feel positive about future relationships; resolve past feelings about her father. All of these goals are
appropriate, but one cannot directly work on them all at once. When
we asked her when some of these things are happening now, she mentioned that they were happening now when she was "in balance." The
rest of the session focused upon times and ways she was continuing to
act in this "in-balanced" way and how she would keep acting that way.

We saw this client eight times. As she continued to have "in-balance" times, she was able to accomplish all of the goals she had listed in the first session.

The Milan team of Palazzoli, Cecchin, Boscolo and Prata (1978) realized the problem with "to be" and instead would describe someone as "showing" depression rather than saying that someone "is" depressed. Their use of a different verb strikes at the problem with labeling and the linear assumption that "to be" fosters.

Use of verbs like *show, become, seem* and *act as if* promote a view that behaviors are temporary and changeable. If we say that someone is acting depressed or depressed-like, the meaning is much different than if we say someone *is* depressed. The presupposition is that she or he is acting that way now, but could be acting in other ways at other times. The change of verb also gives movement to our descriptions.

Another way of avoiding this dilemma of "to be" is just to say, "*The client says* he/she is depressed." This phrasing has the advantage of reminding us that this is merely the clients' view of themselves and their situation at this time, and not a fact.

If we put the assumption that change is occurring all the time together with the previous assumption that exceptions can be created to a problem, we can then begin to search out for those times when someone acts in non-depressed ways. If someone is acting in non-depressed ways sometimes, there may be something different about those contexts or about what the person does or thinks at such times that enables acting differently from the problem way.

As therapists, we need to develop eyes and ears that are flexible in perceiving, and sensitive to non-problem times and behaviors, so that we and the clients can more easily elicit the non-problem times. The process is similar to the experience of looking at the psychology pictures called ambiguous figures in which the figure and ground reverse depending on how you look at them (see Figure 1). In the ambiguous figure, you can see the images of either a vase or the profiles of two faces. At first, some people will see only the image of the vase, and it takes a trained eye to see the opposite picture.

Similarly and metaphorically, clients come in telling us about one side of the image. We try to see both images and invite them to a process of examining the other side of the picture. Change is occurring all the time.

Figure 1. Do you see a vase?
Or is it a picture of two people
facing each other?

4. Small Change Is Generative

Assumption: Small changing leads to larger changing.

Very often, we hear practitioners speak of the "multi-problem" family, or the "severely dysfunctional" patient, or how complicated a case will be. Oftentimes, the practitioner's response to this case will be one of dread of the amount of work or difficulty of it, or resignation at the seeming hopelessness. The assumption underlying the response to these difficult situations usually is that an equally sophisticated, powerful, or long-term answer is required. However, the assumption that small changing leads to larger changing facilitates an easier way and can mean simpler views and actions.

Many cases can appear simpler if one recognizes that people usually use the same attempted solution for all problems. By making a small change in the attempted solution to the problems, clients can change in several different situations simultaneously. For example, many people believe that the way to improve a relationship is by confronting the other person on what they believe the other is doing wrong. The other person, whether a child, a colleague at work, an employee, a spouse, or a friend, usually responds defensively, and an argument then ensues. Those who persist in such attempted solutions by confrontation are likely to gain the reputation of being negative or argumentative, which perpetuates the problems even further. When we suggest that clients begin to say what they want rather than only what they do not like, they can change their approach and therefore change the interaction in many relationships.

Saying that small change is generative also means that we hold to the belief that a client who has experienced some success at achieving something manageable is, therefore, in a more resourceful state to find solutions to other, more difficult problems.

A client came to see us about difficulties in her relationship with a boyfriend. During the course of making changes in the relationship, she realized something about herself. As a consequence of having been abused in the past, she had previously thought that she could not take the risk of asking for what she wanted from someone. She was too afraid that any request would be met with anger and punishment. However, she was now experimenting with initiating requests of her boyfriend. Given that she was meeting with some success, she was now questioning her belief carried over from her past and was feeling a little better. She decided to try this initiation technique with people at work. She was surprised to find that she could make requests there, too, and achieve good results.

The assumption also means that problems are only as big as our definition of them. Our definition of the problem defines our experience and the size of the problem. A client who came to see us had been told by several people that she suffered from depression. She was afraid that there was something terribly wrong with her. Our thinking and initial feedback to her was that we did not think she suffered from depression, but that she was "unhappy and that given her circumstances, it made sense to us that she would feel that way." Depression was a definition that to her meant that there was something drastically wrong with her. Unhappy meant that she was normal and that she did not like her circumstances. The later definition was more manageable and something she could do something about.

Most important, the small-change assumption means that problems, large or small, are solved one step at a time. Recently, a couple came to see us because of repeated fights about the direction of their relationship. She was very upset that he was not willing to give a commitment to a date for their marriage. He could not see how they could do that when they were fighting so much. We asked what they would be doing differently when they were "on track" to making this marital decision. As they considered the "on track" idea, they identified that they would be talking with each other differently. By talking "with" each other rather than clinging to hard and fast positions while blaming the other, they surmised there would be more intermediary experiences of solving problems. This talking "with" each other would be more helpful toward making a commitment than setting a date or breaking up.

The assumption that small changing leads to more or larger changing can have any or all four of the above interpretations and lead to different and simpler approaches with clients. For example: A couple sought therapy as a last resort for their "lack of communication." They stated in the initial session that for the last few years of their 15-year marriage they did not communicate with each other. Their view was that they did not communicate with each other in any area of their marriage and that this communication problem led to chronic, escalating fights.

With solution-focused questioning, we asked about "exceptional" times that when she responded with what she called "positive responses," he did not get defensive or attacking in his usual way. "Positive responses" to her meant responding empathically to his position instead of defending herself right away. She was asked to go home and practice doing these positive responses and notice what other differences that made in him and in herself. To her, this assignment seemed rather insignificant. She was a social worker and accustomed to thinking that behavioral change was only superficial and did not relate to the deep underlying feelings behind their conflicts. Nevertheless, she agreed to give the task a try.

By the next session, there were dramatic changes. She noticed not only that they seemed to understand each other and communicate in a way that was on track to solving their "communication problem," but also that she was no longer taking things personally. This was something she had also wanted to be able to do, but as a person with a long history of personalizing situations, she had not been able to work this through by focusing on her feelings. Her response after three sessions was, "I have a hard time believing that changing these long-standing problems could happen so quickly— but I'll just keep doing it anyway."

Small changing leads to larger changing.

5. Cooperation Is Inevitable

Assumption: Clients are always cooperating. They are showing us how they think change takes place. As we understand their thinking and act accordingly, cooperation is inevitable (*de Shazer, 1982, 1985a, 1986; Gilligan, 1987*).

Working within a solution-focused therapy model, we believe clients' responses to our communication are indicative of how they think change takes place. If clients do not do what we say or if they do something else instead, we do not believe that they are "resistant" but rather that in their thinking this is the best thing to do at that time.

Our assumption that cooperation is inevitable requires that we take clients at their word: they would truly like to reach some solution to the problem. This is contrary to ideas like: clients are resistant; they *really* do not want to change; they like their problem; they are getting something out of their problem; they are denying their problem; they have some secret agenda or are being deceitful. Our experience is that these kinds of beliefs are not helpful in solution construction nor compatible with our notions of trusting people's resources.

A man came to see us fearing anxiety attacks. In the past, he had been in great fear of anxiety overtaking him when he was away from home, so he was now spending most of his time at home. He wanted to change jobs, but was afraid interviews would go badly. He was also angry with his wife for constantly nagging him to spend more time with her. He felt very discouraged.

Just before coming to see us, he had decided to try to get out of the house more. He wanted very much to see his son play basketball on the school team. Despite his fear of anxiety, he had gone to a game.

Initially, we were excited about this change and very encouraging about his doing more things like that. However, we discovered that the more encouraging and suggestive we were of further changes, the more hesitantly he responded, even suggesting reasons why a further step might not work. We discovered very quickly through his responses that his approach to change was different from ours, and that if we were too persistent in our encouragement, he might change less.

He seemed to have his own pace that was different from ours—not better, not worse, just different. Had we wanted to create "resistance" by encouraging change, all we had to do was to continue to be encouraging in the way that he perceived as pushing and he would indeed do less.

Instead, we were very encouraging in *his* way. We told him how impressed we were with his desire to be more active and with his steps in that direction. We also suggested to him that he continue to take things *one step at a time*. We thought that since he tended to be rather ambitious in his thinking, he might want to cut down his expectations of the next step.

This client, like all clients, was very cooperative, and provided clues quickly of how he went about change. We could have created a "resistant client" by suggesting things that he would have regarded as "too fast." Instead, we cooperated with him by urging him to be cautious.

Many of us pick the problem that we would work on first if we were the client. Some of us, because of a diagnostic assumption, decide what needs to be worked on first. For example, we might insist that an alcohol problem be worked on first because we believe that therapy cannot be successful while someone is still drinking. Because we believe that a family problem involving parenting cannot be solved because of marital difficulties, we might insist that the marital problems be worked on first. We try to be helpful by suggesting steps to solve the problem we have selected. Too often, however, clients do not agree with what we have selected as the problem or the route to solution. Therefore, if clients do not think of their situation in the way we do, it actually makes sense in their view that they would not do what we suggest. It also makes more sense for us to believe that they are just being consistent with how they think of the situation than to think that there is something wrong with them or that they *are* resistant. Certainly, in their view they are not being resistant.

A common norm for doing family therapy is that you need every member of the family present. The same norm is used for couples therapy. When we were in our early years of learning family therapy and subscribed to this norm, we lost many of our clients and saw other practitioners lose clients as well.

For example, many times a member of the family may not have believed in therapy at all or may not have believed there was a problem that required therapy. Or, a family member might have some reason for not being able to attend the sessions. These families were at times labelled as "resistant" and the non-attending members were seen as resistant for denying the problem or for not attending. The attending members were seen as resistant as if they somehow participated in an enabling way with the others not attending. We remember being instructed by trainers and supervisors to send the family home, and to meet with them only when the whole family would come in.

We wonder in such circumstances about "Who was being resistant here?" Were the family members being resistant because they did not believe in therapy or had to work at their job? Were *we* being resistant by being so intransigent about our rule? We like to think that the family was telling us how they think changes are made, and that the ones attending were the ones who were available and/or thought therapy might help.

In training workshops, Richard Bandler and John Grinder used to say that there were no resistant clients, only inflexible therapists (Bandler & Grinder, 1979). If we take clients at their word and trust that they want to solve their problem, we can assume that they are trying to solve it in the best way they know at the moment. If some members do not attend sessions because they do not believe in therapy, we take them at their word and assume that rather than resisting, they are showing us how they think about their problem and how they think change takes place.

The burden falls upon us as therapists to find how people think and act upon their problems and to be flexible enough to utilize their unique way. A mutually cooperative relationship is an inevitability.

6. People Are Resourceful

Assumption: People have all they need to solve their problems.

This strongly held Ericksonian assumption is a nonpathology and wellness belief (Bandler & Grinder, 1979; Lankton & Lankton, 1983; Dolan, 1985; Gilligan, 1987; O'Hanlon, 1987). In pathology assessment, a clinician uses some normative model either of an individual or a family as a basis of comparison with that of the client. As Anderson, Goolishian, and Winderman (1984) have stated, these models have been based on the notion that problems result from some failure or dysfunction in the structure of the individual or family. The task of the clinician has been to locate the problem in these structures.

Our emphasis is not upon the cause or maintenance of the problem, but upon the faith that each individual and family are capable of solving their problems and the responsibility is upon us to be flexible and to facilitate change toward what they want. Problems exist in the way people have defined situations and the misdirected actions they persist in taking. Everyone has the ability to change to a different course of action.

By stating that people are resourceful, we do not want to intimate that this approach is a model of attribution or possession. We do not believe that people *have* resources anymore than we believe that people *have* deficits. Stating the assumption in this attributive way is merely our way of highlighting that we believe that everyone is *capable* of doing what they need to do to get what they want.

We recognize that stating the assumption in this way suggests that we believe that people possess resources and that philosophically this is inconsistent with an interactional view and process approach. To be philosophically consistent, we would not talk about deficits or resources at all and we would merely discuss processes and meaning. However, in order to highlight our positive orientation, we have deviated from the interactional level for a moment.

7. Meaning and Experience Are Interactionally Constructed

Assumption: Meaning and experience are interactionally constructed. Meaning is the world or medium in which we live. We inform meaning onto our experience and it is our experience at the same time. Meaning is not imposed from without or determined from outside of ourselves. We inform our world through interaction.

One of the definitions of "inform" from Webster's II New Riverside University Dictionary (Riverside, 1984) is "To give form or character to." This is the usage we intend in this assumption. By the use of the word "inform" we mean that socially and individually, we give form to our experience and existence, that meaning is relative to the participant observer. For example: If someone were to be frozen in a standing position with right hand raised above the head and then be placed in different settings, there would be different meanings ascribed to such behavior.

Thus, a teacher seeing the person with hand raised in that position in a classroom would assume that the person has a question or comment and might call on her or him to speak. An auctioneer seeing the person would assume that she or he is making a bid, and if that were the winning bid that gesture might cost her or him a sum of money.

A cabby seeing the person in that position along a curb would assume that she or he wants a ride and come zipping up to the curb. If the person were standing on a boat and people on other boats were going by, they, following the etiquette of boaters, might assume the person was being friendly and waving, and therefore wave back. If the hand were raised in a courtroom, an observer might assume that the person was taking an oath.

The action of right hand raised overhead can have many different meanings even though physically it is the same gesture. Placed in different contexts, the gesture can have different meanings that are informed by observers as well as by the person performing the action. The performer may inform the event with the same meaning or something other than what others are informing. Neither meaning is right or wrong or a misperception.

We all live in a world of meaning and language. Meaning is informed by participant observers; meaning is ascribed by an observer or participant of an event, not the other way around. The event does not have meaning in itself that is discovered by someone outside of the event. Meaning is relative to the person(s) informing the event. From the point of view of the individual participating in an active way in the world, the individual informs meaning onto his or her world or creates his or her experience. Meaning both informs the experience and meaning is the experience. Meaning cannot be separated from experience or from the person(s) ascribing the meaning. Making the distinction between thought and experience creates an artificial barrier between "inside" the skull and "outside."

Meaning-making is always both inside and outside. It is interactive in the relationship between the individual and his or her experience, as well as in the interactions between people. Meaning evolves and changes in the dialogue between people as they share their experience in language and symbol. There is both a mutual participation in the conversation and an acceptance of influence. For further discussions of the construction of meaning see Watzlawick, 1984; von Foerster, 1984; von Glaserfeld, 1984; Maturana & Varela, 1987; de Shazer, 1988;

for its social construction and application to the therapy conversation, see Anderson and Goolishian, 1988, and Hoffman, 1990.

Problems, goals, solutions all take place within the realm of meaning and are at the same time meanings. A change in meaning is a change in experience. A change may mean for clients that a problem no longer exists, that they can do something different or that they are on a track toward what they want.

8. Recursiveness

Assumption: Actions and descriptions are circular.

There is a circular relationship between how one describes a problem or goal, what action one then takes, how one describes these actions and results, what further actions one might take, and so on. (For further discussions about recursiveness, see Watzlawick, 1974, and Keeney, 1983.)

For example, if a parent describes a child's behavior as bad, the parent will more than likely use punishment as the solution. The resulting behavior by the child (also viewed through the lens of good/bad by the parents) will be used as feedback to judge the success of the punishments.

If the same parent adopts a different frame of the child's behavior and, instead of interpreting it as "bad," describes it as teenage experimenting, the parent may ignore the behavior or give consequences without ascribing a good or bad label to the child. The meaning adopted by the parent both informs how he or she "sees" the child's behavior and also determines what class of solution or action the parent takes. A change in meaning can change how the parent informs further events and what action is taken.

9. Meaning Is in the Response

Assumption: The meaning of the message is the response you receive (*Bandler & Grinder, 1979; Dilts et al., 1980*).

Meaning in the earlier examples of the right-hand gesture is described as if it is created by the observer. There is no absolute meaning to the gesture; it is informed with meaning not only by the person performing the gesture but also by all those others observing the gesture.

A humorous example of the mismatch of these meanings is the old-time movie situation where someone is at an auction and raises a hand to scratch an itch or wave to a newcomer to the room, then discovering that he has just placed a bid in the auction.

Often in everyday life, our interpretation of that example or of other situations is to say that the observer "misinterpreted" what we said or did. In this model, we find it more useful to assume that the onus of responsibility for clear communication is on us rather than on the client. In other words, if the other person makes meaning of our actions that is different from what we intend, the responsibility is upon us to do something different. This is counter to the idea that it is the observer's fault for misinterpreting or resisting our message.

In a family a mother was concerned about some newly emerging behavior in her 13-year old daughter. Mother noticed that her daughter was now dressing in a punk style. She also noticed that her daughter was smoking cigarettes on her way home from school and that her grades had slipped somewhat. To some of us, this may not seem too severe, but to this particular parent in a religious context where smoking was "wrong," these behaviors were serious.

Mother's intent was to remind her daughter that smoking was bad and that her grades were slipping. To mother's way of thinking, she was "reminding" and her intent was to be "helpful." However, to the daughter, the meaning of her mother's message was very different. She saw it not as "helpful," but rather as "restrictive" of her freedom and independence.

The daughter in this case decided to show her mother that she was independent; therefore, she did more smoking and spent more time with her friends than with her homework. This was consistent with the meaning she informed to her mother's actions. Upon seeing her daughter's response, the mother moved beyond reminding and decided that this behavior was "bad" and the suitable response should be punishment by "grounding."

This punishment confirmed in the daughter her thinking that her mother's initial actions were restrictive. So, consistent with the daughter's thinking, she escalated her own actions. This interaction continued to escalate.

In this example, with our assumption that the meaning of the message is the response you receive, the meaning of mother's actions is the response she received: an escalation of the behavior she deplored. From this communication point of view, the meaning of her message ended up very different from what she intended.

So, too, with us as helpers. The meaning of our communication is the response we receive. If the response is different than what we believe to be helpful, then the meaning for us might be that it is time for us to do something different in the communication. If we continue to receive "yes but" responses from our client, the response may mean that it is time to do something different. Meaning is in the response.

10. The Client Is the Expert

Assumption: Therapy is a goal- or solution-focused endeavor, with the client as expert.

The goals of different therapies vary considerably. The most significant distinction in this regard seems to be between those models that attempt to bring about a cure or some personal growth and those that aim at helping the client to solve some problem or achieve some goal.

Models that attempt some cure generally perceive the source of the initial complaint to be rooted in personality and therefore try to accomplish personality change. Models, within the human potential movement attempt to enhance personal growth and self-actualization. Both orientations tend to be rather long-term and usually depend upon insight for change.

These therapy models often tend to use the therapist as the expert in determining what is wrong (diagnosis) and setting the course of treatment. This role and process are similar to those of the physician who makes an observation and conducts tests concerning the symptoms, and then, as the expert in pathology and treatment, prescribes a course of treatment for the patient.

A solution-focused model places responsibility on the other side of the relationship. In this model, the focus is to help clients define goals as precisely as possible. Clients are the experts on what they want to change, as well as in determining what they want to work on. If they recognize other problems in their life but choose not to focus on them at this time, that is their choice. If we, as helpers, are aware of other problems or think that the client could work on some other goal, we might suggest this but still continue to focus on what the client wants.

This position is in sharp contrast to models of assessment or diagnosis which compare the client's behavior or thinking with some normative standard and then suggest that the therapist decide what the client should change and thus determine the direction of therapy.

Given the position that therapy is a goal-focused endeavor, with the client as expert, the distinction of voluntary and involuntary client becomes critical. In this consumer model, the task of therapy is goal-oriented and the involuntary client is initially stating that he or she has no goal. Muddles are created when we as therapists blur this distinction of voluntary/involuntary by our selecting the goal by ourselves despite what the client says, by assuming the responsibility of social control agent, or by trying to motivate the client toward some goal determined by an expert.

By making this distinction of voluntary/involuntary in this approach, we follow two different courses of action. With voluntary clients, we proceed to work toward the goals or solutions they are seeking; these procedures are outlined in the following chapters. With involuntary clients, we explore whether they can still define goals even under their involuntary circumstances; the procedures for this course of action are spelled out in Chapter Sixteen.

We also want to draw distinctions between therapy, education, and support. To us, these are three different and separate domains. Therapy's function is the co-constructing by therapist and client of a goal or solution and the facilitating of that process. Education's function is the process of learning. We do think that therapy is educational in the etymological sense of the word, that is, a drawing forth. We believe that we join clients in drawing forth from them solutions that they want, that come from their own experience, and that they are creating. We do not believe that therapy is educational in the sense of instructional or instrumental. If clients want instruction on parenting skills, they are entitled and we encourage them to seek out instructional classes. We do not think of classes as therapy, however, and we would not refer clients to a class because we thought they had a deficit of skills.

We also do not want to confuse therapy with support. Although we are very supportive and encouraging in our sessions, support as a goal is not sufficient. If clients want support, then perhaps we can explore with them what they think they will eventually accomplish with that support to find out if that can be their goal. We might also explore how they could get support from friends, relatives, self-help groups, or some other source. However, we do not see our functioning in a strictly supportive fashion, with no other goal, as a reasonable use of therapy. Given our assumptions, mere support would be facilitating a dependence that we think is not helpful.

Therapy is a goal- or solution-focused endeavor with the client as the expert.

11. Unity

Assumption: Any change in how clients describe a goal (solution) and/or what they do affects future interactions with all others involved.

We conceptualize problems, solutions, or goals, within meaning. There is a recursive or circular relationship between how one defines a situation and what one does. Thoughts and actions can be described in terms of how one thinks, what one does, and the feedback to one's thoughts and actions. Goals and solutions can also be described in terms of the interactions between people, along with their accompanying thoughts, perceptions, and feedback.

This is a process view of solutions rather than a conceptualization based upon structures. Other ways of thinking assume that problems emanate from a dysfunctional structure of the individual personality, the family, or the marriage.

Rather than using structural labels and focusing on the structure as the locus of the problem, we focus on the recursive process between how one defines a situation, and what one does, and how one defines that, and what one does, and so on. This is a circular view, no beginning and no end.

With this idea in mind, we can assume that any change anywhere in the interaction changes further interaction, whether it be the interaction of how one goes about trying to reach a solution or the interaction between people as they try to reach some solution or goal.

Therefore, it is not necessary to have everyone involved with a problem present in order to bring about a change in the desired direction. In a marital relationship, for example, we can facilitate a change with only one of the members present to bring about a change in the inter-action between the two of them.

Where a husband reports that—despite his attempts to remind his wife to do things that will help her self-esteem and problems—she appears to him to resist and resent him. To him, she appears to defend herself either with reasons why she cannot carry out his suggestions or promises to do it later. He states that he is very frustrated.

We would suggest that he focus for a moment on life without the problem. By focusing on the problem-solved future, he identifies that he would relax and trust that his wife was taking care of herself. In the future, he would just "listen and trust that she would work it out." This is different than his present thinking that she cannot figure this out and that giving advice is the way to help; it has not worked.

We would suggest to him that he do now the things he thought he would do in a problem-solved future. The husband—through adopting a mode of pretending the problem is solved—acts in ways that the wife sees as listening and trusting. She is less likely to act defensively and may even take his listening as supportive. With her actions being dif-ferent, the husband can adopt a different view. He may adopt a meaning that she is different from him, that listening to her is more helpful to her than giving advice.

That simple change on his part leads to different actions on her part, which confirm his taking different actions. The marital problem can thus be solved by our working only with him and by his adopting a dif-ferent solution. By his adopting a different meaning and course of action, the further interactions between them are different.

12. Treatment Group Membership

Assumption: The members in a treatment group are those who share a goal and state their desire to do something about making it happen.

The members may not agree about the problem or goal, the meaning of the problem or goal, or what to do about it, but they do agree that there is a problem or goal and that something needs to be done. Mem-bership, by definition, includes the therapist who has agreed to work with the other members in reaching a solution. The therapy group, therefore, includes a therapist and a client.

Doing therapy may also include people who in other therapy models may not be considered as clients. The client group may include referring persons, protective service people, court-appointed people, school social workers, teachers, work groups, etc. Again, the therapy group or unit includes all those who agree there is a problem they want to solve or a goal they want to reach.

This is different from those therapy models which assume that the client group is a socially defined unit such as an individual, a family, or couple. In other models, the source of problems was assumed to be some dysfunction in one of these defined units. But as Anderson, Goolishian and Winderman (1984) have stated, individuals, families, couples, and court systems do not cause or make problems, nor are problems the result of dysfunctions in any of these systems.

Rather than looking at these socially defined units as the source of the problem, we say that the problem is the problem itself. The treatment group or unit is defined as those who approach us in our role as therapist and say there is a problem they want to solve or goal they want to pursue. This may include family members, some family members but not others, individuals, referring persons, or any number of people sharing nothing more or related in no other way than that they all say there is a problem they are concerned about. This means that there may be others who, even though they are involved in the problem or may be affected by the problem, may not want to do anything about it or do anything about it through therapy.

The advantage of this assumption is that we avoid reifying diagnostic maps of units like individual, family, couple, or psyche. We are less likely to think that our constructs or tools, like enmeshed family or intrapsychic structures, actually exist beyond our using them. This is not an individual therapy and not a family therapy. This is not a model built on organizational constructs. This is a solution-construction therapy that cuts across the distinction of individual and family therapies (Walter, 1989). This is a model that is built on the notion that the people you work with are those who say there is a goal to be accomplished or a problem to be solved. These people are organized around this purpose and this "reality." Their organization, if you will, comes from their joint purpose of wanting to solve the problem or reach some shared goal.

Given that clients are organized around the purpose of a goal or of solving a problem and that goals or problems are relative to the meaning with which the goals or problems are described, the meaning is key to this therapy. We facilitate the evolution of new meaning, a co-constructed solution by which these clients will continue to be organized—or they will disband because the original purpose (the solving of a problem) no longer exists.

Given that the treatment group is defined around those who have a joint purpose, we do not complicate the therapy by trying to bring people into therapy who do not want to be there. We assume that people who do not want to be in therapy are not interested in working on a solution at this time and, therefore, we would not consider them as part of therapy. Because we do not have a diagnostic map of a social unit like a family, we do not consider it necessary to have everyone there. When a person calls about therapy and asks us who should come in, we usually reply that whoever is interested in the situation should come in.

For example, a mother calls because she is alarmed by her daughter's behavior. She says the school social worker and the teacher have told her that her daughter is failing school. Mother and father have decided that the child rearing is mother's responsibility; father does not place much importance on school performance. For him, this is not much of a problem and, to the extent that it is, the responsibility to his way of thinking is mother's. When mother calls, we invite all who want to come in.

Mother comes with her 12-year-old daughter and younger son. As we ask about their goal in coming, we find that the daughter, too, is concerned about school and that the younger boy is there because he is too young to be left home. Mother also reports that the daughter's teacher is concerned. This year's teacher has "adopted" the daughter because she thinks that the daughter has great potential. She has stressed very strongly to mother that she would like to help in the therapy and that mother should have the therapist call because she would like to help.

At this time, in this case, the three who seem to be organized around the goal of improving the daughter's school performance are the mother, the daughter, and possibly the teacher. This is the client group organized around the meaning of "school performance." By virtue of the therapist joining them around their goal, the treatment unit includes the therapist.

In the first session and on the phone with the teacher, we find that the goal is for daughter to be turning in her homework and to be participating in class. We find also that this is happening sometimes whenever the daughter decides that homework and participation are necessary to pass eighth grade, and when mother is consistent about "homework time." When the girl participates in class, the teacher does not worry and is less "helpful."

As the three of them make progress around the school performance, the reason for their being organized in the way they had been diminishes and the system disbands—that is, therapy concludes. The meaning for each of them around the school performance changes. For example, mother redefines the importance of her own consistency; daughter sees school performance as something important to her since she wants to enter high school; and the teacher becomes more confident that the girl is progressing.

The therapy was defined around the goal and the treatment group consisted of the four people organized around that goal, the school performance.

SUMMARY

These 12 working assumptions are the beliefs we use to inform our therapy:

1. Focusing on the positive, the solution, and the future, facilitates change in the desired direction. Therefore, focus on solution-oriented talk rather than on problem-oriented talk.
2. Exceptions to *every* problem can be created by the therapist and client which can be used to build solutions.
3. Change is occurring all the time.
4. Small changing leads to larger changing.
5. Clients are always cooperating. They are showing us how they think change takes place. As we understand their thinking and act accordingly, cooperation is inevitable.
6. People have all they need to solve their problems.
7. Meaning and experience are interactionally constructed.
8. Actions and descriptions are circular.
9. The meaning of the message is the response you receive.

10. Therapy is a goal or solution-focused endeavor with the client as expert.
11. Any change in how clients describe a goal (solution) and/or what they do affects future interactions with all others involved.
12. The members of a treatment group are those who share the feeling that there is a goal and state their desire to do something about making it happen.

These assumptions guide our thinking and our actions and provide the meaning and guidelines for this to be a total approach, a way of thinking, a way of conversing, and a way of interacting with clients.

The following chapters will now give flesh to these assumptions as we spell out more concretely what we do.

DISCUSSION

QUESTION:
These assumptions are very different from what I am accustomed to. Does this mean I have to give up what I presently believe?

We find that it is more useful to us to inform all our actions with these assumptions, and to work in a way that is always consistent with these assumptions. For us, this makes our work and approach a complete package.

We suggest to those who may be learning this approach that in order to avoid the muddles that may occur while they are trying to believe several things at the same time, they suspend beliefs while trying this on. Later, after attaining some facility with this way of working, they can decide how much they want to incorporate in their work and in what way.

We experienced both a gain and a loss as we began working this way. We experienced a loss as we realized that we were giving up that very emotionally close relationship with our clients we experienced using long-term models we previously used. We also found that the satisfaction of seeing people making concrete changes in a short period of time more than made up for our feelings of sadness.

QUESTION:
Do you think this approach works with everyone?

Yes, as long as they define a goal.

3

A Positive Start

■ Focusing on the positive, the solution, and the future facilitates change in the desired direction. Therefore, focus on solution-oriented talk rather than on problem-oriented talk.

This chapter will first describe some rules of thumb that we work by and then how to start out with a solution focus.

RULES OF THUMB

Our way of working involves several rules of thumb, some of which we learned from the Milwaukee Group, that guide us in our actions.

1. If It Works, Don't Fix It (*de Shazer, 1985*)

In other words, if clients are already doing something that is working for them, stay out of the way. Do not—out of some desire to be helpful or sophisticated—suggest something more.

A man came to us because everyone, including and especially his present girlfriend, told him he had "trouble with commitment." He and all his friends had all sorts of explanations for his still being a bachelor and his fears of commitment. According to him, his present girlfriend, however, felt that sometimes their relationship was "progressing." He explained that during these times they both thought he had been open with her and talked to her rather than holding back and keeping to himself. He explained that at those times he "treated her like a friend" and would talk to her about everything, including his doubts and fears about relationships and marriage. This different label of "treating her like a friend" carried with it a very different set of behaviors on his part that encouraged her to think that the relationship was progressing. Clearly, in this relationship, "treating her like a friend" worked. When he thought of her as a friend rather than as someone demanding commitment, he interacted with her in ways that led to further closeness.

In trying to be helpful, and given all the possible explanations or theories about catastrophic fears about commitment, we could have explored all sorts of fears about his commitment. This kind of approach, even though well intended, would have interrupted this man's way of treating her like a friend. So, if something is already working, do not change it; do more of it. In this case, we suggested that he notice what happens as he continues to "treat her like a friend."

2. If Everything You Are Doing Is Not Working, Do Something Different (*de Shazer, 1985*)

Even if what you decide to do seems totally illogical or crazy, do something different. Indeed, what you do differently will probably seem crazy. After all, if you have been doing everything you reasonably can think of and nothing seems to work, the only things left to do will be what seem to be the unreasonable or illogical.

A couple came to see us for sexual problems. The issue as they perceived it was that one of the members of the couple wanted sex all the time and the other did not want to have sex at all. The latter member had some physical problems which caused discomfort and therefore stopped her from having any sex. They explained to us that this had been going on for some time and they had tried everything, including therapy.

In exploring this issue, we found that there had been a time recently when they had had sex; at that time she had said to herself, "Oh, why not!" and continued through her physical ailments, while he let himself be vulnerable instead of questioning. We asked how they had decided to do that and they explained they "had to do something different because what we were doing was not working."

To do something different may seem very obvious. To most of us, the thought of doing something different would seem logical. However, in problem situations, logic seems to go out the window.

Instead, we subscribe to that old proverb, "If at first you don't succeed, try, try again."

3. Keep It Simple

One time, I, John, was working with a man who said he was shy with women and wanted to be more assertive and develop some techniques in making some initial conversation. I had been reading some literature at the time on "paradoxical interventions," so I designed this task whereby he would go to a bar and announce to any woman there that he was doing a survey for a school project on what women looked for in a self-introduction. I further instructed him that since he was concerned about failure and his fears about failure usually got in his way, he should get the failure out of the way with the first woman. By deliberately failing with the first interview, he could then get on with the job of getting some useful information. This seemed like a great intervention and I was rather pleased with myself until I realized, after the client left the session, that he never went to bars. My highly sophisticated intervention was doomed to failure because I outsophisticated myself. Bars were not now, nor ever, a part of his life.

The following is an example of keeping it simple:

A sergeant in the army stated that he was concerned that he was becoming angrier and more violent with his children. Recently, in anger, he had slapped his 12-year-old boy for talking back to him. He was afraid that his frustration was increasing and that he could really hurt his children. When asked how he wanted to be handling the situation, he stated that he wanted to keep things in perspective and not take his children's actions so personally. We asked about those times when he could take it personally, but somehow did not. He said there were no times he could think of, but he wanted to be a disciplinarian with his kids in the same way he was with the men under his command. We asked what was different. He stated that when one of his subordinates messed up, he just thought to himself that the messing up was the guy's problem, (rather than his) and then dealt with the guy accordingly.

To this sergeant this idea that the subordinate was responsible for his own messing up was very different from taking it personally as if he had failed as a supervisor or, in the case of his kids, as a father. To help him out, we suggested that he take notice of how he allowed his subordinates to have responsibility for their actions. We suggested that he also notice how he might already be thinking that his children, too, are responsible for their messing up.

This perspective that individuals are responsible for their actions and the suggested tasks were already within his experience and were very simple to do.

4. If You Want to Do Therapy Briefly, Approach Each Session As If It Were the Last and Only Time You Will See That Client

As you adopt this rule, you will become intensely focused, and notice yourself asking what small difference there might be that will help this client leave this session on track to solving his or her problem.

An example that drove this rule home to us is a case in which we were behind an observation mirror as part of a team approach. The client was a young woman who came in about problems in her relationship with her boyfriend. She began to describe how her boyfriend was a long-distance trucker. He owned a truck with a cab with sleeping quarters behind the seats. Together, they made the transcontinental hauls. As we listened further, we realized that this couple had no fixed home, that their home was this semi-tractor trailer. We further realized that we could not predict when they might have a load that would take them near the office again. This might be the only time we would see her, much less schedule an appointment. Our attention became keenly focused on what we and she could do in just this one session.

5. There Is No Failure, Only Feedback

This rule of thumb is from Bandler and Grinder (1979).

Those of us who are ambitious and want to be helpful have a very difficult time not evaluating our work in terms of success or failure. We all have had the experience of our own feelings getting in the way of our work as we become self-conscious over whether we are succeeding or failing.

There is no one right way, however, or best way to help people. If your task did not seem to work or your question seemed to go nowhere, it does not mean you are a failure. The client response is only feedback and merely means that you need to do something different.

STARTING OUT

When we first meet our clients we want to set the stage for them and explain what we are doing, and the procedures we will follow. They will know what to expect and they can be confident that there will be few or no surprises.

We typically say:

> We would like to talk with you for about 40 minutes about what you want, and about your situation. At the end of that time, I would like to take a break for a few minutes, go behind this viewing mirror, consult with my team, and then come back and share with you our combined feedback or advice if we have any. We work as a team because we believe that two heads are better than one and that this way you will have the benefit of different points of view.

During the break, the members of the team share impressions and points of view and gather our feedback for the client. We usually write out the feedback and the therapist returns to the therapy room and reports the written feedback to the client. Reading the feedback is done in training situations and at times when we want to be precise in our language.

We are not always able, however, to work as a team. Team members may not always be available, nor is a team approach always feasible or cost effective. When we work alone, we still take a break and explain our procedures this way:

> I would like to talk with you for about 40 minutes about what you want and about your situation. After that, I will take a break and leave the room for awhile to think over all that you have said and come back with some feedback, some impressions, and some advice if I have some.

You will notice that we state that we want to talk with the client about *what she or he may want*. We are already setting the stage for a therapy that is goal-oriented and consumer-oriented. We are already suggesting that what they want, their goal, is important to this therapy.

After that brief introduction, we begin.

ASSUMING AND MAINTAINING RAPPORT

Our working assumption is that we have rapport from the moment of contact. We do not assume that we have to do something or something different to create rapport or establish a relationship. By assuming we have rapport, we do not have to take time or sessions in building trust. We do believe, however, there are things we can do or say to maintain and facilitate the working relationship. We have probably all received training at some time in our careers in what to do to help the client feel understood and supported. We have probably learned reflective listening and empathic listening, the restating what the client said, with the same affect and tone.

Different therapy models have defined rapport and empathy differently, or stressed different sides of it. The pioneer of the field, Carl Rogers, in his client-centered approach stressed the feeling side of empathy (Rogers, 1951). He stressed how the therapist should verbally and nonverbally reflect how the person feels. His idea was that the client's feeling understood was very often enough to facilitate change.

Bandler and Grinder (1975, 1979) stressed the notion of pacing. To them, gaining rapport meant matching the primary representational system of the client. If the client tended to speak in visual terms, the therapist should match the client in the use of visual terms. If the client used auditory terms, the therapist was to speak in auditory terms. Finally, if the client spoke about feelings or in kinesthetic terms, then the therapist was to do likewise. The rationale was that both conscious and unconscious rapport was established by using the same information processes as the client. Their thinking was that each of us in processing information tends to use one sensory modality primarily over the others. Some of us are constantly making pictures, some of us depend more on language and sounds, some of us process in terms of our feelings.

According to Bandler and Grinder (1979), as therapists our responsibility is to be the flexible member of the interaction and to match or join the client's way of processing information.

The founders of the Brief Therapy Model of the Mental Research Institute, Paul Watzlawick, John Weakland and Richard Fisch, along with Lynn Segal, stressed the initial support of a client's position (Fisch, Weakland, & Segal, 1982). This amounted to reflecting and supporting the client's world view and, more specifically, initial conceptualizing of the problem.

The thrust of all these models seems to be that people are different—different in their emotional responses to their problems, different in the way they process information, and different in their world views in which their thinking and acting take place. The way to maintain rapport with different clients is to match and pace their unique way of thinking and feeling. The procedure for doing this is to use their language, the key words they repeatedly use to reflect their unique way of thinking and their emotional responses to their situation. For example:

Therapist: So you were saying that you want to do something about your weight?

Client: Yes, I am just too overweight, and I hate myself for it. Actually, I think I overeat because I hate myself. I just eat out of control, you know, as if I just do not care how I look. I am trying to work the Overeaters Anonymous program but I just get so discouraged.

Therapist: So you think that your being overweight is due to how you feel about yourself and you have been feeling discouraged and down on yourself, is that right? And when this is no longer a problem for you what will you be doing differently? (*The first sentence is said with a tone that matches her sadness. The second one is said with a slightly rising tone to reflect some curiosity and optimism.*)

Client: I will be turning this all over to my higher power.

Therapist: So, you will be turning this over and how will you be doing that?

Client: I am not sure. I have a difficult time seeing myself without this problem or weighing what I want.

Therapist: So it is not clear to you yet. (*Matching her visual orientation*) So, if it were clearer to you, what would you guess you would say?

Client: I think I would be eating and doing things in a "slow busy" way.

Therapist: "Slow busy," what will that be like?
Client: I will still be busy because I like to accomplish things, but I won't think it all has to be done yesterday.

In this example, the therapist matches the client's use of Overeaters Anonymous language, her affect and sad tone, her searching for a solution in visual terms and her unique use of the expression of "slow busy," and inquires about the future without the problem.

Of course, we do not want to interact with clients by just matching what they say. Furthermore, we really cannot interact with someone without influencing the direction, process, and content of the conversation. The notion of maintaining rapport and supporting a client's world view and emotional responses may sound as if matching is only a responsive action to what the client presents. As we will elaborate more specifically in later chapters, the interaction between therapist and client is circular, with no individual's actions or words ever being exclusively an initiation or response. Every communication is both a response and an initiation to a newer or different meaning or action. So, although maintaining rapport as a procedure may sound like a passive response to the client, the action is part of a wider concept of conversation (Anderson & Goolishian, 1988). This wider concept includes for us the notion that through the use of presuppositions within our questions and by the direction of our statements, we, as therapists, are already influencing the further evolution of the therapist-client conversation and the construction of the goals and solutions.

The metaphor that seems to apply is that of dancing. When two people dance with one another, an observer might say that one person is leading and another is following. However, on closer examination, one can see that the movements of both dancers are closely matched, calibrated, and mutually influenced. The dancing is a collaborative process, a nonverbal conversation. We would be unfair to evaluate their dancing and to say that it is his dance or her dance, or that it is the result of one or the other's leading. From an interactional view, the notion of "leading" is an illusion.

So, too, we, as therapists, may think that we are setting the direction with our clients or even creating change. But that kind of linear thinking does not take into account the circular nature of conversation. Any dancer who thinks that she or he can unilaterally determine the dancing, soon finds out that cooperation is interactive.

This does not mean, however, that by acknowledging the circular quality of conversation, we do not assume certain actions as part of "roles." Based on our assumptions about change and the value of positively-focused conversation, we will introduce a positive direction and more workable, positive framing as soon as possible within the conversation. We are conversational facilitators. Our job is to facilitate a conversation that opens more possibilities for solution.

The rationale for initially using clients' language and reflecting their emotions is that it provides verbal and nonverbal affirmation. We believe that people are more likely to become more flexible about their beliefs, actions, and even very strongly held beliefs when they perceive their beliefs to be acknowledged. If clients perceive their view as being disqualified or challenged, there is a greater likelihood that the client will withdraw or counter the challenge. Neither withdrawal, defensiveness, or counterchallenges, are responses that we want in our interactions.

Another explanatory principle for the use of the client's language and our lending nonverbal support is the "yes set" from hypnosis (Erickson, 1980). The hypnotic procedure of the "yes set" assumes that by providing an individual with a series of statements that the individual perceives as true, the individual will literally nod in agreement with each statement and then be more likely to accept a question or suggestion to a statement that is slightly different from what was previously believed or a direction that is different than previously followed.

A hypnotist might make a series of statements as part of an induction, with a suggestion added at the end that leads to a deeper trance or to a direction in trance.

As you are sitting here, facing me, your feet on the floor and your arms on your lap, hearing the sound of my voice, while you're breathing in and out, (*more slowly*) in . . . and . . . out, you might be noticing the beginnings of a new thought coming to your mind.

The initial statements that are sensory specific are validated by the individual as she or he follows each statement. The experience is as if the client is checking each statement and saying "yes" to each one. As she or he continues to say "yes," the individual is more likely to give credence to the final, vaguely stated suggestion.

Even if the individual was not consciously thinking of anything new at the time, the mere suggestion at this point that a new thought might be coming to mind is enough to have the client search for the "new" thought. For a further discussion of client searching, see "trans-derivational phenomena" in *Patterns of the Hypnotic Techniques of Milton H. Erickson, M.D.* (Bandler & Grinder, 1975).

In a parallel fashion, this is the purpose of what we do by adopting our clients' language and supporting their emotions. We provide a series of experiences in which clients recognize validation and thus are more likely to accept our suggestion for a new direction. Of course, since we value a solution-focus, we would more than likely suggest, through our questions, a more open frame of the problem or a solution and future-oriented direction.

A POSITIVE DIRECTION

Throughout this book, we discuss the significance of carefully constructed questions. As we discussed in the first chapter, questions contain presuppositions that set the direction of the reply. Questions with different presuppositions invite different classes of answers.

For example, by asking a client "So what is the problem?" we presuppose that there *is a* problem, that the client knows what it is, and that the client can describe it. By asking the question with a "what," we will more than likely receive a noun as an answer. The possible answers will all be members of the class, "problem." The direction will be toward descriptions of problems, toward failures or frustrations. Perhaps, on a more intuitive level in the therapy context, we are also implying that problems are important to therapy.

A more extreme example of the significance of presuppositions is the question, "Are you still beating your wife?" By answering the question, the respondent, even with just a simple "yes" or "no," acknowledges the presupposition that he at some time beat his wife. If he never did beat his wife, it is impossible to answer the question.

With the knowledge of the significance of presuppositions, we tried for a while to create the perfect initial question which would contain all the solution-focused and future-oriented presuppositions that we wanted. We tried, "What is your goal in coming here?" This question assumed that people had a goal, that we thought goals were important, and that clients could articulate them. Also, the question set the conversation in a positive direction. This question fit for some people but not for others. For those who seemed very bothered by their problems or felt the need to describe for us why they were coming in, the question seemed too abrupt.

We tried, "What brings you in?" This question seemed vague and allowed for someone to specify a complaint or a goal. The question had a somewhat passive quality to it, as if something had dragged the client to the session. The other disadvantage was that clients tended to reply with complaints when we would rather be talking about solutions.

Another question was, "What do you want?" This question also set a positive direction. The question assumed that the client wanted something, could specify it, and could articulate it. It also intimated that what the client wanted was important and focal. However, we hoped we could find a more process-oriented question.

We tried, "How would you like to be acting, when therapy is over?" This seemed to contain most of our assumptions but was too cumbersome.

"How will you know when you do not have to come here anymore?" was very focused and oriented toward a brief therapy. However, it also seemed cumbersome and premature for some clients.

With varied success with each of the questions, we decided that no one question could be perfect or optimal with everyone. We concluded that the *interaction* was primary, rather than just one question. So, if a very positive question was not the right start for one client who wanted very strongly to talk about the problem first, we could do that and then ask more positive and future-oriented questions as we went along. If a client accepted our positively oriented questions right off, so much the better.

We were reminded of our rule of thumb that "There is no failure, only feedback." We gave up the search for the perfect question. We now ask, "What is your goal in coming here?" and trust that if the question is too abrupt or not a fit, we will adjust the conversation with succeeding comments and questions. On the other hand, if this positively oriented and goal-oriented question avoids discussion of complaints and problems, so much the better.

DISCUSSION

QUESTION:
These ideas about carefully designed questions and "yes sets" seem a bit manipulative and underhanded. Do you not think so?

The notions of manipulation and underhandedness seem to imply that one is attempting to do something *to* someone else with some unstated agenda of one's own. Of course, our agenda is to help our clients reach what they want—their goal or their solution. If it becomes apparent to us that the client wants something we do not do or cannot provide, then we say so and sometimes end the therapy. If someone asks for intensive, psychoanalytic psychotherapy or states that he or she just wants someone to talk to, we might state that we do not do that and see if we can agree on another acceptable goal.

We also make it very clear that our interest is in helping clients get what they want. We are not interested in tricking people, nor do we feel that "the end justifies the means." Ours is a consumer-oriented model. Rather than making some diagnostic assessment of what is wrong with the client or the family, we work with them on what they want and only on what they want. We are very upfront and direct about what we are about, which is helping people construct solutions in as short a time as possible.

The notion of manipulation also implies that somehow someone exerts some control over someone else. On a philosophical level, we subscribe to Maturana and Varela's concept of structured determinism (1987)—that people do what they do and that we, in communication, at most provide the opportunity for their doing what they do. To use a mechanical example, when we turn the key on our car, we do not make the car start. By turning the key, we merely provide the means for the car to do what it does. The car usually starts; on the other hand, we all know from experience that it may not.

So, too, with our interactions with our clients. Although, in our grandiosity, we may occasionally think we changed our clients, the most we do is provide the opportunity and context for them to do what they may do or choose to do in that context.

Because we believe that people change by focusing on what works and on the future, we communicate with them in that way.

Perhaps this notion of manipulation has been perpetuated by the counterbelief that, somehow, we as therapists should be totally neutral and that we can be totally neutral and objective.

Psychoanalysis has attempted to perfect this notion of neutrality and objectivity by removing the analyst's influences upon the free association process. By remaining out of view of the patient and providing only minimal comments, the analyst hopes to receive pure and uncontaminated information.

However, we subscribe to the communication theory assumption that in interaction one cannot not communicate (Watzlawick, Beavin, & Jackson, 1967). We are always communicating and interacting. If we are upfront about what we are doing, we should use the tools of our profession—language and communication—in the ways that are most likely to help our clients attain what they want.

QUESTION:
You mentioned the "yes set" of hypnosis. Do you use trance?

No and yes. In the sense that we do not use formal inductions or formal trances, we do not use trance. In the sense that we believe that all conversation is trance-like, we believe that we do use trance. We do not use formal inductions, but we do believe that as we pace the conversation and ask questions that require the client to search inside their experience and memory or to create some new experience for themselves, the client is in trance.

More to the point, we are not sure that the distinction between trance and something else is useful in this domain. If we were to use the distinction of trance and non-trance, we would then have to develop criteria for when to use trance and when not to. We do not think that the distinction or the developing of criteria is useful. It appears to only complicate matters and introduce a distinction that is not necessary.

EXERCISES

1. *Maintaining rapport.* In order to sharpen and enhance your reflecting and rapport-maintaining skills, find someone who will practice with you. Have one of you be the storyteller, the other the designated listener. As one listens and reflects back for the storyteller, the

teller should use a graduated thumbs up to indicate when they experience themselves as more understood. This is not an exercise in success or failure, only in what works better with this person. The thumb is to be used only from a position of nine o'clock to 12 o'clock, not a thumbs down. In other words, it only indicates what is working or what is working better. The exercise is to facilitate a positive focus on what works and to experiment with different forms of feedback to see what might work even better.

As the listener, listen carefully for the client's language and reflect that, even if it is not your own natural language. If the client talks in abstractions and you are used to talking in terms of affect, try abstract talk.

2. Solution talk versus problem talk. Again with a partner, for five minutes try to engage in problem talk. Notice the questions you ask and your feelings as you listen to your partner's responses about problems. Ask your partner to take note of his or her affective response.

For the next five minutes, concentrate only on solution talk or times when the problem does not happen. Take note of any differences for you in terms of the questions you ask as well as in your own affective response. Ask your partner to take note of his or her affective response and any other differences.

Compare the differences, both for you and your partner, between the problem talk and the solution talk. Some of you may experience a lightness and optimism as you talk about the more positive times as opposed to a heaviness with problem talk. On the other hand, you may feel sadder or more discouraged as you talk about solutions as you are more reminded of the difficulty.

For the listener, take note of the questions you ask. Write them down and later examine the presuppositions you are using.

3. Just one session. With a partner, pretend as the therapist that this is the only session you will have with this client. Take note of any differences in your approach.

4. First questions. Experiment with different questions enumerated in this chapter for starting the first session and notice what response you receive.

4

Well-Defined Goals

■ Therapy is a goal or solution-focused endeavor with the client as expert.

This chapter is designed to help you understand and develop skills in forming well-defined goals.

MOVIEMAKING

We like to think that the therapy process is similar to creating a movie. We are assisting clients as the directors of their own solution movies. The clients simultaneously are both directors and the principal actresses or actors.

In chapter two, we mentioned an example of the East German bob-sledders and how they rehearsed their run down the hill. Metaphorically, we want to take our clients through that type of process. We want to assist them in simulating the making of movies of themselves in the process of solving their problems, movies that are complete with soundtrack and internal dialogue. We want these movies to be of their creation that they can step into in order to experience themselves solving the problem or doing what they want in a positive sense.

In the succeeding chapters, you will find out how clients frequently tend to start describing their solutions in the subjunctive mood or the future tense. For example, they may say subjunctively, "If I were parenting the way I want to, I *would be following through* on what I have said." Or, they may say in the future tense, "When I will be parenting the way I want to, I *will be following through* on what I am saying." Within these two forms of speech, you can assume that clients are creating representations of themselves solving the problem. When their

51

sentence mood changes from subjunctive to indicative and/or from future to present tense, you can guess the clients are likely to be stepping into their movies and rehearsing their solutions, or are reciting present experiences of solving the problem. An example is, "When I am following through, *I am speaking calmly and telling* the children the consequences of their behavior." This movement from future tense and subjunctive mood to present tense is optimal. The movement to present tense comes about in conversation as we move from talking about some hypothetical solution to times in the present when clients are performing their goal somewhat already.

We use the words goal and solution in a unique way. Many of us commonly interchange these words with words such as end result, objective, or outcome. Our use of the words goal and solution connotes processes and movielike, not static things or finished results. An end result for our bobsledders would be a still picture of them as they cross the finish line or receive their medals. A process is more like movies of their going through the entire run. Perhaps, if it were not grammatically clumsy, we should use words such as "goaling" or "solving" to enhance the process connotation.

Keeping this movie metaphor in mind will help to facilitate your using the tools of this and the following chapters.

THE CRITERIA FOR WELL-DEFINED GOALS

A solution-focused brief therapy is a consumer approach. We endeavor to help clients get what they want. Other models built on normative models of mental health or of a well-functioning family or marriage take an expert position and state what the goals should be. On the other hand, a solution-focused approach focuses exclusively on what the client states she or he wants to be doing.

Given that we focus on what the client wants rather than on what we think the client *should* want, client goals are critical. We have found not only that the notion of a goal is critical but that applying certain criteria in developing goals is also critical.

The criteria for a well-defined goal are as follows:

1. In a Positive Representation

By this, we do not mean good or bad, moral or immoral, healthy or unhealthy. We do mean that the goal needs to be stated in a linguistically positive form, that is, in terms of what the client *will* be doing or thinking, rather than what they will *not* be doing or thinking. The reason for stating the goal in a linguistically positive way is that we want the client to be developing a representation of the goal in her or his mind and experience. This can be a visual representation, it can be words or sounds, it can be feelings or sensations. The representation will likely include some or all of these sensory modalities. The critical piece is that the representing has to *be* something rather than the absence of something.

We want a positive representation because to form a representation of something that is stated in the negative is impossible. Think about the previous statement for a moment. If we were to ask you in the next few seconds not to think of a piece of cake, you would more than likely picture a piece of cake in your mind and begin salivating. You might then do something to that picture such as try to make it disappear or cross an X over it in order to "not think of a piece of cake." However, you will picture it before you do anything else.

In exactly the same way, should clients state that their goal is to not be depressed anymore, it would be impossible for them to make that representation. They will more than likely recall feeling depressed first, and then tell themselves that the feeling should not be felt or that the feeling is not necessary. Clients might also picture themselves being or acting depressed or repeating depressing comments to themselves. In fact, the more clients try to make themselves not depressed, the more likely they are to think about depression and, as a result, feel more depressed.

One of the major inadvertent drawbacks to problem-focused approaches is inherent self-reinforced affirmation of the problem. The clients are very often talking about the problem and making representations of the problem. The more the clients talk about the problem, the more they renew the same feelings and create further images of the problem.

This reinforcement of the problem is not what we want our clients to be doing. We do not want them to have to think about the problem first every time they want to think about achieving their goal. However, if clients begin to develop a representation of what they want to be doing, the representation can be very compelling in itself and act as a movie for where they want to go.

Returning to our story of the bobsledders, you will notice the considerable advantage for these athletes to have formed a representation of themselves successfully maneuvering the difficult course. They not only formed a representation of their goal but also became part of a positive representation of the goal and made the representation a rehearsal for the actual event.

When your client outlines a *negative* representation, the key word for you to use in evoking a *positive* representation is "*instead.*" For example, if the client says, "I do not want to withdraw from my husband," your question to use is, "So what do you want to be doing *instead?*" This juxtaposition will evoke some description of what they *will* be doing or thinking differently in a positive form.

2. In a Process Form

By this, we mean that the goal should be stated as if the description were movielike, a process, rather than a still picture. Nouns used as goals are static. Nouns represent still pictures; while better than a negative statement, stills are not nearly as compelling or effective as movies with sound tracks.

One good way to know that your clients are describing goals in a process way is when they use verbs with "-ing." This ending indicates that they are sequencing actions, thoughts, or representations. The processing can be in the future tense or present tense.

For example, the client might say, "I *will be listening* to what my child has to say before I tell him what I want him to do." The client might describe the exchange more conditionally by saying, "If I were handling this the way I want to, I *would be listening* to what my child has to say before I told him what I want him to do." The client might also state the goal in the present tense as, "When I handle the relationship now the way I like to, I *am listening* to my child first, before I tell him what I want him to do." All of these examples are process descriptions with "-ing" verb endings and suitable for defining the goal.

The word for you to use to evoke a process description is "how." The client will more than likely give you either "-ing" descriptions or a sequence of actions. "What" questions usually evoke nouns and are not useful for process descriptions.

3. In the Here and Now

Process in the here and now means that the client can start the solution *immediately* or continue with solution actions. Many clients talk about what they want as if the goal were some object in the far future. For example, a client might say, "I want to make a decision whether to stay married or get a divorce." The problem with this definition of behavior as a goal is that the goal is usually too far into the future, and too removed to feel any control over. The way the goal is stated as a "decision" takes the form of a noun, a static object, something removed from them. It is usually thought of as an event that is usually far into the future.

We want to define the goal in a process way as something they can be on track with, immediately. So we would ask, "So if you were *on track* to making a decision now, what would you be doing or doing differently?" Another way of saying this is, "As you leave this session and you are on a track to solving this, what will you be doing differently, or saying to yourself differently?" ". . . saying to yourself differently," may invoke a different meaning. These questions bring the goal into a process form and can be substantially more immediate. The client might respond with, "I would be bringing up the topic of separation with my wife and talking with her about separation rather than avoiding the topic."

As therapists, we do not think necessarily that we have to continue to see this client until she or he makes whatever decision that will eventually be made. We basically need to help the client more into the process and feel inherently convinced that she or he is on track to making a decision.

The problem with goals so far out in the future is that they are far away. Experientially, they can seem to be remote and, therefore, less under the client's control. By bringing the goal into a process form right into the present, the client becomes more focused on things she or he can do right *now* or perhaps may be doing already.

In addition to those clients who want a completed action such as a decision, there are clients who state what they want as a difference of condition. For example, a client may state that she or he wants to be 50 pounds lighter. This is stated as a static state, that is also too far into the future. If such a weight loss were stated as the goal, we would want to bring the solution process right into the here and now. We would ask, "So if as you leave the office here today, you were on track to becoming lighter, what would you be doing differently?" This question brings the distant object of a 50-pound weight change into a process form in the here and now.

An answer such as, "I would be eating differently and going through my day differently, not so hectically," would be a good start. The person is describing eat*ing* differently and go*ing* through the day differently. These are process words and have more potential for being done right now.

4. As Specific as Possible

The more specific a description, the more compelling the description is for the client. The art of the therapist comes into play here as you use all your skills to help clients develop even more specifics about what they will be doing or thinking. What we mean by "doing and thinking" is the definition by clients of concrete behavior and what they would be saying to themselves or to other people. What clients say they will be saying to themselves provides the meaning or new meaning they will be using to describe the situation.

Keep in mind that if some clients do not immediately come up with specifics, they are not being resistant. If you consider for a moment that clients have probably been overfocused on the problem and on what they do not want, they probably have never thought, or only rarely thought, of what they *do* want. So clients may need some coaching and patience on your part in focusing on the positive—what they do want and, specifically, how they might be doing what they want or will be doing what they want.

The chief way to evoke specific answers is to be direct. For example, "Can you tell me more *specifically* how you will be listening more to your child? What will you be doing differently? What will your child notice specifically that will tell her (or him) that you are listening as opposed to not listening?"

5. Within the Client's Control (Meaning That the Action Can Be Started and/or Maintained by the Client)

This criterion is critical and should probably be starred. Many of our clients come in with complaints about how they want *someone else* to be different or how they want something to be different that they can do nothing about. If we engage with clients about goals of changing someone else or having someone else change, we will be participating in an endless and fruitless effort.

We want to help clients identify a goal that *they can start and maintain by themselves* even now in our office. The goal cannot be contingent on something or someone else changing or changing first. We may be able to help clients bring about some change in relationships with others even without the other person being in therapy, but we cannot join in the notion that someone else has to change first.

Clients who state their goal in terms of a change of condition not within their control or state their goals in terms of someone else changing first may be working under the assumption that these changes have to happen *first* in order for something else to happen that they want. The clients may view this type of change (something out of their control or a change in someone else) as a means or condition for something else that they ultimately want to happen. For example, in a cocaine case, a woman thought she had to first rid herself of the taste for cocaine in order to stop using it. She thought that she had to dislike the cocaine in order to stop using it. Ridding herself of the taste, however, was not within her control.

Clients often think that in order for "B" to happen, "A" has to happen first. Acting in accord with this assumption, they persist in trying to make "A" happen so that they can have "B." However, if "A" is out of their control, they end up very frustrated.

For example, a man may believe that he needs to have more self-confidence in order to act more directly in asking someone else for a date. As he tries to make himself feel more confident as a first step or to remind himself that he has to be more confident, he, of course, is even more aware of the times when he does not feel confident. As he puts off talking with women until he feels more confident, he feels worse about his lack of confidence. He believes that "A"—more self-confidence—has to happen first before he can do anything toward what he wants, that is "B"—talking to women and getting a date. The problem is that trying to make himself feel more self-confident is out of his direct control. Ironically, the more he focuses on his lack of confidence as a condition for action, the less confident he feels and the less likely he is to ask someone out for a date.

Another example is a husband who thinks that a change by his wife is a condition for their having more intimacy. He thinks she should want to be spending more time together. He, therefore, tries to convince her that her desire for space is unrealistic and not loving. He tries to convince her that she should want to be together with him more because that is what married couples do who love each other. Ironically, the more he tries to convince her that she should want to be together, the less she feels like being with him. He continues to try to change his wife, a goal that is not within his control. He continues to focus on the means (the change in his wife's attitude) rather than on the end, intimacy with his wife.

As clients persist in attempted solutions that fail, they continue to see ultimate goals (or ends of the means) as being further out of reach. When clients state a goal that is out of their control as a means to something they want, we help them reverse the assumption about the means to the end. Where clients think that "A" leads to "B," or "A" has to happen first, we often suggest the opposite assumption, that "B" can lead to "A." Very often, "B" involves some action or change of thinking on their part which is within their control.

Reversing the assumption and having the man mentioned above act as if he were confident or the husband act as if he were already more intimate provides each with options that are within his personal control.

As the man *pretends* to be confident, he takes actions that yield some of what he wants. He may approach a woman and engage in conversation. He may not get the date he is looking for and the conversation may not be all he wants, but he does have some experience for feedback about his next course of action. As he continues to take actions and to adjust his actions as needed, his self-confidence will more than likely change and/or he may discover that self-confidence is not so crucial as a means to talking with women.

As the husband focuses on the occasions when he now has close times with his wife and on what he does at those times, he notices that he is more relaxed and not so pushy with his wife. She perceives him as being more relaxed and tends to be more welcoming. With success at focusing on what he is enjoying with her and on having intimate times, he can give up his belief that she has to change first.

6. In the Client's Language

This criterion is a check on us, as therapists. We want to be sure that we are working toward a goal that the client wants, not what we want or what we think the client should want. Many of us have received training about what is good or normal or healthy. We find it easy to slip into thinking that a client has a variety of problems that the client is not talking about or is denying. So we start thinking about all the things that the client *should* be working on.

Many of us have been trained to "read between the lines" of what people are saying and to interpret what they *really* want, even if they do not consciously know it yet. Many of us have made interpretations like, "This child's failing in school is really a cry for help about his family" or "This boy's refusal to go to school is really a request for limits." By making these assumptions or interpretations, we can easily attempt to define goals *for* clients rather than focusing on what clients say they want.

If children you think are crying for help by failing in school do not want help with school, do not try to convince them that they *should* want help in school. Ask them what they are coming in to see you about and write it down in their words.

When we find that sessions do not seem to be progressing, we usually discover that we are off track on the goal. Sometimes, we consult with each other. When we consult, our first question to the other is, "What does the client want?" Sometimes, the answer may be, "Well I think the client wants better communication skills." The consultant of the two of us will ask again, "Is that what the *client* says he/she wants?" We usually discover then that we have assumed what the client wants or made the decision ourselves about what the client should want rather than making sure we have the client's explicit statement. We have been pursuing action on some goal that the client has not defined as his or her want.

To make sure that you know what the goal is, write down in the client's words *what they say they want*. It is not unusual for the final form of what clients say they want, to be quite different from their initial statement. Through conversation about and clarification of the goal in terms of criteria of a well-defined goal, the form of the goal may well change. Clients may realize through defining processes that they cannot change another person or may discover that the goal may be something other than what they initially stated. Just make sure that in the final form, the goal is what *they say they want and in their words.*

THE CRITERIA FOR A WELL-DEFINED GOAL WORKSHEET

Below is a checklist for a well-defined goal. This is a useful tool for making sure the goal is continuing to be developed. Each statement of the client can be compared with the criteria. The key words will give you some hint about whether the statement meets the criteria or give you a shorthand clue of what to do. If the statement is not yet well-defined, use one of the questions provided on the right to help your client develop his or her "movie" according to that criterion.

CRITERIA	KEY WORDS	SAMPLE QUESTIONS
1. In the positive	"Instead"	"What will you be doing instead?"
2. In a process form	"How" "-ing"	"How will you be doing this?"
3. In the here-and-now	"On track"	"As you leave here today, and you are on track, what will you be doing differently or saying differently to yourself?"
4. As specific as possible	"Specifically"	"How specifically will you be doing this?"
5. In the client's control	"You"	What will you be doing when that happens?"
6. In the client's language	Use the client's words	

Figure 2. Criteria for Well-Defined Goal Worksheet

DISCUSSION

QUESTION:
What is the difference between goals and solutions?

We think of solutions as a type of goal, or solving as a type of "goaling." In other words, the endeavor between therapist and client is goal-oriented. Within this larger frame, clients and therapists may sometimes frame the goal of the therapy as the construction of and solving of some problem. For other clients, who focus immediately upon what they want, the goal may never be mentioned in the context of problem or solution.

Within this model, we do not believe that problem information is needed in order to be helpful. A better title for this approach would be goal- or outcome-oriented therapy. However, most of our clients and most of us are working in situations where clients perceive the goal and function of therapy as solving problems.

The important thing to remember is that goals and solutions are processes. Even though the words, goal and solution, are nouns and it is easy for us to think that goals are some static thing or end result, we want to emphasize again and again that goals and solutions are movie-like, not finished results.

QUESTION:
What about issues the client has not mentioned but we know are a problem? What about deeper or unresolved issues?

Except for problems that are bound by law and ethics, such as abuse or the risk of danger to self or to others, we respect clients' ability and responsibility to focus on what is a goal or problem for them. We trust that if a change is necessary for someone to obtain what they want the problem will come up on its own or be solved on its own. For example, if parents come in about their child's school behavior, we trust that any marital problems that may exist will surface as we focus on how the parents are going to solve the school problem. We do not have to confront the parents head-on or label their difficulties as a marital problem. We trust that if the parents are going to solve their child's school behavior together they will have to work out their differences either directly or indirectly. We also trust our assumption that small change leads to larger change and, therefore, the marital problem might solve itself.

We also do not make the distinction between surface and deeper issues. We take each problem, solution, or goal *at face value* with no one change dependent on another and no one problem as a sign of others.

EXERCISES

1. Pick a difficulty that you are struggling with now. Ask yourself, "What do I want to be doing instead?" After you have begun that process, go through the checklist for a well-defined goal, one by one. Watch and listen for how your personal movie changes. If your solution does not meet the criteria, adjust your solution so that it does.

2. With a partner playing a client, ask him or her to tell you the goal in coming to see you. Keep the exercise framed in terms of goals rather than problems in order to make it easier to use the six criteria. Write down your partner's responses and compare the goal statements with the criteria. Practice using "instead," "how" questions, and "specifically" to focus the goal.

3. Go through your present case records and identify the *client's stated goal*. Go through the worksheet for well-defined goals. Does the client's stated goal match the criteria? If not, ask yourself what questions you may need to ask in the next session. Make sure the goal is the client's and not yours for the client.

5

Pathways of Constructing Solutions

■ Meaning and experience are interactionally constructed.

This chapter overviews the map of pathways of constructing solutions. After introducing the paths in this chapter, succeeding chapters will describe the paths in more detail.

POSITIVE PATHS: POSITIVE CONVERSATION

The conversation between therapist and client based on constructing solutions, can be described as taking many different paths. Just as getting from Chicago to New York can be mapped many ways, so too with mapping the varied processes of constructing solutions. No one way is better or right under all circumstances. No one way gets you there all the time in the way you want. There are an infinite number of ways and conversations.

Figure 3 is a map of possible pathways to move along through a possible conversation. It can guide your thinking and actions in the process of developing goals/solutions. (This map is a development from the "Central Map" created by de Shazer, 1988.)

This map is a simplified guide to the conversation in our therapy sessions. It visually actualizes four assumptions:

1. Focusing on the positive, the solution, and the future facilitates change in the desired direction. Therefore, focus on solution-oriented talk rather than on problem-oriented talk.

63

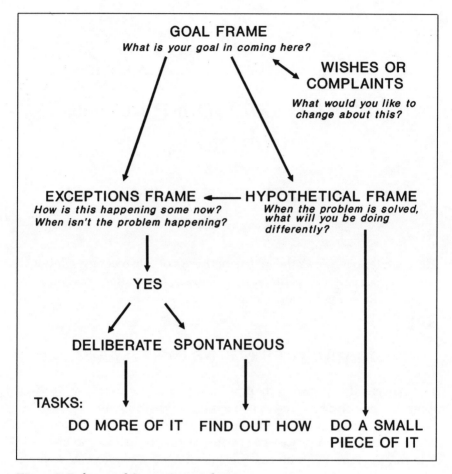

Figure 3. Pathways of Constructing Solutions

2. Exceptions to *every* problem can be created by therapist and client, which can be used to build solutions.
3. Change is happening all the time.
4. Meaning and experience are interactionally constructed.

The map suggests focusing on the positive by: first, identifying what the client wants (the goal); then focusing either on how that is happening now (exception times when the goal is happening already) or how the problem is not happening (exceptions to the problem times); or how the goal/solution will look in the future (hypothetical solution). The map (and the assumptions built into it) assume that change is happening all the time and that new meaning and experience of change are constructed through the therapeutic conversation. The paths merely suggest different ways for new meaning and experience to evolve from the interaction of therapist and client(s).

With this quick overview of the map, let us now walk through it in greater detail.

WISHES AND COMPLAINTS, OR GOALS AND PROBLEMS

We begin an initial session with the question, "What is your goal in coming here?" Clients often state what they want in a way that implies that some action can be taken by them. However, they sometimes begin by saying something in the form of a complaint or a wish, rather than a goal or problem.

These distinctions are useful at the beginning of therapy. Wishes are some affective statement by the client of how she or he would like things to be. These wishes may be cravings or desires, but are not goals. Complaints are the opposite side of the same coin. Complaints are statements of how the client is unhappy with the way things are. Complaints are usually statements of discontent, grief, pain, or resentment. The statements, wishes, or complaints do not include implications of solutions or that anything can be done. They are usually statements of affect about some situation.

Clients may also report a diagnosis either of their own making or by a professional. Diagnoses are not goals or problems. Diagnoses tend to be labels that describe a state or condition. As such, the diagnoses do not imply any action or solution.

A diagnosis also confuses logical levels. A diagnosis can confuse the person with the problem implied in the label of the diagnosis and states the situation as if the person and the problem were the same. White and Epston (1990) have written about the disempowering aspects of confusing the person with labels of the problem. In their model, they use a procedure called "externalizing the problem" to achieve the separation of levels. We also want to separate the person from the problem, but more importantly we want to focus on the goal or solution as separate from the person.

As we previously stated in our assumptions in Chapter Two, we would not assume that a person *is* anything, or that the person acts in certain ways *all* the time.

So when clients come in and make a self-diagnosis or state that they are unhappy, or the children are unruly, or they wish the children were happier, or they were more confident, or the spouse were nicer, we begin to wonder, "What can *we* as therapists do about it?" Since wishes and complaints are only affective statements, we can do very little. If we accept such statements as goals, we will engage in an endless pursuit of trying to change clients' feelings about their situations.

What we aim to do is help clients change their expressions of unhappiness into statements of goals. With wishes or complaints translated into goals, clients can formulate indications for activities or solutions.

For example, a client comes in and in response to the question, "What is your goal in coming here?" describes how depressed she feels and how she has always had very low self-esteem. She proceeds to tell us a long history of broken relationships with men and how she has just been let go from her job. She states she is feeling very low and wonders whether she will ever have a successful relationship or be happy. As the client is telling us this, a question forms in our mind: "This is all very sad, but how can we help her with all this or what does she want out of coming to therapy?"

This question coming to our mind is our clue that we and the client are still on the wish or complaint level, and that we need to "Do something different." The following questions can be useful in moving from wishes or complaints toward a statement of a goal or problem:

1. Possible question: "I am very sorry to hear how things are going. Can you tell me what about this you would like to change or in what ways you would like to be handling things differently?" This question supports the client's feelings and asks a goal-oriented question in which she or he is invited to state the goal in terms of changing or an action response.

   For example, the previously mentioned client might say, "Well, I want to work out some ways in which I can make my relationship work, so I do not continue to be rejected." This statement is closer to a goal about which she can do something.

2. Another possible question: "I am sorry to hear how badly things have been going. Can you tell me what about this I can help you

with?" This question invites a statement of something more specific and in terms of how you, as therapist, can be instrumental.
3. Still another question: "I am very sorry to hear how badly things have been going. Can you tell me again what you would like as a result of coming here?" This question sympathizes with what the client has said and further restates our goal-oriented question.
4. Another possibility: "This may sound like a strange question given all that is going on, but how is this a problem for you?" This question does not have the advantage of orienting a client to a positive statement, but sometimes the question can be useful in obtaining a problem statement as a pace for someone who is presenting his/ her situation negatively. Even a problem statement implies something can be done.

If the client were to say, "I do not want to be doing things that cause me to be rejected," the statement implies that there may be things in the opposite direction of action. She or he may be able to do things to get more acceptance. We would then ask, "So, what will you be doing instead?"

Moving from a wish or a complaint to a goal is a move from merely an expression of affect towards some definition that implies possible action can be taken. Once the client is stating something on the goal or the problem/solution level, we are in a position to use the conversational frames and pathways towards solution constructing as outlined in Figure 3.

CONVERSATIONAL FRAMES

Three tools that we use in conversation with clients are the frames of goal, exceptions, and hypothetical solution. We use these as co-constructive frames, invitations for both the client and therapist to enter. The frames are not just constructive or perceptual frames for us as interviewers to help us filter information. By asking questions of the client in the form of these frames, we invite the client to construct a story, or "reality," within these areas that make up the frame. When the client responds within these frames, both the therapist and client are co-constructing new stories of their experience. Both therapist and client are engaged within the frames.

We use the words goal frame, exceptions frame, and hypothetical solution frame on two different levels. We use them on the perceptual level to describe how we filter what we see and listen to from the client, as well as how the client filters what she or he sees and hears. On the interactional level, we use these frames to describe the mutual framework that everyone is involved in as we converse. They become the frame of the conversation.

White and Epston (1990) have written about how the narrative metaphor is a useful analogy for therapy. They propose that people make a story of their experience; problems arise when the story does not fit their lived experience. They further propose that the goal of therapy is the co-authoring of new stories that allow for experience that is helpful, satisfying, and more open-ended.

We find this metaphor of "storying" useful; our metaphor of moviemaking is consistent with "storying." We use the frames of goal, exceptions, and hypothetical solutions to enhance the process of generating new stories or movies.

We use these frames for different purposes. The "goal" frame is used to invite the client into conversation about what the client wants to be doing and what will be the task of therapy. This frame is used in variations on this question: "What is your goal in coming here?"

The "exceptions" frame is an invitation to converse about the time when the goal or solution may be happening already or when the problem does not happen. This frame is used in variations of either of the following two questions: "How is your goal happening somewhat now?" and "When doesn't the problem happen?"

The "hypothetical solution" frame is an invitation to brainstorm and pretend the goal is happening or the problem is solved. It is used in variations of this question: "When you are doing what you want (or when the problem is solved), what will you be doing differently?"

All three frames are intertwined in the paths to goal development or solution construction.

A MAP OF SOLUTION-CONSTRUCTING PATHS

We want to know *what the client(s) wants to be doing* in a well-defined way—and the "logic" of the map (Figure 3) helps both the therapist and client construct the goal in a well-defined way. We help the client construct her or his goal by focusing the conversation on *how they are doing their goal now* (exceptions of either when the goal is happening already or the problem is not happening) or *how they will be doing it in the future* (hypothetical solution).

This map of pathways to constructing solutions is used concurrently with the checklist for a well-defined goal to guide the conversation around to the development of new meaning and goals or solutions. As the therapist, we are following the paths of the map and we compare each statement made by the client with the checklist for a well-defined goal in order to enhance and sharpen the goal development.

A solution-focused approach boils down to the interweaving of these three frames and their accompanying questions. Most of the questions we ask the clients are variations of these three questions. They are used in an open-ended manner in the sense that we make no predetermination what the answer should be. The expert is the client and the solution or goal is his/hers to construct.

In sum, our first question to the client is, "What is your goal in coming here?" To this question, the client usually gives us a goal statement. However, sometimes clients give us a complaint or wish and we need to help them redefine their statement into a goal. If the client responds with a wish or complaint, we use one of the four questions from the previous section in order to help the client move to the goal level. We might ask, "So, tell me what about this you would like to change," or, "Tell me how I can help you with this." We pursue this until we have a statement on the goal/problem level.

We are then ready to pursue paths of constructing solutions. The paths we outline below are only suggested ways to think about goals and conversation. We do not want to suggest that these are the only paths or that the paths embody a structure that must be followed. We believe that each therapist is different and each client is unique. Each conversation between therapist and client, as well as each path of constructing solutions, is unique and open-ended. There is no set way.

Path I: Goal Statement and Exceptions

When clients respond to the question, "What is your goal in coming here?" with a statement of their goal—or when we have helped clients redefine their complaint or wish into a goal—the map suggests that we adopt either the exceptions path or the hypothetical solution path. The exceptions path orients clients around times when the goal may already be happening, even though not to the full extent or in the exact way they may want.

As the client states her or his goal, we check with our criteria for a well-defined goal to determine if the statement is linguistically positive—that is, what the client wants rather than what the client does not want.

When we take the exceptions route, we need to keep in mind the other criteria and invite more statements from the client that are specific and process-oriented in the here and now. For example, if a client stated that she or he would like to be *acting more securely or confidently in a love relationship*, we would follow up this statement with questions such as: "Tell me about the times when you act a little that way now" (Request for exceptions, times when the goal is already happening) or "How are you specifically doing that, when you are acting a little more securely?" (A specific and process-oriented question).

Assuming that clients identify times when they are doing some of what they want (exception times when the goal is already happening), the next fork in the map is centered around the distinction of control (the fifth criteria of a well-defined goal). Distinguishing according to control is based on the client's frame of reference. We assume that if clients are already doing what they want to be doing, they are doing it within their sphere of control. However, they may perceive their actions as totally spontaneous and seemingly out of their control.

Clients may perceive that being able to *act* more securely in a love relationship is dependent on their mood or possibly on the actions of the other first. Another possibility is their not knowing how to explain their performance within the exception times.

If clients perceive their actions to be within their control or as deliberate actions, we would then pursue how they will continue to do these things. If they perceive their performing of the goal as spontaneous or out of their control, we as therapists would facilitate their making what seems to them out of their control as in their control and repeatable.

You may have noticed that this stated goal of *"acting* more securely" comes close to being stated in a wish form. If the client had stated that she or he wanted to *"be* more secure," this statement would be only a wish for a feeling. If *"being* more secure" were the initial statement by the client, we would have to use questions to get the statement in a goal form that implies some action can be taken, such as, "What about this can I help you with?" or "If you were feeling that way, what would you be doing differently?"

Path II: Goal Statement and Hypothetical Solution

If the client maintains that there are no occasions when the goal is already happening or if she or he has a difficult time stating a goal in a positive form, we use the hypothetical solution frame to find out more details about the goal. Should the client who wanted to be acting more securely maintain that there were no occasions when acting more securely happened even a little, we would ask about a hypothetical future when the goal will be happening; for example: "So, if a miracle happened and you were acting the way you want to, how would you be *acting* (client's word) differently?" (Goal orientation in the hypothetical) or "So, if, as you leave here today, you were on track to acting more securely, what will you be doing differently?" (Goal orientation in the hypothetical and in the here and now).

Once the client enters the hypothetical solution frame and answers the question, she or he usually comes up with details that enable a switch to exceptions and identification of times when she or he is accomplishing the goal somewhat, right now. For example, in response to the hypothetical solution question, the client might say that if he were acting more securely, he would be pursuing his own interests rather than waiting at the phone for his lover to call. This statement is more specific, and allows the therapist then to ask, "So tell me about those times when you get into your own thing even if you are tempted to wait by the phone." This brings the client into exception times when the goal is already happening. You then pursue the example with criteria for a well-defined goal.

Path III: Problem Statement and Exceptions

When the client presents a problem rather than a goal, we can help her or him move to a positive direction by asking an exception-oriented question: "When doesn't the problem happen?" This form of the question will orient the client into a search for positives. This question remains within the "problem frame" rather than the goal frame, but leads the client toward the other side of problem time and into the present when the problem is not happening.

We can pursue relatively the same "exceptions" path that was used with the client who began with a positive statement (Path I, Goal Statement and Exceptions), by inviting the client toward "exceptions to the problem." We pursue this path of the map without initially getting a goal statement. For example, suppose the same client came in and stated that the reason he was coming in was that he was acting too insecurely with his lover. He stated that he repeatedly pursued and nagged his lover with questions about whether she loved him or not. His initial statement is in the form of a problem. We can pursue the exceptions frame by asking, "When doesn't this happen?" We thus invite and pursue exception times but still remain within an "exceptions to the problem" frame. After finding some exception times, the client may be more able or ready to define what he *does* want as opposed to what he does not—how he *wants* to be *acting* rather than how he does not want to act. He may also be in a better position to adopt a more positive definition of the exceptions.

Initially, the same client may have been so overwrought that he could think and say only what he did not want, that is, to not be insecure. By our pursuing times when he acted not so insecure, we invite him to look at contexts or times of some success. If he thinks that signs of his acting insecurely are times when he pursues his girlfriend with questions of "Do you love me?" "How much do you love me?" and "What are you thinking of me?" we would invite him to look at times when he resists asking those questions or does something different. After identifying the exception times, he may be in a better position to talk about what he does want, a goal in a well-defined way. He may then be able to say that he wants to act "more self-dependently" rather than being dependent on his girlfriend's reactions. This latter frame of "acting dependent on himself" is in a positive form and the beginning of a more workable goal.

While pursuing this path, we still use our checklist for a well-defined goal. The difference from Path I (goal statement and exceptions) is that initially we stay within the "exceptions to the problem" frame, not in a goal frame, until clients seem to be in a better position to define what they want. Clients then are more in a position to create movies of themselves, and refine such movies in terms of what they *do* want to be doing. We still help the client describe exceptions more specifically, in a process form, and as close to now as possible. We also pursue the distinction of the map between deliberate and spontaneous exceptions, and then help the client describe what they want as within their control.

Path IV: Problem Statement and Hypothetical Solution

Sometimes, in beginning therapy with a client, switching to a hypothetical future with the problem solved is a more workable path. If a client seems to have difficulty stating what she or he wants or in finding exceptions, the "hypothetical solution frame" can be useful.

A hypothetical solution path can be useful with many clients, especially couples who arrive so angry or resentful that they have a difficult time identifying anything positive. A hypothetical solution path is also useful for clients who are overfocused on the problem or on their present attempted solution. For example, parents may be so focused on a child's misbehavior that they have lost track of what life will be like when the problem is solved or even of what they want. Another example are clients who are so focused on their means of losing weight that they have lost track of what they want out of losing the weight.

We invite them into the "hypothetical solution frame," life without the problem, with this typical question: "If a miracle happened tonight and you woke up tomorrow with the problem solved, or at least you thought you were on track to solving it, what would you be *doing* differently?" This is a variation of the "miracle question" of the Brief Family Therapy Center (de Shazer, 1988).

This new framing invites them to suspend their reality of the moment and enter a hypothetical reality of miraculous. When they enter a hypothetical reality, anything goes. Their "reality" framing of the problem does not have to apply and they can begin to define what they want or will be doing within a "miracle" frame.

A couple who come in stating that they always fight can be focused toward a miraculous future when the problem is solved. They may reply that they will be talking *with* each other as opposed to *at* each other. By suspending the frames and distinctions they apply to now and "reality," they can speak of what they want in a "nonreal" or "miraculous" future.

Clients who binge and purge in order to lose weight can focus on what they will be doing when at their desired weight. They may respond that they will be acting more assertively with people on the job or in social relationships.

Often, the hypothetical solution question brings out a more workable definition of a goal or solution than the problem "reality" the clients had been working under. The couple who had said they had always fought can now focus on talking "with" each other. Clients complaining about being overweight can now focus on what they ultimately want beyond controlling the weight—that is, acting more assertively.

The next step on the map is to guide clients to exceptional times in the present—that is, when the hypothetical solution happens now "a little bit." This step follows the arrow from the hypothetical on the right to exceptions on the left. This step brings the miraculous into the present, where it can be used to build on. With these new and more workable definitions of a goal, clients will have an easier time finding "exceptions."

The fighting couple would be asked to identify times when they talk *with* each other now *a little bit*. Within this frame of talking with each other rather than that of their problem, the couple is now more able to find positives and to identify what they do that works at those times.

If time does not permit your pursuing the hypothetical into exceptions, tasks can be constructed for the client for "Doing some small piece of the miraculous solution." This will be explained further in Chapter Six on the hypothetical solution frame.

The progression of the map from top to bottom involves the development of goals and solutions within the criteria for a well-defined goal. At the bottom of each path are suggestions for tasks that can be outlined at the end of the session. The map thus leads not only to goal and solution development, but also to actions that clients can do at the end of any session.

The next two chapters will discuss specifics on how to use the different paths.

DISCUSSION

QUESTION:
Is this map not imposing too much structure on the interaction?

This map of possible paths to take in conversation with clients is only a conceptual schema. Although we teach it rather strictly at first, we expect that each therapist will use it eventually within her or his own personal style. The map is never imposed at the risk of losing rapport. It is a map only of possible conversations and does not impose what the goal should be or what the client should do. The map and criteria for a well-defined goal make therapeutic conversation different from casual conversation or other types of conversation.

The criteria for a well-defined goal offer guidelines for solution construction without specifying the content. If you find yourself supplying the goal for clients or trying to force the conversation toward what you think they should want, you are off track. Go back to what they say they want.

EXERCISES

1. With a partner, ask the first question of a first session: "What is your goal in coming here?" Then, ask yourself if the response is a complaint or wish statement or if it is a goal statement. Do this several times, with your partner playing different clients. Practice identifying when you have a goal or problem statement, as opposed to a wish or complaint statement.

2. Go over the status of your present cases and ask yourself whether you have complaints and wishes or whether you have goals.

6

The Hypothetical
Solution Frame

■ Focusing on the positive, the solution, and the future, facilitates
change in the desired direction. Therefore, focus on solution-oriented
talk rather than on problem-oriented talk.

With the checklist for a well-defined goal and the map for solution construction in hand, we are now ready to look at the hypothetical solution
frame in more detail. The hypothetical solution frame is the easiest to
start with. By using this frame, you are more likely to evoke a linguistically positive statement; with a solution stated in the positive, you are
already constructing solutions.

The hypothetical solution frame is used under these circumstances:
when we seem to have difficulty with clients coming up with a positive
framing of their goal; when we seem to have difficulty with clients coming up with exceptions since they seem to be having difficulty viewing
their situation in any way other than the problem frame; or when we
want to check how the exceptions compare with how clients imagine
the solution to be.

As we mentioned briefly in the previous chapter, the advantage of
the hypothetical solution frame is that it enables clients to free themselves from the confines of how they have defined the problem. The
confines of the problem definition very often allow for only a limited
number of options for solutions.

For example, if clients define their problem as binge and uncon-
trolled eating, they usually define solutions in terms of trying to control
their desire for food and their eating. They sometimes say that they
cannot control their appetite and their desire for all the wrong foods.
They spend much of their time, therefore, worrying whether they will

stick with a food plan and stay away from sugars and other "bad" foods. The problem in the clients' view is defined as lack of control and their efforts are classed under attempts to control desires and appetite. If you were to ask for exceptions at this point, you would get exceptions about when clients are "in control" of the desires for food. These exceptions are not particularly useful because the clients are still within the unworkable problem frame. These are times when clients think they are able to control their desires and make themselves not think about something.

When we ask clients what they will be doing differently when the problem is solved, they often report that they will be thinking about other things in their life rather than worrying about their appetite and eating habits and will have a perspective on food in relation to the rest of their life. This frame of thinking of other things in life and thinking differently about food is much more open. It does not involve control of desires, that is, trying to *not* think of food. The frame allows clients to think in a more open way of the many different things they may think about instead of their worries about food. They can also consider in what ways that perspective might be different or useful.

Introducing a conversation around a life without the problem allows people to enter the realm of possibility. Their previous frame offered only a restricted view that was not working.

VARIATIONS OF THE HYPOTHETICAL SOLUTION FRAME

The hypothetical solution frame can be introduced in many different ways to match the client's worldview. The form articulated by the Brief Family Therapy Center in Milwaukee is the "miracle question," which goes as follows:

"Suppose that one night, while you were asleep, there was a miracle and this problem was solved. How would you know? What would be different? How will your husband know without your saying a word to him about it?" (de Shazer, 1988, p. 5)

This was an adaptation of Erickson's crystal ball technique (Erickson, 1954). The idea behind the technique was to have the client create a representation while in a trance of a future with the problem solved or without the problem. The idea was to have the client look backward from the future toward the present and identify how she/he reached a solution.

Using the hypothetical solution frame carries out the same idea, although no formal trance is needed.

The hypothetical solution frame can be introduced in various ways, depending on the worldview of the client. If the client is likely to accept the notion of miracles, then we use our variation of the original miracle question of Brief Family Therapy Center.

If a miracle happened tonight and you woke up with the problem solved, or you were reasonably confident you were on a track to solving it, what would you be *doing* differently?

This question invites the client to enter the frame of the problem as solved or on track to being solved. The "on track" frame allows for a more process-oriented answer. We also use the verb *doing* almost exclusively. As much as possible, we want clients to answer the question in terms of *actions* or of things they will be saying to themselves or to others, that is, *the meanings they will be making.*

This does not mean that we discount affect or feelings. We certainly support whatever feelings a client may be experiencing. For the sake of solution development, however, it is much easier to *act* your way to a feeling than to feel your way to a new action. It is easier to take an action and your feelings may change. If you wait for a feeling first, you may wait a long time. If you try to force a feeling, you may para-doxically produce the opposite of what you want. Anyone who has made an effort to feel relaxed or to feel happier when feeling down knows how counterproductive it is to try to force the feeling.

We elicit, whenever possible, statements that include some action, some behavior, some new framing, or something clients will say to themselves or to others.

Some clients answer the hypothetical solution question with a solution that will be an accomplished fact several months from now. Clients give us responses such as, "I will have decided whether or not to stay in my job" or "I will have a good self image." These responses are stated as accomplished facts and are not nearly as useful as process descriptions. So we ask the miracle question again, this time stressing the "on a track to solving the problem" part of the question. We ask the question in this way:

> So, let us say tomorrow you wake up, and you have not decided yet about your job, but you are thinking you are on track to making an eventual decision, what are you *doing* differently?

This will invite a response that is more here and now, more process-oriented, and broken down into smaller behaviors than a "decision."

If clients tell us that they will *feel* differently, we respond with an acknowledgment of the feeling and a restatement of the question. For example: "When you feel that way, what will you be *doing* differently?"

If clients still have difficulty speaking out of their own frame of reference, shift to someone else's. For example,

> If I were a fly on the wall and watching you, what would I see you doing differently? What would *I* see that would tell me that you are feeling differently? How would *someone* in your family *know*?

These questions include an acknowledgment of the clients' initial statement that they would be feeling differently. Without denying that, we accept that there will be a difference, and still ask for information in terms of actions or thoughts.

Other ways of introducing the hypothetical solution frame are as follows:

For little children, the notion of magic is useful, so the question would be introduced in terms of magic.

> If we had a magic wand and the problem went away, what would you be doing differently?

We might also use the notion of pretending.

> Lets pretend the problem is solved and you are having better luck with (getting along with the kids at school, getting better grades at school, getting to school on time . . .). What are you doing differently?

For the practical minded client for whom miracles or magic would not fit, we might introduce the question in a more down-to-earth way . . .

If this were the last session and you were walking out of here with the problem solved, or you were at least on track to solving it, what would you be doing differently?

For clients who come in blaming their last six therapists and saying there was no progress, we might start with this:

If coming here was useful, what would you be doing differently?

If such clients answer the question as asked, they will enter the frame of *their* doing something differently, rather than one where the therapist is different.

For clients who do not think they will be "doing" anything differently, we might ask . . .

What do you think you might be *saying to yourself or someone else* that is different?

This question will invite a change in meaning around the situation even if the behavior or actions are no different.

There are as many ways to introduce questions within the hypothetical solution frame as there are clients or therapists. The thrust behind the different introductions is to utilize the worldview of clients in order to make it easier for them to enter the hypothetical solution frame.

When you ask questions within the hypothetical solution frame, you will run into all kinds of responses that may initially seem to be roadblocks. Clients may say, "I will not be doing anything different. I will just be feeling different" or "It is not I who will be different, it is my husband who will be different." These are not signs of "resistance." The client is entering new territory and may be struggling. Expect to go slowly and patiently. The client's response is feedback to you and will tell you what to do next.

Usually, you need only to acknowledge the response and ask the question again, just as we discussed above with the "feeling different" response: "So, if you were feeling different, what would you be *doing* differently?"

If the client responds with a long pause and an "I don't know," accept the response at face value. The client probably has not thought about possible solutions before and probably does not *yet* know. Acknowledge the response, and ask the question again even when the question sounds totally illogical. "So, if you did know, what might you say?" The question on the surface makes little or no sense. When we first heard Insoo Berg use the question, we thought it was laughable. You will be amazed, however, that most of your clients will accept the question, sometimes with a smile, and then go on to answer it.

Some clients will respond with a statement that *they* will not be doing anything differently; their spouse will be different, or their children will be different. Acknowledge what they say and ask again.

So, when your husband is acting more the way you want him to, what will you be doing differently?

If they maintain they will not be doing anything differently, they probably believe from their frame of reference that they will just be themselves. Change the frame of reference and ask:

"What will your husband say you will be doing differently?"

In most cases, acknowledging what clients initially say and asking the question again or from someone else's point of reference will ultimately obtain a workable response. Clients want to comply with our requests. This is usually a new way of thinking for many clients and you need to be patient.

FOLLOW-UP QUESTIONS

The responses you receive to the hypothetical solution question need to be measured against the criteria for a well-defined goal. You will ask yourself whether what the client stated is linguistically positive, in a process form, in the here and now, as specific as possible, and in the client's control. All the questions you have already learned with regard to developing the goal according to the criteria are relevant at this point.

According to our map, we now want to bring our hypothetical solution into the present and check out how the client imagines a solution may already be happening now. Attempting to bring the client's hypothetical solution into the present may initially seem to not make sense to you. You might be wondering, "If we elicited a *hypothetical* solution, how could the hypothetical be happening now?" or "If the client constructed a solution within a 'miracle' frame, how could 'miracles' be happening now?" You might also be wondering how a client is going to report exceptions now if they did not before. As strange as it may seem, if we scale down the hypothetical, clients will search and find times when the hypothetical is happening now. To help scale down the hypothetical solution, we usually ask the question in this form.

So tell me about some times when this (the hypothetical solution) may be happening *a little bit* now.

With the insertion of the words "a little bit" or something similar, clients will be able to find exceptions now—that is, times when the hypothetical solution is happening now. Also, by instructing clients to "tell you about some times," you assume that there are such times and they will search for them. In contrast, if you were to ask, "Are there some times when this happens a little bit now?" a client could easily say "no." By instructing them to tell you about some times, you will more than likely get a response of exceptions.

Asking for exceptions or for times when the hypothetical solution is happening now is really a test of your conviction about the assumption that exceptions to every problem can be created by you and the client. As you gain more skill using the hypothetical solution frame and become more accustomed to asking for exceptions, you will find additional evidence for the assumption.

Often, with the difference in framing associated with the miracle question, clients can now find exceptions that they could not find before within the problem frame. From the earlier example about binge eating, the hypothetical solution of "thinking more about other things in my life" or of having a different "perspective" about food provides frames that are more workable than controlling thoughts and desires for food. With these new frames, the therapist and client have a better chance of identifying exceptions. We would ask for exceptions in this way: "Tell me about times now when you 'think more about other things in your life' or have more of the 'perspective' that you are looking for." The client will begin to search for times in the present with this new frame of "thinking more about other things in my life" and "having a perspective on food in relation to my life."

When the client responds with an exception, our conversation centers on the hypothetical solution *in the present*. The advantage of identifying the solution as occurring in the present—even if the identification is marginal—is that the goal of therapy can then be framed as "keeping this going" rather than as "solving a problem."

Another advantage to locating the hypothetical solution in the present is that clients will start using present tense verbs, which usually means that they are stepping into their "movies." In the hypothetical solution, the representation of the solution is often like a movie that clients appear to be watching as observers. This means at this point that they are still apart from the movie. By bringing the movie or hypothetical solution into the present with exceptions, clients may no longer be only watching. They may be reporting as if they had stepped into the movies and are reporting their experience.

If our bobsledders had watched movies of themselves only going down the run, their experience would not be as compelling as when they put themselves into the movie and experienced the run. The bobsledders in fact experienced the run visually, auditorially, and sensationally.

As clients report exceptions in the present, they are doing the same thing as the bobsledders. They are reporting in the present tense from their experience rather than as observers of an experience.

CASE EXAMPLE

A couple complained of a competitive and conflictual relationship. The couple had been married for several years and stated that most of the time the relationship was bad. They also stated, however, that since they seriously discussed divorce two or so weeks before, the relationship had improved a bit.

The wife explained this improvement as a result of her "backing down" rather than fighting as she had most times and the husband explained it as a result of her listening rather than interrupting. We continued to discuss these better times to find out more about what they did that worked.

She reported that she was treating herself nicely by accepting a hug from him once in awhile and he stated he was trying harder.

She was skeptical, though, about these exceptions continuing because she felt that all the improvements were due to her efforts at "backing down" and that he thought the problems were all her fault. Although she could identify exceptions, she framed them within "backing down." The "backing down" frame was likely to be only a short-term solution in her mind. If she thought she was backing down, she probably would continue to feel resentful of having to do that and would return to fighting. As long as he thought that she was doing all the changing and the problems were basically hers, he was not likely to do anything different or feel that he was part of the solution.

We asked the hypothetical solution question: "So, let's say a miracle happened and your relationship was going more the way you want, what would you be doing differently?" She stated there would not be any more competition. Since this was linguistically negative, we asked what would be going on *instead*. She stated there would be "understanding and tolerance." This was positively stated, though still vague and not in a process form.

When we asked him what he thought he would be doing, he said he did not know. We accepted this statement and then utilized it in the following question: "Well, if you did know, what would you say?" He responded that there would be "more balance" in their relationship between time together and time apart. He thought they were feeling threatened by the time now spent apart. His answer of "balance" was positively stated, but it was still vague and not in a process form.

Our choice at this point was whether to get these statements of *understanding, tolerance,* and *balance* to become more specific and in a process form or to follow the map into exceptions and find out how understanding, tolerance, and balance may be happening a little bit now.

Looking for exceptions is usually the first choice. The advantage is that the search brings the hypothetical solution, with its more positive and workable frames, into the present where the client can be specific and give us a process description. Within these frames of "understanding and tolerance," the wife could now look at those times when things went better, when she did not see herself as "backing down," and when he did something different. These exceptions of understanding and balance, would be more workable and he might have an easier time identifying what he did differently at these times, rather than thinking that all the good times were due to his wife's being different.

These new frames of "understanding, tolerance, and balance" introduced with the hypothetical solution question were more open and positive than the initial problem frames. Within these frames, the couple could have a different "search" in the present. They could now have an easier time identifying things they were doing in the present that were already under their control, and that worked better.

Another advantage of bringing the hypothetical solution into the present is that clients will usually give you answers that are more specific and in a process form. They are, thereby, furthering the solution development according to the criteria for a well-defined goal.

When asked about how some of the hypothetical solution was happening now, this couple said that there were times when there was this "understanding" going on. She said that during these times she thought she listened more rather than trying to rebut everything he said, and that he did not walk away. What did he do *instead* of walking away? She stated that he was quiet and made it possible for her to say what was on her mind.

When we asked him what he was doing during these times, he did not know. Before we could ask, "Well, if you did know, what would you say?" she responded and said that he was more verbal and nicer. She previously became fearful of what he might be thinking of her when he was quiet or walked away. She liked his staying on and letting her know what he thought. This he could understand and he thought he could do more of it.

We gave the couple feedback at the end of the session that highlighted what they had identified as working within the more workable frames from the hypothetical solution. We told the couple that we were very impressed with these better times of "understanding, tolerance, and balance." We were struck by how they did that and we wanted to know even more about those times. We, therefore, asked them to notice what other things they were doing during these times that they had not noticed *yet* so that they could tell us about such experiences next time.

THE SOLUTION CONSTRUCTION WORKSHEET

The worksheet (Figure 4, p.87) is a visual schema which includes the three main questions of a solution focus and the criteria for a well-defined goal. The worksheet will facilitate your keeping track of your client responses and what questions you may want to ask.

DISCUSSION

QUESTION:
I have asked clients what they want or what will be different when the problem is solved, and the clients tell me things like, "I will have lost 75 pounds," or "I will have made a decision about whether to stay married or get a divorce." When I try to explore what they need to do, we are stuck with all the diets that have already failed or with talk about their conflict and ambivalence about their marriage. What do you do in these situations?

Many clients respond to the hypothetical solution question with answers that describe remote solutions. Clients describe situations that will be occurring several months or longer from now and that describe a state of being or the conclusion to a process. The answer is helpful in that it describes what they are ultimately looking for. All we want to do, however, is facilitate the clients getting on track or in process. We do not want to make the goal of therapy an ultimate conclusion of lost weight or a decision. That might happen within the period they are seeing us, but we do not want to make the end result the goal. The goal is the process, a process of eating differently or of making steps toward some eventual decision about a marriage.

To make this clearer, remind yourself that this model is focused on "goaling" rather than on goals, or "solving" rather than on solutions. The "-ing" will be a reminder that we are interested in clients being in process.

So, when clients reply with a non-process answer such as, 75 pounds lighter, we ask,

So when you walk out of here today and you are not your desired

GOAL OR PROBLEM

*What is your goal
in coming here?*

WISH OR
COMPLAINT

*What would you like
to change about this?*

EXCEPTIONS

*How is this happening now?
When doesn't the problem happen?*

HYPOTHETICAL
SOLUTIONS

*If a mircle happened, and the
problem were solved, what would
you be doing differently?*

CRITERIA FOR WELL-DEFINED GOALS

YES	NO	
---	---	1. In the positive
---	---	2. In a process form
---	---	3. In the here-and-now
---	---	4. As specific as possible
---	---	5. In the client's control
---	---	6. In the client's language

re 4. Solution Construction Worksheet

weight yet, but you are *on track* to getting what you want, what are you doing differently?

Another question would be: "When you are on track, how will you be acting differently?"

The answer we receive to these questions is usually a more process-oriented answer that is more in the present. All the clients' circumstances may be the same, but they are *doing or thinking differently*. This kind of answer focuses not only on what they are doing but also on things within their control. For those clients who tend to think that there are only two states of being, the problem time and the wonderful solution time when everything else outside of them is different, this questioning builds an understanding of process, of solv*ing* the problem or reach*ing* their goal.

There are other possible approaches. We may ask, "When you are at your desired weight, what will you be doing differently?" Clients may then answer with what they will be doing or thinking differently after the hypothetical solution. If the client says something like, "I will be more assertive with people and likely to socialize more," you can then ask, "How does this happen now a little bit?"

With the answer to this question, you are now talking about exceptional times when the client is already doing some of what she or he is ultimately looking for.

As mentioned in Chapter Four, many clients think in terms of A leading to B, and miss that B can also lead to A. If clients think they cannot be assertive or outgoing (B) until they lose weight (A), they miss out on the other side of the solution. That is, they may also lose weight (A) by doing more of what they ultimately want, acting more assertively or outgoing (B).

QUESTION:
You seem to be stressing a great deal of precision in your questions. Why is precision so important?

We think clients are cooperative, and they will often answer in just the way you ask the question. If you ask what will be happening (rather than what will they be doing), they will tell you about differences outside of themselves and in their surroundings. If you ask how they will be feeling, they will respond with statements of feeling. If you ask how the situation will be different, they may give you a very vague answer or describe how someone else will be different. Clients will usually answer the question just as it is asked, so you want to think about *what it is* that you want to know. Do you want a feeling statement, do you want a statement of behavior, do you want a statement of the meaning the client may ascribe to the solution?

Conversing with a client is a little like working with computer software. If you were to *cooperate* with the computer by typing a certain direction according to the syntax of the software, the computer cooperates with that communication. If you are not precise with your typing or with your direction, the computer is not being resistant when it does not cooperate. It will respond appropriately to your communication. You must be precise in your direction or you will not receive the response you seek. You need to cooperate with the rules of the software.

EXERCISE

Step 1.

With one of your clients, ask the hypothetical solution question and take notice of what they tell you. The first time you use the question, resist the temptation to do anything more with the reply. Just take note of what the client says, or how the client says it, or what the client does with it. When you feel you can no longer resist responding to the client's replies, then ask the client to tell you more about the hypothetical solution.

Step 2.

As the client tells you more about the hypothetical solution, write down the answers on the solution construction worksheet (Figure 4) and begin to use the checklist of criteria for a well-defined goal. Use the words "instead," "how," "specifically," and "on track" to help the solution become more well-defined. Take the criteria checklist for a well-defined goal into the session with you.

If you feel somewhat hesitant about bringing the sheets into the sessions with you, use worksheets in between sessions to gauge the client's progress in solution construction. You may then have some ideas about what questions you may want to ask in the next session.

Step 3.

Ask your clients to tell you about times when that hypothetical solution may be happening now even a little bit. This may seem initially like a slow and tedious process. It may seem too cognitive if you are somewhat affectively oriented. Be patient. The rewards will be more than gratifying.

You are now ready for the "exceptions frame."

7

The Exceptions Frame

■ Exceptions to *every* problem can be created by the therapist and client and used to build solutions.

By using the word "problem," all of us distinguish problem times from all the other times when the problem does not happen. Unfortunately for all of us, once we make the distinction but the problem does not get resolved, we tend to focus even more on the problem time and on what does not work.

We tend to create or apply some rule or belief that we then use to filter all succeeding experience. Once we decide, for example, that fear of flying is a problem that we need to rid ourselves of, we look for the cause of the problem. We then tend to focus our attention on all the times we are afraid. Our fear escalates as we pay more attention to it.

The exceptions to the problems rule invite us to look at the other side of the distinction between problem time and everything else. When we do something else, we are probably doing something more workable. Therefore, we would like our clients to do the same.

With the next sequence of questions, we invite clients to enter the exceptions frame. Much of the early articulation of this sequencing of questions was done by Lipchik (1988a, b) and Lipchik and de Shazer (1986).

The basic sequence we use is as follows:

Exceptions *elicitation*:

"When are you already doing some of what you want?" (*Used in response to a goal statement by the client*)

"When doesn't the problem happen?" (*Used in response to a problem statement*)

Contrasting for *contextual differences*:

"What is different about these times?"

Specification:

Within the client's frame of reference:
"What are *you* doing differently?"
"How are *you* thinking differently?"

From outside the client's frame of reference:

"How are you perceived by *others* as acting differently?"
"If *they* think you are acting differently, how then do *the others* act differently with you?"

Bridging the exceptions as the goal of therapy, and *framing* the goal as continuing to do the exceptions:

"So, as you continue to do these things, will you think that you are on the beginning of a track to getting what you want out of coming here?"

Pursuing the goal of continuing to perform the exceptions:

"How will you keep this going?"
"How do you predict that you will keep this going?"
"How will others know that you are keeping this going?"

The thrust of this sequencing of questions is to create exceptions to the problem times, find out what is different, bridge the exceptions as the goal of therapy, and then pursue the exceptions.

There are several advantages to talking about exceptions rather than about some hypothetical future or something else. The first advantage can be explained in a metaphorical way. In going through a revolving door of a building, all of us have had the experience of having to push the door from a dead stop. The door is heavy and sometimes difficult to start moving from a dead stop. We have to overcome all the inertia

of a large glass and metal door. However, if we come to the door immediately upon someone else just leaving and the door is still moving, we
have a much easier time because all we have to do is add our efforts
to the momentum.

This is true for our clients. If the client thinks she or he has to solve
a problem from a dead stop, the process can seem like having to overcome all the inertia of the problem. However, if we help the client to
think about exceptions and to frame the goal of therapy as continuing
to do more of what he/she is already doing, inertia of the problem does
not exist. The client only has to keep the "door moving."

Another advantage is that the exceptions put the solution in the
realm of the possible and into the present. The present is a much more
compelling time than the remote past or far distant future. The experience is at hand and easier to bring to mind for details of usefulness
and success.

Exceptions can be created in several ways:

1. When the client has stated a goal rather than a problem, ask,
   "When are you doing *some* of what you want to happen already?"
2. When the client makes a problem statement, ask, "When doesn't
   the problem happen?"
3. At times, in the course of saying why a client is coming in to see
   a therapist, the client mentions that things are a little better or
   mentions something that is different. In that case, the way to elicit
   the exceptions is by asking, "How is that different or better?" By
   asking this "difference" question, you will set the client to talking
   more about these exception times.

Here are some examples:

1. Goal Statement and Exceptions

Therapist: What is your goal in coming here? (*Goal frame*)
Client: I thought about this on the way over here and I want to be acting more effectively with my kid. I just divorced and I have custody of my 15-year-old boy. (*Goal statement*)
Therapist: (*With empathic tones*) Sounds like quite a time of change.

(With curiosity) How do you mean "acting effectively?" *(Specification)*

Client: Well, sometimes he goes to school and sometimes he does not. I think if I were acting effectively, he would be going to school and doing other things I tell him to do. I would be using discipline better. *(Goal statement, "acting effectively" and "using discipline")*

Therapist: So when you are acting more effectively, you will be telling him what to do and you will be using discipline better. *(Clarification)* When are you acting more effectively now or using discipline more the way you want to? *(Exceptions frame around the goal)*

Client: There are some things that I am absolutely sure about, like curfew, for instance. With that, I am convinced of what a good time is for him to be home, and I can ground him if necessary. But there are other times when he says that his mother lets him do it or he argues with me and then I give in.

Therapist: So, are there times now where you act somewhat effectively even when he says those things or argues? *(Exceptions frame to a problem statement)*

Client: Sometimes. Sometimes, I know that it is just my guilt or my fear that he will want to go back to live with his mother that is getting to me. *(Contextual difference, knowing he is responding to guilt or fear)*

Therapist: How does that make a difference, knowing that you are responding to guilt or fear? *(Contextual difference)*

Client: Well, then I stay cool, and do what I know I should.

Therapist: So, as you continue to recognize when you are responding to guilt or fear and continue to do what you know you should, will you think you are on track toward getting what you want? *(Bridging the exceptions as the goal of therapy)*

Client: Yeah. I just have to catch myself.

Therapist: How will you continue to do that. *(Pursuing the goal)*

In this example, the man started with a goal stated in the positive. We assumed that there are times when he is already performing his goal and we asked about those exceptional times. We asked for the differences in those times, and found out that he is already doing what he wants to—"acting effectively" and "using discipline"—when he is sure of what is needed and when he catches himself responding to his guilt or fear. The remainder of the session then focused on how he would continue the exceptions.

2. Problem Statement and Exceptions

A young man came in complaining of hearing voices. Voices are not necessarily a problem in themselves.

Therapist: So I am a little confused. How are these voices a problem for you? (*Shifting from complaint level to problem*)

Client: Well, these voices tell me that people are after me and that I'd better be careful.

Therapist: That could be good advice in some cases. So how are they a problem? (*Shifting from complaint to problem*)

Client: Well, people at my residence hall are telling me that I am acting pretty weird and paranoid.

Therapist: Oh, so the problem is that you act differently and then people treat you differently? (*Clarifying problem*)

Client: Yeah, they are getting real suspicious of me.

Therapist: So, are there times when you do not listen to the voices or you do not act that way? (*Exception elicitation*)

Client: Well, the voices are there all the time.

Therapist: So, do you listen to them all the time? (*Exception elicitation*)

Client: No, not all the time. Sometimes, I am just too busy or I trust my own opinion rather than the voices. (*Contextual difference*)

Therapist: So, sometimes you trust your own opinion and you act differently. Those times go more the way you like? (*Specification*)

Client: Yes.

Therapist: How do you do that? (*Specification with a presupposition of his directing his choice*)

Client: I just ignore the voice like a radio station I don't like. (*Specification*)

Therapist: Are there also times when you want to listen to the voices telling you to be careful? (*Exception elicitation*)

Client Yes, some of my old crowd, back when I used to deal dope, still want to get back at me and I need to be cool.

Therapist: So, sometimes you think the advice is good and you choose to listen. So, if you continued to make choices of when you wanted to listen to your own opinion and when you wanted to take this other advice, would you think you were on track to getting what you want from coming here? (*Bridging the exceptions as the goal of therapy*)

Client: That would be all right.

Therapist: So how will you continue to make these choices? (*Pursuing the exception of "making choices" as the goal of therapy*)

In this example, the complaint was first moved from the complaint level of "voices" to the problem/solution level of "his acting weird and people treating him differently." Hearing voices is not necessarily a problem. So, we needed to move the statement to the level of goal or problem before we asked about exceptions. He stated the voices were a problem because he then acted weird and people treated him as if he were weird.

Within the problem definition of how the voices led him to do things that make him appear weird to his friends, we could then ask for exceptions indicating when the voices were not a problem or when he did not act in the problematic way.

In pursuing the exceptions, we found that he makes choices, and that by choosing when to follow his own or some other person's opinion, he is more satisfied that he produces more of what he wants.

3. Recent Changes or Differences

A couple who had been married 13 years came to see us.

Therapist: What is your goal in coming here? (*Elicitation of a goal*)

Wife: We have been having difficulties. A few years ago, my husband quit his job to go back to school, and I took over the financial responsibilities. Lately, I have been feeling overwhelmed with all the responsibilities. In addition to the responsibilities, I used to think of his needs first all the time, but last weekend I decided that I had enough. I felt overwhelmed. I left him and went to stay with my sister. (*Despite the goal-oriented question, sometimes clients will begin anyway with complaints or problems. Often, within these statements, there are hints of exceptions and differences.*)

Therapist: Was that different for you to take that kind of action? (*Exception elicitation and looking for contextual differences*)

Wife: Yes, very much so, and things have been a little better since then. I have moved back in but I told him that there were things I wanted him to do differently. And since then, he has been better. We need to communicate differently and he has listened and been more open with me. (*Client expands on the exception and how this action on her part is very different.*)

Therapist: Really? (*With encouraging tones and curiosity*) How have you seen him do that? (*Specification*)

Wife: Well, in the past he would walk away, and now he really listens, and actually is encouraging me to say more. I also wanted him to come to therapy, and get a job. He has been looking for a job and the fact that he is here means a lot to me.

Therapist: I guess it does; (*with encouraging tone*) it is not always easy to come to therapy. Well, let me ask this: If you continued to have these good talks, and you continued to think more often of yourself first, would you think you were on track to getting what you want from coming here? (*Bridging the exception as the goal of therapy, and using her words as much as possible*)

Wife: Yes.

Therapist to husband (with enthusiasm): Is this true, have you been doing all these things? (*Exception elicitation*)

Husband: Yes, I have. But it has been hard. For a long time, the role reversal has been extreme. She has been taking care of the bills and sometimes not too well. When she would mess up the bills, I just did not want to know. I figured that if she messed them up, then she would have to clean them up. But lately I figured that we have to work together, so I got myself involved again. (*Expands on exception, and offers the new meaning he is operating under, "We have to work together."*)

Therapist: So you decided that not being involved was not working and so you are getting more involved with the finances. That is really great. How are you doing that? (*Eliciting contextual differences and specification*)

Husband: Well, when she left for those few days, I realized how important she is to me, and that I cannot just leave all the headaches to her anymore. (*New meaning*)

Therapist: Well, how has she been different? (*Exception elicitation about her*)

Husband: Well, I have pushed for more of what is going on and no more keeping things from me just to keep peace. She has told me more about what she wants me to do and how bad things really are financially.

Therapist: I guess her leaving was quite a shock to you?

Husband: Yes, it was.

Therapist: Well, I am impressed that you went ahead and did something about it. Not everybody does and you could have just let her go. (*Encouraging and reinforcing*) So, are there other things you are doing that she has not noticed yet? (*Elicitation and specification with the expectation that there are other exceptions*)

Husband: Yes, I contacted my sister about a loan for us. I had to eat my pride because I am a pretty private person.

Therapist: I can see that it was hard. I guess that indicates how serious this situation is to you and how much you care to get things back on track. If you continue to do these things and the two of you continue to have these open and good talks, even if talking is not always easy, would you think you are on track to getting what you want out of coming here? (*Bridging the exceptions as the goal of therapy*)

Husband: Yes, I think so.

Therapist: Well then, let me ask, how are the two of you going to keep doing these things? (*Pursuing the exceptions as the goal of therapy*)

This case example typifies what can happen when, as therapist, we listen with great care for exceptions and differences. By asking how her leaving was different, we opened the discussion for many other differences that had occurred in the previous few days. These differences in the problem area were expanded upon and then bridged as the goal of therapy. If we had not asked about the recent change of her leaving, the potential of these recent actions could well have been lost.

A new, more virtuous (as opposed to vicious) cycle can be enhanced wherein the wife will continue to think of her own needs rather than of his first all the time and he will continue to involve himself with the affairs of the family rather than leaving them all to her.

Bridging these recent actions as the goal of therapy enables the couple to see their tasks as continuing to do things like they have been achieving in the past week, that is, keeping change going. Remember our metaphor of the revolving door, and how difficult moving a revolving door from a dead stop can be and how much easier the door is to move, if it is already moving. Metaphorically, the clients' goal of continuing to do what they are already doing becomes roughly equivalent to keeping the revolving door moving. The task of the conversation from this point on is to elicit more of what the couple is doing that is working and to recycle through the exceptions sequence as necessary.

In the session just described, the wife responded to the "How will you keep this going" question with a concern. She said she found that her anger and resentment from the past sometimes got in the way. When she wanted to talked with her husband in this more frank and honest way they were developing, she would sometimes be stopped by her anger.

Rather than assuming the anger or resentment was a problem or that the anger stopped her *all* the time, we assumed that there were exceptions to this also. We asked, "So are there times now when the anger is less of a problem?" She responded that often when she would get angry, she would just become quiet and then stop talking to her husband. However, there were times now when she was dealing with the anger.

"How?" we asked. She said there were times now when she would consider dealing with her anger versus being quiet and not talking. At those times she decided to deal with her anger by letting him know how she felt and then to move beyond it. He had said to her that he could not change the past. She said that sometimes now after she had said what she felt, she could let go of the past, and talk some about the present.

This concern the wife had brought up with regard to our question about how the couple was going to keep the changing going was cycled through the exceptions sequence and the already emerging ways of her dealing with resentment were discovered. Again, if we had treated her resentment as a "problem" and had not focused on exceptions, we may have created a situation wherein she thought the resentment was a problem that she had to solve rather than continuing to express her feelings and put her needs first more often in ways she was already doing.

This notion that there are exceptions to every problem might not seem quite so strange if we consider that many clients come to see us in response to a crisis. The problems may have been going on for some time, but often there is some threshold that is reached when somebody says, "This has to change," or the problem is moved to the fore by a school counselor or someone else. When confronted by a crisis, many people respond by calling a therapist as one of several steps they take action on. They have already taken steps other than calling the therapist on which the client and therapist can capitalize.

A supervisor once told us that he believed that clients came to therapy not because they needed a solution, but because they realized what the solution was and were terrified. This is another explanation of exceptions. People may already have ideas of what they need to do and may have already made a start. All we have to do is normalize their fears and support their continued actions.

WHAT DO YOU DO WITH THE EXCEPTIONS?

Many newcomers to this approach say that they can identify and construct many exceptions but that either they do not know what to do with the exceptions or the exceptions do not seem to be significant enough to make for successful therapy.

After you have elicited exceptions, it is useful to check off three aspects of them. Exceptions should . . .

1. Meet the criteria for a well-defined goal.
2. Be bridged—and accepted—by the client as the goal of therapy.
3. Have a meaning from the client's point of view that is likely to make the exceptions endure.

DO THE EXCEPTIONS MEET THE CRITERIA FOR A WELL-DEFINED GOAL?

The map, the goal frame, the exceptions frame, and the hypothetical solution frame are all tools for goal and solution development. Regardless of the path we follow, we want to compare the client's responses within the goal frame, the exceptions frame, or the hypothetical solution frame to the criteria for a well-defined goal.

As clients report what they are not doing during exception times, we ask what they are doing instead. We have then a linguistically positive representation of what they are doing. We also want clients to state the exceptions in a process form—that is, how they are doing what they are doing or thinking the way they are thinking.

Oftentimes, clients explain their exceptions as a result of activities or relationships other than their being different—that is, someone or something else is different. We want to redirect such responses in order to find out what the clients are doing that is within their control. (cf. Chapter Ten on enhancing agency)

IS "CONTINUING TO DO THE EXCEPTIONS" ACCEPTED AS THE GOAL OF THERAPY?

When clients report exceptions to problem times, we need to review with them whether or not continuing to make the exceptions happen is acceptable to them as the goal of therapy. As we,mentioned earlier, to frame the goal of therapy as doing more of what clients are already doing makes the task of therapy seem much easier. However, we want to have an explicit understanding with clients that that is their goal for their therapy. We do not want to be pursuing a goal if that is not what the client wants or if the client believes that continuing on the particular track will not lead to solution.

We also want to bridge other concerns or goals to the exceptions. An example might be a mother who comes in with concerns about her four-year-old having behavior problems in preschool. She may say that what has been different lately is that she has given up trying to substitute for his missing father and that she is taking care of her own needs more. The continuation of these recent changes (exceptions)—her deciding she could not make up for the father; her taking care of herself more rather than devoting her attention almost exclusively to her son—needs to be bridged as the goal of therapy. It would be helpful to extend the bridging to her concern for her son. We might say, "Are you thinking—as you continue to take care of yourself more and give yourself a break from the pressure—that in the long run you will be more effective with regard to your son and his preschool situation?" If the answer is "Yes," then we would ask, "How will you continue to decide to take care of yourself?" If the answer is "No," then we would explore the concern or objection and check to see if the exceptions could be bridged in some other way.

ARE THE MEANINGS OR FRAMEWORKS OF THE EXCEPTIONS WORKABLE AND LIKELY TO LAST FROM THE CLIENT'S POINT OF VIEW?

Clients sometimes outline exceptions that are working; the meaning that surrounds their actions is likely to keep the exceptions going. Clients may say that they recently decided that worrying about things they could not do anything about just did not make sense and so they turned to focusing on problems they could do something about. This new decision contains a more workable framework, a distinction between things clients can do something about and those things they cannot. If they say they are confident they can continue to make this distinction, there is no further need on our part as therapists to coach them to some other framework.

On the other hand, a client who thinks that things are better between herself and her husband because she is "giving in" and may have trouble in the future. Even if she continues to avoid fights, she may still believe she is losing and will either feel bad or gather her strength to fight again. This framework of "giving in" is something you and she may want to redirect to some other framework.

EXCEPTIONS WORKSHEET

Figure 5 is a worksheet that contains a sequence of questions for constructing exceptions. This is just a suggested order. The actual conversation with your client may not need certain questions or you may find yourself skipping around. Spaces are provided for your client's response.

EXCEPTIONS ELICITATIONS
With a goal statement:
When are you already doing some of what you want?

With a problem statement:
When doesn't the problem happen?

CONTEXTUAL DIFFERENCES
What is different about these times?

SPECIFICATIONS
Within the client's frame of reference:
What do you do differently?

How do you think differently?

From outside the client's frame of reference:
How are you being perceived by others as acting differently?

If others think you are acting differently, how do they act differently?

BRIDGING AND FRAMING
So, as you continue to do these things, will you think that you are on the beginning of a track to getting what you want out of coming here?

PURSUING THE GOAL OF CONTINUING EXCEPTIONS
How will you keep this going?

How do you predict that you will keep this going?

How will others know that you are keeping this going?

Figure 5. Exceptions Worksheet

DISCUSSION

QUESTION:
What about those problems that the client describes as happening all the time?

With most problems that clients bring up, scaling down the exception question will get you added results. For example, instead of saying, "Tell me about the times when your husband does not ignore you," you might say, "Tell me about some of the times when this is a little less of a problem." This scaling down of the frame with words like "a little less" or "not as much" will enable the client to enter the exceptions frame.

At other times, when the client says there are no exceptions, you want to ask the hypothetical solution question in order to advance thinking in a more positive direction or obtain a more workable frame. After obtaining a more workable or open frame through the use of the hypothetical solution question, you can again try to elicit exceptions. Remember to scale down the response to the hypothetical solution question, with words like "a little bit" or "slightly." For example, with the client who thinks there are no times when he does not act fearfully in getting on a plane but thinks he will be thinking and acting more assertively when the problem is solved, you would then ask, "Tell me about those times now when you act *a little assertively* or *at least not so fearfully.*"

The expression "not so fearfully" is a way of scaling down the framework by staying in negative language as a pace for the client's thinking. It might be too big a leap for the client to think he was acting even a little assertively. He may think he is never assertive in any way. He can imagine, however, that sometimes he does not act quite so fearfully. This scaled-down negative framework may elicit exceptions. After talking about exceptions "of acting not quite so fearful" and after you have facilitated his building on these exceptions, he may be more able to identify his exceptions in a positive way and even use the word "assertive."

EXERCISES

1. Use the Exceptions Frame Worksheet with a colleague, initially, so that you can become used to using the worksheet and hearing yourself asking the questions. Asking the questions with a colleague will be helpful before you begin to use the questions with your clients.

2. Use the Solution Construction Worksheet (Figure 4, p. 87) in your session. Take note, during the session, of the goal or problem statements and of any exceptions that the client mentions. After the session, examine your worksheet and compare the client's responses with the criteria for a well-defined goal (Figure 2, p. 60). Prepare the questions you want to ask next time. As you become more facile in using the worksheet, you will not need to wait for the end of the session to use the criteria.

8

Positive Feedback

■ Small changing leads to larger changing.

So far, we have been concentrating on conversational pathways for constructing solutions and outlining the criteria for a well-defined goal. We have also discussed how the questions we use are highly influential because the questions include the assumptions we work under and tend to be suggestive to clients of new avenues of thought and action. While we believe that creating solutions through the conversation the client has with the therapist may be enough, we also believe there is a tremendous advantage for the client to receive positive feedback.

Very simply, we believe that a little positive support and encouragement can go a long way. Clients, in the midst of change, can often experience confusion or fears—and a little encouragement by someone outside of the problem can be reassuring.

This chapter focuses on more direct forms of feedback that we offer— that is, cheerleading, compliments, messages, and tasks.

CHEERLEADING*

In general, we use cheerleading as support and encouragement for positive things clients are doing and, most especially, for their changing and solving. Cheerleading may be emotional support that comes across through raised voice tone, gestures, excited expressions, or the choice of words. In the session, we want to respond immediately to any mention of change, however small. Trainees are often surprised by how much we

---

*This term, cheerleading, was originally used as a research code for process research on interviewing. We are using the term here to describe any supportive expression by the therapist. Cf., de Shazer et al., 1985.

use emotions. Trainees may mistakenly expect us either to be more cognitive or to show more restraint with the clients. However, our interviews are hardly flat inquisitions. Conversations with clients are very much affectively supportive and encouraging for further changing.

Recently, we worked with a family with a seven-year-old who was having trouble keeping his bed dry all night. The boy seemed rather embarrassed at the beginning of the session as he heard his parents talking about his failures.

We asked about the times when the boy makes it through the entire night without wetting. The parents said there were several nights during a week's time without wetting.

We asked him:

Therapist: Is this true, there are some nights when you keep your bed dry the whole night? (*Said with a slightly rising tone of curiosity*)

Boy: Yes. (*With some embarrassment and shyness*)

Therapist: Well that sounds pretty good. How do you do that? (*Cheerleading as well as seeking specification and contextual differences*)

Boy: Sometimes I wake up and go to the bathroom.

Therapist: You do! (*Said with excitement and surprise*) That sounds like a pretty grown-up sort of thing. How do you do that?

Boy: Welllll, I don't know. I guess I just don't want to have to sleep in the wet.

Therapist: Really! You say that to yourself at night? (*With continued enthusiasm*) How do you get yourself to remind yourself of that and then get up? Aren't you really sleepy?

Boy: (*With more excitement*) Yeah, but I can do it.

Therapist: Well, I guess you can but that seems like a very grown-up kind of thing to do. (*Keying on his desire to be seen as more grown up*) What do your parents think of you doing such a grown-up thing?

As you can see, we are very affectively involved in news about positives and change, and try to use curiosity and excitement to the client's advantage in the session.

Cheerleading also includes several presuppositions that we embed. We believe that individuals are in control of their actions—that is, individuals are the ones who produce their changing, even when they think initially their changing is either spontaneous or out of their own control.

We, therefore, embed responsibility and "in control" assumptions in cheerleading with the use of questions and statements, such as . . .

1. "How did you decide to do that?"
2. "How do you explain that?"
3. "That is really great!"

1. "How Did You Decide to Do That?" (Lipchik, 1988b)

This may be asked about an exception. "How did you decide to do that?" is usually asked with a rising tone and excited curiosity. Clients may not initially think that they consciously decided to do the exception or change, but we invite them to think in terms of conscious control and personal responsibility.

For example, in the above interview with the boy, he may initially not have thought that what he was doing was different or good or mattered. With the question of "How did you do that?" however, he tends to search for or create what he did that brings about the better times.

Clients may also think that their doing something may have happened because of a confident mood or because someone else did something first. We nevertheless want to cheerlead the client's action and embed the idea that what she or he is doing is "responsible."

For example: "So, you think that your looking through the job ads was just because you woke up feeling more anxious. But how did you decide to do that? Other people would respond to anxiety by going back to bed."

With someone else who thinks she or he was only responding to some other person, we might ask: "So, I know you are thinking that you responded only because she was friendlier, but how did you decide to respond at all? You have been burned in other relationships. How did you have the courage to take a chance again? How did you decide to do that?"

2. "How Do You Explain That?"

This question may be used with people who are not aware of the positive things they have been doing. The point of the question is not so much to get an actual explanation as to highlight for clients their doing something positive. The question can be more rhetorical than literal.

"How do you explain that?" is usually asked with a rising inflection that hints at encouragement as well as curiosity.

3. "That Is Really Great!"

Any complimentary phrase may be used in the conversation to support new or positive behavior. Positive cheerleading is used to facilitate the resourcefulness of the conversation and the further searching for additional examples of exceptions or positives. Clients often are tentative about change, especially if they think this is something entirely new for them. This kind of support is warming and expansive because it allays fears and facilitates a positive track.

Cheerleading has to be paced and timed properly. Sometimes, when therapists are new to the solution focus, they try to point up all the positive behaviors of the client before the client is emotionally ready to accept the compliments. The therapists may be "too much in front of their client." You will recognize these situations when the client begins to disqualify your compliments, or argue with you that things are not really *that* good.

These situations remind us of a story told by a friend and colleague, Kevin O'Connor. Kevin told us about a nurse who worked in a physical rehabilitation center. Each day, she would take for a walk patients who were still weak and unsure of the strength of their legs and their ability to walk. The nurse would take them by the arm and begin walking with them down the hospital hallway. She learned that as long as she walked just a little bit behind while supporting the patient's arm, the walk seemed to go well. If she was just a little ahead of her patient in the pace of her walking, however, the patient would express uncertainty about walking or say that maybe they were walking too fast. The nurse quickly learned that the walks went better when she was perceived by the patient as just slightly in back, rather than out in front and pulling.

So, too, in therapy cases, the therapist can be perceived as if trying to convince clients of all the positive things they are doing, before they are at the point of being able to recognize or accept them. They are not being "resistant." More than likely clients sincerely believe that what you think are positive actions or changes are not that significant and that you have a misperception. Therefore, the more you try to point out the positives, the more they try to help you see that the changes are really not that significant.

The conversation can become an argument between the therapist as the more positive person and the client as more negative or realistic, depending upon your reference point. The meaning of the message, however, is the response you receive. Therefore, if the conversation continues in this fashion, with the therapist citing positives and the client saying "Yes, but," you need to do something different.

In these situations, the therapist has chosen language or frames that do not match the client's view or that may present too big of a leap for the client to accept *yet*, or *at this time*.

For example, a therapist might say:

Therapist: Well, Beth, it sounds like you are doing a number of good things for yourself. You reached out to some friends and got out of the house during the weekend. You are letting go of that bad relationship and are thinking of yourself.
Beth: Not really. I think of him all the time and I am not happy. When I went out with my friends, I was feeling really down and hardly talked.
Therapist: Yes, but you did some things rather than sitting around and it sounds like you even talked to another man.
Beth: Yes, but he was boring and I was still thinking of Michael.

When your client or you start to use "Yes, but" or you sense that you are trying to talk your client into something, you can suppose you are too far ahead of your client. Therefore, scale down your compliments; use the same complimentary words, but toned down in meaning and affect.

Cheerleading is more effective when used in response to what the client has stated rather than to something you see. For example, the therapist with the client who was preoccupied with Michael might say:

Therapist: So, despite feeling terrible you tried a few things but not with overwhelming results. (*Said with curiosity but low and matching affective tones*)
Beth: Yes, I know it will take time to get over Michael and I just cannot stay home. I just wish I did not think of him so much.
Therapist: (*With low affect and tone*) I guess you are right. It can take

time. Given that you were feeling low about the breakup, how did you decide to get out of the house rather than just sit around and think about him? (*With curiosity but muted affect*)

The therapist matches the client's tone and the meaning around the changes the client reports. Rather than responding with seeming over-excitement, the therapist affirms her feeling and the fact that she did *something*.

More matching of tone, affect, and language will be discussed in the chapter on cooperating.

THE CONSULTATION OR "THINK" BREAK

From the Brief Family Therapy Center of Milwaukee, the Brief Therapy Center of the Mental Research Institute, and the Milan Model, we learned the advantages of taking a consultation or "think" break in our sessions. The break involves taking time out of the therapy conversation to think over or brainstorm about the progress of solution construction, and to prepare some direct feedback for the client.

Even if we already believe during the session that we know what we want to say to the client and can define what task we will suggest to her or him, we take a break. There have been too many occasions when we skipped the break and, after the client left, realized what we wished we had said. The break gives a little distance and time to think through what we want to offer as feedback.

As we mentioned briefly in Chapter Three, we usually meet with clients anywhere from 30 to 45 minutes in conversation. When we work as a team with a mirror, the partner in front of the mirror explains to the clients at the beginning of the session that she or he will be taking time to consult with others behind the mirror and then return with feedback and possible advice.

If we are working alone, we explain that we are going to leave the room for a few minutes in order to take some time to think over what has been discussed and that we will then rejoin the client with some feedback.

Originally, while we were using a problem-focused approach, we thought of the break as providing a boundary between the interview and the intervention delivery. The initial part of the session was focused on "gathering information" about the problem and the attempted solutions. We thought of ourselves then as "interviewing" for information. We would take a break from that phase called information gathering and create an intervention. At that time, we thought of the intervention as the agent of change and we spent a great deal of time mapping the patterns of the attempted solution and creating tasks that would intervene in the pattern. At that time of our model development, we thought of the intervention as all-important. The phases of our sessions were conceptualized as (1) the interview part where we gathered problem information, (2) the consultation break part in which we designed the intervention, and, finally, (3) the intervention delivery part.

With a solution-focused approach, we no longer believe that we are gathering information. As discussed earlier, we now believe that we as therapists are co-participants in solution construction. We no longer believe that there is this objective thing called information. We believe that we have participated in a continuing conversation through which new meaning and, therefore, solution(s) have evolved.

On the break, we no longer wonder about the patterns of the problem of an observed system. We focus on the treatment group of therapist and clients, and on how solution construction is evolving. The break now is used to reflect on the solution construction and the feedback we can offer the client to facilitate the process.

Whether we are working as a team or as an individual therapist, the advantage of the break is that we can take time apart from maintaining the conversation in order to think more precisely about what feedback may be helpful for the client. When involved in the conversation, we can be distracted by the needs at the time for being empathic, maintaining the conversation, choosing and constructing questions, and monitoring the solution process. During the break, we are free of those responsibilities.

If we as therapists have unwittingly joined the clients in a framing of the problem/solution that is not working or if we have become involved with the client in an interaction that is not productive, the break provides the opportunity to step out of the role of therapist and take a more distant view. We can readjust when we rejoin the client.

The break also offers us a time when, as a team or as a therapist working alone, we can pool our perspectives and brainstorm on the feedback. Oftentimes, we find that the perspectives are different. The therapist in front of the mirror may be more affectively touched by the client because of the physical closeness in the session. Those behind the mirror often experience a more detached perspective. Even working individually, we experience the break as offering a detachment that we do not experience in the session.

Recently, I, Jane, was seeing a couple for several sessions about marital problems without a team behind the mirror. The couple did not seem to be making progress in reaching what they wanted and they decided to take time off from therapy. About six weeks later, the couple called for therapy around problems ascribed to their child. Since the couple thought a male therapist would be helpful for their boy and since I felt discouraged about the lack of improvement in the case, I suggested that John be the partner in front of the mirror, with me as the member of the team behind the mirror. The couple and child agreed. During the initial session with John conducting the session, a lot of things became apparent to me from behind the mirror. I became aware that a lot of changes had occurred in the marital relationship which I had not seen while I had been the therapist in the room with the couple. Having the perspective from behind the mirror gave me some distance that proved helpful. Not getting caught up in the negative emotions of the present in the therapy room became easier and enabled me to see that in the longer perspective the couple had made and were still making a considerable number of changes. Without feelings of discouragement from the previous therapy, John, in front of the mirror, could ask questions about how things were different since the last time. The couple reported exceptions not only with regard to the problem about their child but also how they were acting more as a parental team, and getting along better.

With a team approach, there are many different perspectives, given the different personalities, genders, ages, and so on. These different perspectives provide a richness to the process in that each person is contributing from his or her position in the conversation. We really believe that "two heads are better than one."

We like to think that the break also offers time for clients to think about what was said and about the questions that were raised during the conversation. Do not be surprised when clients offer you their thoughts and reflections during the break after your return.

The clients also seem to be more expectant when we return. Given that we have framed the break as a time for us to think about what they have told us, clients appear expectant of the results of this "thinking" and "brainstorming."

The break now offers us a boundary between the conversational feedback of the initial part of the session and a more formal feedback. While we no longer think of ourselves as interviewers gathering information, we like the break as a time to gather our own thoughts and provide clients with a more formal feedback time. The break creates a specialness to the feedback time.

The feedback is organized around compliments, message, and a possible task (de Shazer, 1985; O'Hanlon & Weiner-Davis, 1989).

COMPLIMENTS

Compliments are statements of praise or support that we offer the client and that are usually focused around the stated goal or solution process.

Tomm (1985) has stated that one of the most basic distinctions that we make in language is the distinction between good and bad. That distinction tends to create different climates. A "bad" label tends to be restrictive and people tend to close in and become defensive. On the other hand, a "good" label tends to free people. They become more open and expansive. They are more likely to generate new ideas and actions, to be more open to new or different ideas.

This idea is consistent with the basic thrust of the model, that focusing on the positive and on solutions facilitates change. Our feedback, therefore, is positive. This positive focus works for both the clients and the therapist(s). All the members of the treatment group focus on what is working and how what is working can be enhanced.

The central idea of offering compliments is to facilitate the solution construction. More specifically, compliments facilitate solution processes by (1) creating a positive context or climate, (2) highlighting the positive things clients are already doing in the solution area, (3) alleviating fears of judgment by the therapist, (4) alleviating fears about change through the support, (5) normalizing events and feelings, (6) framing the responsibility and credit of changing as the client's, and (7) supporting each person's view, if the client system is more than one person. This is a modification of the first listing of the purposes of compliments by the Schaumburg Group of Wall, Kleckner, Amendt, and Bryant (1989).

1. A Positive Climate

While a positive climate has probably been set or facilitated by questions and cheerleading in the conversation, the direct compliments often cement the positive focus of the therapy or carry it one step further.

Therapists have to look for positives. This has the obvious effect of focusing our attention during the conversation and the break on positives or changes of the client.

Giving compliments to clients offers a context of "good" as Tomm (1985) explained. This has effects for the whole treatment group, both for the therapist(s) and the clients. Therapists have to keep eyes and ears open for positive changes or for things that are working, while clients are left more open by the setting of a positive tone.

Clients generally respond to the positive nature of the entire session with more relaxed body postures and voice tones, and with more positive language. During the feedback of compliments, the response may be even more pronounced. Clients will generally relax more and may even spontaneously suggest that the compliment is a new way of looking at the situation. Clients who may have thought that they were doing nothing right will spontaneously say, "I guess I have been doing some things right," or "I did not think anything was working but now that you mention it, I guess there are some things."

A woman came to see us after being in therapy for over eight years. She was clearly accustomed to analyzing herself and her problems, but had sought us out because she now had only this one problem she wanted to solve. Our cheerleading in the session and the feedback at the end of the session were filled with compliments about all the positives we perceived her doing. She looked at us and said, "You know, this is so different from my other therapy in the past. You are so positive, I felt so down before I came, and now—I feel good!"

At this time, the clients may offer even more "exceptions" that they thought of during the break or that the compliment reminded them of. In the above case, she continued, "I had not thought I was handling things as well as I am."

2. Highlighting Recent Changing

If you believe in positive reinforcement, this should fit very well. We facilitate continued changing by highlighting things we think the client is already doing that are helpful or working. Often these compliments are no more than our saying how impressed we are with the things they are already doing. We then go on to list all the exceptions to the problem or all the recent changes we found in the first part of the session.

For example, a couple came to see us about how to handle their "chronically mentally ill, adult child." During the session, there were several examples of how the parents were able to maintain distance from the adult child and let her make her own decisions. In the feedback, we complimented the parents on all the things they were doing as parents that were helping the situation. The feedback was:

> We are very impressed with how both of you have been able to maintain your distance and let her make her own decisions. For example, it is striking how you, mother, told your daughter that she would have to manage her own money and are holding firm that she needs to support her own apartment. It is striking how you, father, walked out of the kitchen, instead of yelling and getting into a power struggle. We are impressed how each of you is showing her that you have confidence that she can learn from her choices, both successes and mistakes.

These parents apparently took our compliments as affirmations. They returned the following session with even more examples of how they were backing off and showing the daughter they had confidence that she could learn from her choices.

3. Alleviating Fears of Judgment

In the initial part of the session, clients have told us many things that they feel ashamed of, embarrassed about, or vulnerable about in some way. Clients often feel exposed and fearful of the judgment an "expert" may be going to make. By returning after the break with compliments, we can set their minds at ease.

For example, a woman came to see us about her marital relationship. We conducted the first session by eliciting the positives and exceptions to the problem. We complimented her on the exception times. When the woman returned for the second session, she started by saying,

> Things have been much better this week. You know, I want to say that I was very nervous about coming here last time. When you went out of the room to consult with your colleague and came back, I thought you were going to scold me—you know, slap me on my hand, but you did not do that. You told me how well I was doing and that made me feel so good.

Rather than being critical, as some may fear, we are complimentary and encouraging.

4. Alleviating Fears About Change

Many people are fearful of the consequences of change, of what may happen, or of what they fear change may mean. Some clients fear that you are about to tell them that they have to do even more although they may feel they are already doing as much as they believe is possible. Compliments can serve to alleviate fears through the implicit message that you recognize their struggle and the tremendous amount of effort they have put into trying to solve their problems. Compliments can be affectively empathic and supportive as you let clients know that you understand and that you are joining them in their efforts.

A woman came to see us because she thought she had an "eating disorder." She said that she binged several times a day. She was reluctant to give us details because she felt so embarrassed and ashamed. She cited several diet programs she had used and how discouraged she was that she had always failed. She felt bad because, after each program, she not only went back to her old weight but then surpassed it.

When we changed to talking about the future, she was reluctant to do that. She later explained that she was afraid that we would ask her to promise to do something and she did not want to disappoint us, or to be disappointed again with what she thought was her lack of willpower.

Our compliments to her included how impressed we were with her persistence, that she had not given up despite the weight programs not working out. We also told her how impressed we were with how much she cared about herself to be working so hard on this and that it was obvious to us how serious this was to her. We told her that with something important like this, it was extremely important to go slowly and cautiously. After all, she did not want to be disappointed again.

These compliments served to reassure her about her fears of jumping into another crash program and about her concerns about criticism for her lack of willpower.

5. Compliments as Normalizing

When involved with a problem of losing perspective, many clients feel that they are the only people who have this problem, or that there must be something wrong with them for not being able to solve the problem. Compliments can be so worded as to let clients know that the problem is common, or expected, and that there is nothing wrong with them. For example, with someone who is feeling depressed and overwhelmed, we might say:

> We are actually very impressed that given all the things that are going on—your son in trouble at school, the divorce pending, your tight finances, and your boss putting more pressure on you—that you are handling things as well as you are. We would expect you to be feeling overwhelmed and sometimes wanting to just leave it all.

Or, for a single parent who is overwhelmed with all the responsibilities, we might compliment her or him in this way:

> We are very impressed with how you are managing all these things for your children, actually going above and beyond the call of duty. We would think there would be something wrong with you if you did not occasionally wish you had never had the children and that you were responsible only to yourself.

Complimenting parents for the responsible approach taken allows them to back off from the pressure they are putting on themselves and to accept as normal that sometimes they may wish they were alone or may even hate their children for the moment. Putting the feeling in a positive way allows parents to back off by their choice and do so more effectively than if we told them that they were being overly responsible and that they needed to back off. With the latter negative way of putting it, they could very easily take the comment as a criticism and respond defensively.

Normalizing allows clients to stop blaming themselves, or someone else, and then to do something different.

6. Compliments as Responsibility Enhancers

Compliments are an excellent way of reminding or framing the responsibility and the credit for changing as the client's. In this approach, we want the client to recognize her or his own resources and responsibility in changing and we want to promote independence. In traditional models, the client's dependency on the therapist is seen as a vehicle for processing the transference by the client. The processing and analysis of the relationship is conceptualized as the vehicle for change. In contrast, we want clients to get on track to solving their problems or to reach their goals. We, therefore, want to minimize as much as possible their thinking that we as therapists are responsible for the change. If clients thought that we were responsible or that they as clients were dependent on therapy in order to change, they might return to therapy every time they run into a snag rather than reassuring themselves and looking to their own resources.

We use compliments like these to enhance independence and a sense of their responsibility: "We *agree with your* idea that it would be better for the children in the long run for you to take care of yourself with a day off occasionally." This framing of ". . . agreeing with you" makes clients the experts and reinforces their constructing their own solutions. For example, with parents we might say:

We are very impressed with your coming up with this new idea this week for taking care of yourself rather than only taking care of the children all the time. It looks good on you. (*This compliment also reinforces the client's generating his or her own solution.*)

With others we might say:

> We know that you will probably credit us for the improvements
> in your relationship, but we think you should have all the credit
> for your solving these problems. While we sometimes offer advice,
> not everyone takes it or uses it in the way you two are.

This compliment legitimizes their accepting our suggestions but also
credits the couple for being open to the advice and utilizing it to the
betterment of their relationship. The compliment also preempts their
disqualifying their responsibility and credit for the changing.

7. Compliments Used to Support Many Points of View

Compliments are used to support each individual in a couple or family.
Frequently, a person will come in feeling alone or alienated in the family or feeling that the family conflict means that only one person can
be right or okay.

Compliments can be used to support each individual, and still enable
you, as the therapist, to keep your neutrality (Cecchin et al., 1987). By
complimenting everyone, you acknowledge everyone's view or position
and demonstrate that many views can coexist.

For example:

> We are impressed by your coming here tonight, Steve. We know
> that it was not your idea and that you have had unfortunate marital
> therapy experiences in the past. It seems to us a sign of how much
> you care about Kathy and making the relationship work, that you
> would take this risk and respond to her request to come to marital
> therapy.

> We are impressed with how you, Kathy, showed that you cared
> for Steve so much that you drew the bottom line and insisted that
> he come with you tonight and talk about how you want things to
> be between the two of you.

Compliments can be directed to individuals or they can be made to
the relationship or to the family. Sometimes, we may want to normalize

the situation for the couple and sometimes we can help draw a family together through a compliment. For example, we might say to a couple discouraged by their fighting:

> We are impressed how the two of you are hanging in there even though you feel discouraged at times. They say the first year of marriage is the hardest and that more divorces happen in the first year than in any other. Given this first year can be a difficult period of adjusting, we are that much more impressed that you are keeping your faith that the two of you will work this out.

Or for a family who thinks they are working against each other, we might say:

> We are struck by how each of you is showing your concern for the family in your individual ways; how you, Dad, are putting in such long hours at your job; how you, Mom, are sacrificing your own time for the kids; how you, Jerry, are keeping to yourself so as to not rock the boat; and you, Kathy, are worrying about your Mom and Dad. We are touched by how much you all want what you think is best, and helpful for the family. It would be easy when individuals have different ways of helping to think that maybe you are in conflict when you are all trying to reach the same thing.

Compliments vary depending on the timing in the process of solution construction. With some clients, you may have elicited many exception times; the primary purpose of the compliments may be to reinforce what the clients are doing. In other situations, you may have spent an entire session listening to and supporting the client who is in a terrible situation and is upset or fearful. You may not even have had the chance to discuss goals. In these situations, your compliments are directed towards alleviating fears and normalizing the client's feelings. Compliments directed to reinforcing will wait for further sessions after a goal has been established.

MESSAGE

The message part of our feedback is organized around one of four purposes. It can be (1) educational, (2) normalizing, (3) suggesting a new meaning, or (4) most often, a rationale for the task.

1. Educational

Sometimes, in addition to compliments, we want to offer some difference that comes from formal disciplines. The function of the message is the difference of meaning that it suggests and, by implication, a difference of action. Usually, these messages are statements about research or expert opinion (that clients might or might not know) that will help them think differently about their situation or solution. These messages might also be used to affirm what clients already believe or are doing. For example, we might say to a couple who are intent on resolving *all* their issues before they can have trust or enjoy their relationship:

> In a recent research study of couples going through conflicts, the researchers found that some stayed together and some divorced. With the couples that stayed together, the researchers found that they had just as many fights as those that did not stay together, but unlike the other couples, they were able to put the issues aside for awhile and go have some fun or good times.

With parents we might say:

> We have found that some children are action-oriented at different ages and some are reason-oriented. With action-oriented children, consequences work best. With reason-oriented children, discussing and giving reasons for doing what they are told work best. Neither orientation nor response is better than the other. Children are simply different in this way and sometimes the orientation changes back and forth as they grow up. We think that your child may be at an action stage and he may have to have con-

sequences first for awhile before he sees the value of the reasons that you have been giving him.

2. Normalizing

Just as when we give compliments, sometimes we want to give a normalizing message to a client or family. The purpose is to affirm what the clients are doing and enable them to acknowledge their efforts.

For example, to parents in a newly blended family, we might say:

> You know it is not unusual when two families are coming together after having been used to being separate that there is a stressful time of adjustment. And when parents think they have failed in their previous marriage, they can easily fall into thinking that the normal fights and conflicts that go with adjusting are signs they are failing again. The fact is, when family members are saying what they want, as people are doing in your family, that is actually a good sign that the adjusting is happening and the family is on track.

3. Alternative Meaning

The message can also provide clients with a different meaning for what is happening. For example, we saw a family concerned about their daughter who was considered a "problem child." She often cut school— and when she did go to school, the teachers thought she did not listen or work. The school counselor recommended family therapy. From behind the mirror, it was clear that this was a teen who valued nontraditional ways and being different from everyone else in a traditional suburban family and school system. She came to every session dressed radically different from her parents and talked with excitement about anything that was different or new. The parents, however, had interpreted her behavior as a sign of character defect. In the feedback message, we suggested: "Clearly, both of you parents have been doing something right in producing a daughter who has the courage to go her own way and to be an alternative learner, someone who learns in nontraditional ways." This difference of meaning made it possible for the parents to view the daughter as someone who used other ways to learn, not someone who was bad or crazy.

In another case, the parents complained that their son was argumentative. Whatever they said, he had to "question them" and "fight back." The father, who valued education and wanted his child to be successful, thought that his son's behavior was an indication that he would not be able to conform and achieve as he grew up. Our message to the parents was, "We are actually impressed with how expressive your son is and we think he has the makings of becoming a great trial lawyer . . ." The father clearly liked this thought, and after this point he was able to engage his son in discussions instead of trying to get him to listen and behave. Of course, as you might predict, that son no longer wanted to be adversarial with so encouraging a father.

4. Rationale for a Task

Most often, our message to clients is a rationale for a suggested task. The messages are simple and straightforward. If clients report several things they are doing within the solution, we tell them we think they are on track and, therefore, should continue. If the solution is less developed, we say that we would like to know more about the better times and thus want to suggest that they observe the better times so they can tell us more about them. These rationales simply follow the rule of thumb, "If it works, don't fix it. Do more of it."

TASKS

As we mentioned in Chapter Five on pathways of constructing solutions (see also Figure 6), homework tasks flow from the path of the session and are aimed at furthering the construction of solutions.

Our use of homework assignments flows from the decision tree and tasks developed by de Shazer and Molnar (1987), further developed in *Clues* (de Shazer, 1988).

The basic tasks are:

1. Observe for positives.
2. Do more of the positives or exceptions.
3. Find out how the spontaneous exceptions are happening.
4. Do some small piece of the hypothetical solution.

The first task is a general task and can be used almost anytime. Tasks

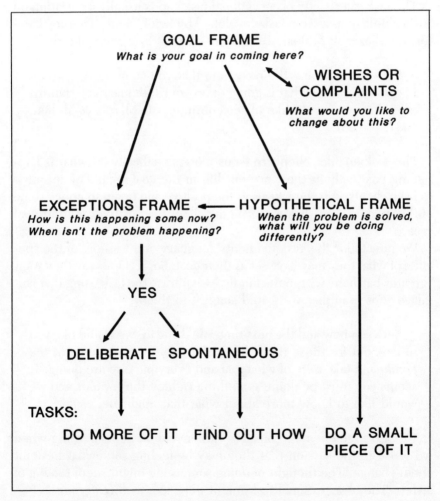

Figure 6. Pathways of Constructing Solutions

two through four, you will notice from Figure 6, flow directly from the progression of the pathways of constructing solutions.

1. Observe for Positives

This is the most general task that we suggest. It can be used regardless of the path of the map we used. We use "Observe for positives" by itself or in conjunction with the other three tasks.

The task is a strictly observational task and is usually a variation on the formula first-session task developed by Brief Family Therapy Center (de Shazer & Molnar, 1984). The original task went like this:

> Between now and the next time that you come in, we would like you to notice what is going on in your life (marriage, family, etc.) that you would like to see continue. (de Shazer & Molnar, 1984, p. 298)

This task enables clients to focus more specifically on what is happening positively in their present life in the goal area. The intent is to have clients shift their focus to the positive and begin to notice some of the specific ways they are bringing about the positives in their goal area.

We now tailor this task to clients' language and to some of the specifics of what they may have set as their goal. So, if clients say they want "greater harmony within the family," we phrase the task using that language. For example, we would suggest to them:

> Between now and the next time you come in, we would like you to look out for those times when there is some *harmony in the family* and take note of what you and everyone else are doing. It seems you must be doing something right at those times and we would like to know more about what that might be.

We also urge clients to observe rather than to *do* something when we sense in the session that they may be feeling somewhat hesitant about change. The thought of *doing* something might seem too big of a step. The observational task might not seem as threatening.

For example, a man came in who had just lost three teaching jobs in a row and was concerned about starting another for fear of being fired again. His employers had fired him because of his lack of control and discipline in his classes.

When asked what he thought he would be doing differently when he was on track in having more control and discipline, he replied that he would be taking things slower, and in a more planful manner. He thought he got in trouble when he began to act in impulsive or desperate ways. To his way of thinking, he was in danger of escalating this activity and feeling more and more out of control.

We asked if "taking things slower" was happening now. He said that on his present job, which was as a temporary clerk, he reminded himself from time to time to slow down. How was he doing that, we asked. He said that when he would say that to himself, he would take a breath and look at what he had written out as his plan for that day.

We offered him this feedback and task:

(Compliments)

We are struck by your dedication to teaching, that despite some very disappointing experiences you are still dedicated to helping young children and keeping the faith that you can learn more of what to do with them.

We are also impressed with your insights about what you are doing that are helping you do even more of what you want. We can see how taking things more slowly would enable you to use more of your skills and feel somewhat more in control.

(Message, a rationale for the task)

We are also impressed with your doing some of this already in your present job. We are curious about how you manage to do this given that this temporary job has its own pressures.

(Task)

So, we would like to suggest that between now and the next time you come in you notice what you are doing or what is different when you are acting even the slightest bit more slowly in the way you want. Make mental notes, if not written ones, so you can tell us about it next time.

This task assumes that he is already doing some of what he wants and does not require him to do anything in the areas where he is fearful. Since he does not have the pressure to do anything different, he might be more likely to observe what he is already doing. By doing this, he will find more exceptions to enumerate in the next session.

For other clients who like to *think* about changes first before they take action, this observational task seems to be a good fit.

2. Do More of the Positives or Exceptions When These Are Perceived as Deliberate and Within the Client's Control

If the interview produces exceptions to the problem or already occurring changes in the solution area that clients would say are deliberate and within their control, then we instruct them to continue to do the exceptions and observe what happens.

For example, a young woman came in complaining about feeling depressed and discouraged about a recent break-up in a relationship. She had been engaged and her parents had disowned her over her choice of a husband. Despondent about the turn of events and feeling there was no hope, she had tried to kill herself.

After joining and empathy, we asked what she wanted from therapy. She stated that in the relationship and the storm with her parents and fiancé she had "sort of lost herself." She now wanted to think *for* herself and *of* herself. She thought she needed to be taking care of herself and not get so wrapped up in what other people thought or wanted.

When we asked how she might already be doing that, she stated coming to therapy was one thing and that she was looking for another job because she had lost her job. She further stated that her job search was different in that she was looking for what she thought might be interesting for her, rather than for what she thought she should do. She was not pressing herself to call her fiancé and was letting go of some of that sense of desperation that she had to get married now.

These were all exceptions within the area of her goal of thinking for and of herself, as well as taking care of herself. She would say these were all deliberate things and within her control. Even if these were not all consciously thought out beforehand by her as "thinking of and for herself," she would say that she could repeat all of the actions she was taking.

We therefore gave her this feedback and task:

(*Compliments*)

We are very impressed that you are choosing life over death, that despite what has been happening you are choosing to make your life worthwhile to you by thinking about yourself and doing what is good for you.

We are struck by how you are already doing some of that by coming to therapy, by looking for a job that interests you rather than for one you think you should do, by relaxing your expectation that you have to get married *now*. We agree with you that these all seem to be steps in the right direction and helpful for you. We are curious about what else you are doing or thinking differently about that you have not noticed yet.

(*Message, a rationale for the task*)

We think this taking care of yourself is great and want to encourage you to continue doing it at a pace that seems right to you. We know that you have been ambitious in your thinking in the past and you might be tempted to take more than one step at a time, but we would urge you to take it slow.

(*Task*)

So keep up what you are doing that is "for you" and take notice of what you are doing so that you can tell us about it next time.

This simple message complimented her, reinforced what she was already doing in the solution or goal area, suggested that she continue to "take care of herself" (her words) and notice what else is happening (the implication is that there is more she is doing that she has not noticed *yet*). Because she had placed demanding expectations on herself in the past, we suggested that she move ahead at a more comfortable pace.

3. Find Out How the Spontaneous Exceptions Are Happening

If the exceptions clients talk about in the session are seen by them as out of their control or spontaneous, or if clients cannot explain how the exceptions happened, we suggest a task that focuses their attention on how the exceptions are being accomplished. The most common task to bring out what is working for the client is pretending.

For example, a woman came to see us because she was feeling depressed. She stated that she did not feel like a productive person and that even with her husband's support and encouragement, she was not able to do anything more. In fact, his encouragement only made her feel worse by reminding her of what she was not doing.

She stated that when the problems were solved (hypothetical solution) she would be acting more organized and scheduling her day when she got up. Right now, she thought her antique business and managing her household were failing because she would stay in bed or just sit around all day.

We asked whether any of this being organized and scheduling her day happened now, at all. She said there were days when she would be productive for half a day or sometimes longer. How did she explain this? She said she could not; some days she just felt different. When she felt different as she woke up, she was more organized on those days. We gave her this feedback:

(Compliments)

We are very impressed with your setting these goals of being more organized and acting more productively in your business and home life. Other people have been content to let others do it and take advantage of them or else they have just given up. In contrast, you definitely want to be contributing your share.

(Message, a rationale for the task)

We are also struck that some days you act more productively and organize your day. Somehow you get yourself to do that, but as yet you are having difficulty explaining it. We think there is something to these days when you feel different.

(Task)

So, what we want to suggest is that on the odd-numbered days of the week you pretend to feel different and see what happens. We know that you might not always feel that way. In fact, you might even feel the same old way. However, we think there is some potential in how you act and think different when you do. So, every other day *pretend* to feel different and on the even-numbered days just do as you normally do. Let us know what differences you notice.

This feedback message very simply complimented her, gave her the message that there was some potential for solution in the exception times, and asked her to pretend to do what she said she was doing and notice what worked.

We asked her to pretend to do this every other day in order for her to be able to contrast the results with what she did "normally." It is hoped that the difference between her experiences will give her more clues as to how she can have control over what initially seemed out of control to her.

4. Do a Small Piece of the Hypothetical Solution

Sometimes we have no information other than the hypothetical solution. That may be because there was not enough time to get exceptions or maybe, despite our best efforts, there were no exceptions that were articulated. All we have is a description of the hypothetical solution. More than likely, we cannot tell clients to go home and practice the hypothetical solution because to them it is still in the realm of miracles or magic. We suggest to clients, at that point, that they go home and experiment with some very small piece of the solution.

The reason for scaling down the task to some small piece of the solution is that usually the solution has so far been discussed only within the frame of the "miracle" question. Therefore, in the client's mind, the solution may still be very remote and unreachable.

In order to fit our task within their present framing, we suggest that clients go home and "experiment" (if that word is a better fit with their worldview) or "pretend" (if that word is more fitting) with some small piece of the solution and let us know what happens.

For example, a young woman came to see us about some problems she was having with her mother. She thought of her mother as always being critical of her. She felt frustrated that no matter what she did to please her mother, the mother never seemed happy.

We asked how we could help her with this. Initially, this was quite a puzzle to her because she was hoping her mother would become different and she had not thought of what she wanted from therapy or what *she might do differently.* She thought for a moment and then said she would like to be taking a "pro-active" stance. We asked how she would be acting (hypothetical solution) if she were being "pro-active" now. She said that when she was spending time with her mother who lived out of town she would be "setting her own agenda and taking charge more" of the time with her mother. She could not think of any exceptions, times when she was doing that even a little bit with her mother now.

We asked how that would be for her if her mother did not always like what her daughter did as part of the "pro-active" stance. She said that it would be hard for her to be "pro-active" when her mother disagreed, but at least she would have the satisfaction that she had voiced what she wanted rather than acting passively as she did now. She stated that what she did now was always to ask her mother what she wanted to do. However, she resented always having to ask or having to do what her mother wanted.

We asked what her mother might say about her taking a more "pro-active" stance if she were here in the session. She thought for some time, and then said that she thought that maybe her mother might even like it. She might like seeing her daughter state what she wants.

At the end of the session, we had no exceptions, no recent examples of the client being "pro-active" with her mother. So we asked her to do some small piece of the hypothetical solution.

(Compliments)

We are very impressed with how much you care about your mother and about your time with her. Someone who did not care as much would just blow off the time and it would not make any difference whether it was a good time or bad time.

We are also impressed by how you respect yourself and how you want to have a good time for yourself and how you would like to have a better relationship with your mother.

(Message, a rationale for the task)

We are very struck with your idea about being more "pro-active" and "taking charge more."

(Task)

We would like to suggest that you might want to experiment with this new idea. Because you tend to be a giving person and being pro-active might seem a bit awkward at first, you might want to do just a small piece of it to try it on for size.

The idea of this task is to help the client create experience for herself with the new meaning that has evolved from our conversation—that is, being "pro-active" and "taking charge more." With this new meaning, she can experiment with the solution. This does not mean that she *has* to succeed with it. She is only to experiment to find what about it she might like to continue. Since it is new, we suggest she do only a small piece of the hypothetical solution and we leave it up to her to decide what a small piece might be.

While all these tasks flow from the map, each task must be framed by the message. The message provides the context for the task. If the interview has produced exceptions that are deliberate and the client seems likely to do tasks, then usually we try to have the compliments, message, and task all flow with the same theme and momentum. The compliments will highlight the exceptions; the message will frame the exceptions as being on track to solving the problem and will indicate the control the client has over the exceptions; the task will tell clients to do more of what they are already doing.

Similarly, if the exceptions are perceived as spontaneous, the compliments, message, and task will all be organized around the theme of spontaneous exceptions and how clients will find out how they brought them about.

All four of these tasks assume that a goal is being developed and solution construction is in motion. However, even when a goal has not been established yet, there are times that we give tasks that focus the client on distinguishing between complaint and goal or on defining what the client wants.

For example, some clients come to therapy with a misconception of what the therapist can do. Couples may come in with each mate expecting that the therapist can and will be able to change the other. Other clients may have a list of wishes or of things they do not want, but they have not as yet thought of what they *do* want. In such circumstances, we might suggest that clients take the time between sessions to think about what they want from therapy. For some clients, that may require their having to think about whether they want to put the energy into their marriage or divorce, or do something that involves some risk. A message and task might be like this:

(Message, normalizing and a rationale for the task)

It seems very apparent that the two of you are very clear about what you have not liked and that you are very frustrated with how things have been going between the two of you. It would seem to make sense that you would be torn about whether or not you want to take risks or steps to make things better.

(Task)

We would suggest that you give some thought this week as to how we can help you if you decide that you want to try working things out or how you would like us to help if you decide that you do not want to work things out.

This task does not require a decision about marriage or divorce, but does ask the clients to think about what they might like from coming to therapy. Since there has been no agreed-upon goal as yet, we cannot ask them to *do* anything.

Another example is a mother who came in about her 16-year-old son. The mother was concerned about the repeated fighting between the two of them. She was a single parent and they lived in a dangerous part of the city. Mother was concerned about her son's safety with all the gangs in the neighborhood and wanted him to stay home much more than he was willing.

The son was also concerned about the fighting, and wanted to be talking and getting along with his mother. He just wanted her to trust him more to be on his own and pick his own friends.

In the first session, mother and son identified some times when they talked and he felt trusted. At the second session, they reported that things were much better. Mother was very pleased that he was not arguing with her and was doing the things she asked.

At the third session, they reported that things were much worse. The boy was very discouraged that despite his trying to please his mother and do what she said, she seemed just as restrictive and overly protective.

In talking with mother, we found that she thought that the burden for the solution was all with her son. Mother seemed to have criteria only for when to punish or restrict him and not for when to trust him. She had not thought out how she would know when to let go of him more, now that he was getting older. Her goal had been defined thus far only in terms of what *her boy* would be doing differently and did not include what *she* would be doing differently.

We gave mother this message and task:

(Message, new meaning and a rationale for the task)

We are impressed how you are managing to be a single parent in such difficult circumstances and how you have raised a boy who so wants to have a good relationship with his mother. You have obviously been doing a good job of encouraging respect and responsibility. It seems to us that now that he is getting older you also want him to be developing more trust in his own judgment. If he is going to make mistakes, we suppose it is better that he make them now when he has you for advice and counsel.

(Task)

Since it is important to both of you that he know that he is earning your trust, we suggest you think about how you will know when to let him do more things independently and how he will know that you are trusting him.

This task was designed to facilitate the mother's defining a goal rather than a complaint. At the beginning of the session, she had still been defining a goal that was out of her control—that is, her son being different. She was not, as yet, recognizing how she could facilitate his further changing in the way she wanted.

DISCUSSION

QUESTION:
Are not clients put off by your leaving the room and taking a break?

When we first started taking breaks, we carried with us all our assumptions from earlier models. We were afraid that clients would think we were rude, that we were cheating them of their time, or that we were not really working.

We have found the opposite to be true. Clients have told us how much they appreciate the direct feedback before they leave. Some clients comment that they frequently had felt frustrated with previous therapies that were so nondirective that they did not know what the therapist's thoughts were.

Some clients have even commented that they really appreciate that we are taking separate time to really think about what they said.

QUESTION:
Have you found clients objecting to receiving only positive feedback?

Some clients do. For them feedback that is only positive does not seem "real." Other clients think the way to reach a solution is to plunge into the problem or they think they have to know why the problem is happening.

For those clients who want "reality," we might preface what we say with "You probably will think this is too positive, but . . ." We might also tone down our feedback or bring in our cautions or worries to match whatever concerns might be behind their desire for a more negative or balanced feedback.

We might say:

We are really impressed that you are taking a firmer stand with the children, being direct, and following through. However, we are also concerned that since you are such a loving parent you might mistakenly think that the consequences are a sign of meanness on your part rather than a way to prepare the children for the responsibilities they will face in the real world.

For those clients who are problem-oriented, we might explain that our style is to focus on what works. We might further explain that if focusing on what works does not help, we can then get into the problem material.

QUESTION:
What about the mirror? Is it necessary to use one or to work as a team?

The mirror is not necessary and working as a team is not necessary. They are both advantages. The mirror gives the team the advantage both of being apart from the session and of having the detachment to have a different perspective on the client's situation, as well as on the interaction between therapist and client.

The team is a tremendous advantage if you have that luxury. The additional perspective of each person of the team and the distance created behind the mirror provide a melting pot of feedback for the client to choose from and take advantage of.

However, when I, John, used to do home visits, I obviously could not use a mirror or team. However, I would still ask the client for a "think break" and use some time to think out my feedback. Co-therapy in our experience provides the additional perspective, but does not provide quite as clean a detachment as the use of a mirror.

At first glance, using a team approach can hardly seem to be cost effective. However, the learning that takes place by all the members seems to more than compensate for the added time. The reputation of your therapy is enhanced by the effectiveness added by use of the team.

QUESTION:
Do you always give a task?

We almost always give a task or suggestion unless the client has somehow indicated that a task does not fit or we simply do not have one. We do not necessarily expect the client to do the task and we never ask directly if the task was done. We used to ask clients about their task, but when they had not done the task they were usually defensive. Now, we just ask our beginning question of "What is different or better?" and assume that in the course of the reply the question of whether or not they had done the task will be answered.

EXERCISES

1. Keep a journal for yourself for a week. Look for the things that are going on in your life that you would like to continue and write them down. At the end of each day, write out one compliment to yourself based on the journal. This will provide you with an experience roughly similar to that of your clients.

2. In beginning to give feedback to your clients, start by giving the client three compliments. Notice the differences in the client's responses both then and in the next session. Enjoy the change. Use the compliment worksheet (Figure 7) to generate your compliments.

3. Use the solution construction worksheet (Figure 4, p. 87) to determine where you and the clients are in constructing solutions. Based on where you think you and the client are, pick a solution constructing task that flows from the conversational pathway toward solution and tell the client directly and straightforwardly what your suggestion is.

This worksheet is designed to help you construct compliments and feedback for your clients. When taking your break in the session, read over and answer the following questions. Your answers will provide positive reinforcement for your clients and may lead to messages that you want to use. Ask yourself:

1. What can I say positively about the client that can promote a *positive atmosphere*?

2. What things is the client doing that are already working, positive, or exceptional that I can highlight and *encourage*?

3. Are there *fears about being judged* that I might want to support or alleviate?

4. Are there apparent *fears or expectations about change* that I might want to alleviate?

5. Is there anything about the context that I might want to *normalize*?

6. How can I give *credit* to the client for changing?

7. If there is more than one person present, how can I *support each individual*?

Figure 7. Compliment Worksheet

9

What Do We Do Next?

"Every Session Is the First, Every Session Is the Last"

■ The meaning of the message is the response you receive.

Sometimes trainees ask us, "What do I do after the first session?" While this is not an unusual question and while we do think that constructing solutions can be described in a sequential fashion, we do not want to promote the notion of stages or phases to therapy. We also do not want to promote the idea that subsequent sessions need to be much different than the first. What we do want to promote is the idea that constructing solutions is a way of thinking and interacting with clients. Every session is the first and every session is the last. Constructing solutions may extend over 15 minutes in a first meeting, possibly over an hour of a first meeting, over several meetings within a short period of time, or over a few meetings over a longer period of time.

To the extent that you are looking for positives, the exceptions, and solutions, and to the extent that you are promoting change by maintaining rapport and offering positive feedback and encouragement, every session is a first session. To the extent that you are asking what this client needs to be doing differently at the end of this session to be on a track toward what she or he wants, every session is a last session.

The duration of therapy is not predictable. Trying to predict the duration of therapy or the number of sessions usually gets in the way of creating successful solutions. The clients will tell you through their actions and feedback what to do next and whether or not another session is necessary.

140

This thinking about the span of time and need for sessions is very different than "short-term" models which determine beforehand what the problem is and how long therapy should be required.

When one approaches therapy one session at a time, there are no phases or stages. Every session is the first; every session is the last. Describing the solution process, however, as a sequence of interactions and procedures can be useful for organizing our thinking and actions, regardless of how brief or how long the time span may be. Describing the sequence of interactions and procedures will also help you decide what to do in the next session—if you think one is needed.

WHAT DO WE DO NEXT?

So far we have described solution paths in terms of therapist and client utilizing the goal, hypothetical solution, and exceptions frames to create client movies of themselves solving their problem. The paths include using the criteria of a well-defined goal to develop the movie and the client's experience. We further invite the client not only to construct her or his movies but also to recognize their solution movies in their present experience. As the client does this, we offer positive feedback and further suggestions.

As change occurs, as solutions evolve, and as we and the client progress down the solution-constructing paths, one of the questions we as therapists ask ourselves is, "How will this client know she or he does not have to come here anymore?" or "How will this client know that her or his changing is for real and lasting?"

To some of you these questions may seem premature or you may ask why these questions would be relevant so early. In a "goaling"-oriented therapy, however, we want to know not only what clients may want to be doing but also how they will know when they are doing what they want to do. The question is relevant very early in the solution process because we want to make sure that clients not only get what they want but that they have some way of recognizing the fact of their getting what they want. If they are solving their problem but do not know how to recognize the solution, the solution is of little or no use to them.

We also believe that clients' notion of the future can propel the present for them. So we want to help them construct a solution that is recognizable and convincing now.

Once the client is talking about changing (whether in the first or subsequent sessions), we ask, "How convinced are you that your changing will continue?"

Some clients respond unequivocally that they are solving the problem or there is no longer a problem. They may even spontaneously mention that they do not think there is a need for additional sessions.

Some clients will respond more hesitantly. We ask how they will be acting differently or what will be different when they are saying goodbye to us. They may tell us what more they need to be doing. Some will indicate an objection to the present solution. Others may say there is still a troubling aspect, usually around the meaning of the solution. Some will respond that they just need more practice or need to see the results over time in order to be convinced they are on track.

The answers to "How will you know you do not have to come here anymore?" and to "How convinced are you that your changing will continue?" lead us to one of the following conclusions?

1. The client is convinced she or he is on track and, therefore, therapy is completed.
2. The client thinks she or he is on track and thinks that more practice of the solution is needed.
3. The client thinks she or he is on track and will be convinced by success over time.
4. The client appears to be struggling and further solution development is needed.

1. The Client Is Convinced She or He Is on Track and Therapy Is Completed

A family came to see us because the family thought their 13-year-old son was depressed. He had suffered a broken leg several months ago and had not been able to play football that past fall. It was now winter and the family thought he was depressed because he was not doing as well as he wanted in his hockey performance.

In the family session, we asked each member's goals in coming to see us. Both mother and father wanted their son to be feeling better and to change his attitude. To them, he seemed either depressed or irritable. They both thought these problems stemmed from his being depressed and discouraged about his injury. Father, especially, thought his son's irritability was due to poorer performance in sports. Father was the assistant coach for his son's hockey team.

The son thought that he might be depressed, but he was not sure if he was or not. He was not sure what "being depressed" meant. What he wanted was for his parents to be treating him differently. This was a surprise to the parents. He said that his father was treating him too much as if he were a "gofer." This meant that at home his father was always telling him to "go for" this and "go for" that. He also thought that his father was treating him harder than the other boys on the hockey team.

At the end of the session, we complimented them all on being so open and frank about what each wanted. We thought the family's openness showed a great deal of caring and trust in one another that permitted each to be so direct. Since the family's goal was to have more times when the family was getting along, we asked them to take notice what they were doing when the family was in part getting along better.

The family called to cancel the next session. They said that things were going very well. They were impressed by the notion that being direct was a good thing. Since each member of the family was now continuing to be direct, relationships were going quite well. Father and son felt they had reached some new understanding and the son said he had learned that he could speak his mind to his father.

They were convinced of the solution and therapy was completed.

2. The Client Thinks She or He Is on Track and Thinks That More Practice Is Needed

Often, we will see sudden change in the solution after the first session, but the client still feels she or he needs to practice the solution for a longer period of time. In response to the question, "How convinced are you—in percent—that you will continue to do what you did this past week?" clients may suggest a fairly convincing percentage that they are on track but not convinced yet that they can keep the solution going without continued practice. The percent suggested is not at the level expected when therapy is concluded. They have no objection to the track of solution. They just feel a need to repeat the solution because it is seen as a new skill.

A man came to see us for therapy for the problem of repeated masturbation in public washrooms. Prior to his entering therapy, this behavior happened almost every day and he was feeling ashamed. After the first session, the behavior did not occur during the following week. He was actually on a solution track, but not convinced that he would continue this change until he had achieved his solution on several occasions in different places. He knew that he was still tempted to perform the old behavior and so he wanted to experience more and possibly different situations without the behavior.

We saw him for a few sessions more, with a month between these sessions to allow him time to try out his new skill and continue to get reinforcement.

3. The Client Thinks She or He Is on Track and Will Be Convinced by Success Over Time

The client's evidence for success is several successes or some marker the client has selected.

A couple came to see us where the wife had been afraid to say what she wanted or to say she was angry for fear that her husband would get defensive and start calling her names. Within the first two sessions, the couple had identified exceptions and ways of talking to one another whereby she could say what was on her mind without his taking it personally. She, however, was not yet convinced that this would continue because of their years of marriage when communication did not go this way. She felt a need to come in once a month over several months as a safety check and to use the time to build convincing experiences of being direct while he listened. Because she had been disappointed before, she wanted to build a history of success she could use to reassure herself when she was tempted to go back to her old ways of self-righteous silence and withdrawal.

Other clients think they are on track, but for them there is some context or event that will mark success. For example, parents who are concerned about their children's school performance may be more convinced that their solution of being firm about homework is working when their child brings home a better report card. The report card serves as the marker.

4. The Client Appears to Be Struggling and Further Solution Development Is Needed

A couple described repeated conflict in their relationship. However, the relationship had been better in the past week. Each credited the change as due to the other person's being more giving. In other words, each explained the change as due to the other's change rather than to her or his own change. Although they were doing better, we worried about this solution process because the solution was not well-defined. Each saw the solution as resulting from something out of her or his control, the other person's change. Further solution development was needed for the couple to identify what each of them individually was doing that was making things better and to recognize how solution development could continue even when the other slipped back into old ways.

SUBSEQUENT SESSIONS

We start each session after the first with the question, "So, tell us what is different or better?"' This question presupposes that change is happening and that something better or, at least different, is happening. This question sets the tone for the session on a positive note and continues from the previous session the process of looking for positives, exceptions, and solutions.

In this way, we let our clients know what we think is useful and important—that is, positives and solutions. Figuratively, we "train" our clients to recognize what is useful and expected. We do not think that we instrumentally or literally train our clients. We believe, however, that as a result of our acting in accordance with our assumptions, clients learn to expect certain questions from us and our positive orientation. "Training" clients is not unique to this approach. If we thought that feelings were primary, we would probably start our sessions by asking clients, "So, how are you feeling today?" If we thought that dreams were important, we would probably start with, "So, tell me your dreams of the past week." Clients would thus learn that we thought feelings were important or that dreams were important.

By asking positive-oriented questions, we continue a solution process. At times, we may not have accomplished much in identifying the goal or in developing a solution during the first session. Time may have been restricted because of lateness, because the clients were still too angry to focus on solutions, or because of a need to clarify the reasons for the referral. Many situations may interfere with the solution process at the first session and we may find that the task of the second session continues to be clarifying what the client(s) want. We may have elicited only half the goal or, as happens with couples or families, we may not have had time to talk with everyone as fully as we wanted.

The statement of the goal in the first session may have been stated only vaguely. In any case, we want to use the exceptions and changes from the time between sessions to sharpen the definition of the goal. We want to continue to build on the changes and keep in mind the criteria for a well-defined goal.

Client responses will run the whole spectrum from dramatic change and unbounded optimism to feeling that the situation is much worse and downright discouraging. Do not be discouraged or surprised when the client says the situation is the same or even worse.

When clients report the situation is the same or even worse, keep in mind this absolute rule of thumb: Never believe them! Keep in mind your assumption that change is occurring all the time and *do* believe that this is how clients have experienced the time and that it is their view as well. Their responses, however, may merely indicate that the goal or solution is still being developed and that this session is still like a first session. Their response may also indicate the size of the measuring sticks they have been using for success or the meanings they have applied which would account for their thinking there was little progress.

Therapist: So, how have things been since I saw you last? What is different or better? (*Exceptions frame*)

Client: Well. . . . things have been pretty bad . . . the stress and pressure I am under is not any better; matter of fact, the deadlines I am under are getting even worse.

Therapist: I am sorry to hear that and that your deadlines are all the same. How have you managed to cope with all the deadlines since I saw you last? (*Exceptions frame within the client's frame of "stress and pressure"*)

Client: That is not all of it. Things with my husband have gotten worse since I saw you.
Therapist: I don't understand. Along with your deadlines, things with you and your husband are not going well either? (*Clarification*)
Client: My husband is really pissed at me because I put my foot down. I told *him* to take care of the kids so I could go work out. I decided I had to have time for myself and that meant that I had to pull back the reins.
Therapist: You mean things became difficult with your husband because you decided to do something about the pressure, to take time for yourself, and he did not like that change?
Client: Right.
Therapist: So, actually things seem worse because you took some steps in the direction you wanted, reducing stress by taking care of yourself.
Client: Yes, that is true. I am taking care of myself and looking out for my needs. My husband is not used to it, I guess.

The client may initially have thought that the week was worse and she was not making progress. She may have hoped she would be feeling different already, she may have hoped her husband would have welcomed her change, she may have hoped the stress would have gone away by itself. Regardless of the explanation, more than likely her initial criteria and evidence for progress did not allow her to notice the difference in her actions of the week. By assuming the exceptions can be created in the conversation and by being sensitive to nuances of change, you and the client can continue constructing solutions.

You may find that the client's experiences have been better for the whole time right up to the day of the appointment. However, because of a reoccurrence of the problem the day of the session, the client has lost track of all the good time.

When clients say that things are the same or worse, this is the time for you to accept what they say as their view of the situation and then use all your exception-oriented skills to find any differences.

For example, for a client who says that the week has been about the same, acknowledge what the client says and then utilize the response to ask about exceptions.

Therapist: What is different or better?
Client: Well, things are about the same.

Therapist: So, things *seem* about the same. Are there times when you would have expected things to be even worse, but they were not? (*Exceptions frame*)

Client: Well, actually yes, I guess. We could have had a fight about my mother. Normally, when I say my mother is coming to visit, my wife and I get into a big fight about it. I don't know why we did not this time. I guess we have been so tired of fighting, we just did not do it this time.

Therapist: So you might have had a fight but you did something different. What did you do rather than fight? (*Specification and contextual differences*)

Client: I guess I was not going to try to talk my wife into being nice to my mother or getting involved in my mother's visit.

Therapist: So, that was different. How did you decide to do that? You could have tried things that you have done in the past that do not work. (*Specification and contextual difference*)

Client: Well, I guess I am learning that I cannot change her. Trying to make her enjoy my mother was not making it.

This sample session demonstrates how to remain true to the assumptions that change is occurring all the time and that exceptions can be found or created. First, the therapist accepted the client's view that things were the same. Then the therapist asked about times that the relationship could have turned worse, but he and his wife did something different. The client searches for occurrences when the problem could have happened but did not or when the problem could have been much worse but was not so bad.

The idea that keeping matters from becoming worse can actually be a change can be used even more explicitly. For example:

Therapist: So, what has been different or perhaps better? (*Exceptions frame*)

Client: Oh, things are about the same.

Therapist: Really, I would think that given your circumstances, it could be expected that matters would be worse. How are you managing to keep things from being much worse? (*Exceptions frame*)

Client: Well, you are right. I am having a terribly hard time just keeping my head above water.

Therapist: So, you have been having an extremely difficult time. How have you been keeping your head above water, even though you have been separated only a few weeks? (*Exceptions frame*)

In this session, the therapist again accepts the client's presentation of his circumstances and then frames the exceptions question in terms of why things are not worse. The assumption that keeping things the same despite overwhelming circumstances can be an accomplishment in itself is made explicit.

Often, clients will come back and report that their situation is much worse. After supporting their frustration and feelings of anger or discouragement, use the hypothetical solution frame in the context of the "worse" frame.

Therapist: What is different or better? (*Exceptions frame*)
Client: Our relationship has been much worse. We fought all week and we have not talked to each other the past three days.
Therapist: Wow, things must have been really tough. I guess, with such a week, feeling discouraged and hopeless would not be unusual. Yet you are still here. Does that mean you are still hoping to make things better? (*Rechecking the stated goal*)
Client: Yes, we do not want to divorce, but our relationship has to change.
Therapist: I am very sorry to hear that the week has been so rough. The time must have been very rough and frustrating. I guess you do not want to have another week like that again. Are there actions or words said that you would do differently if you had the week to do over again? (*Hypothetical solution frame within their report of a worse present*)

This conversation typifies the therapist accepting the "worse" frame, rechecking whether working on their relationship is still their goal, and then using the hypothetical solution frame. Once you have elicited some examples of how they might do things differently, you can then ask about times when they are doing that "somewhat" now. The exceptions that the couple may have missed earlier might come out.

In the sessions subsequent to the first, we may also ask the "confidence" question in order to make further decisions about the feedback at the end of the session, the timing of the next session, or concluding therapy.

SPACING SESSIONS

Many of us who have been trained in traditional therapy models are accustomed to scheduling one or more sessions regularly every week. In this solution-focused approach, we schedule each session on its own merit. The criteria we consider before scheduling the next session are:

1. Time needed for the performance of some homework task.
2. Promotion of confidence in the solution.
3. Promotion of independence from therapy.
4. The client's responsibility for therapy.

1. Time Needed for Performance of Some Homework Task

Some homework tasks take more time to do or more time for the client to perceive some meaningful difference. A task of asking a client to pretend to be in a good mood on the odd-numbered days of the week is intended to give the client the experience of difference when acting differently. Acting as if she or he is in a good mood on the odd-numbered days while going about things normally on the other days provides the client with a contrast. To do this task for only a couple of days does not provide the client with enough experience or feedback. This type of task generally takes two weeks.

Tasks take varying lengths of time and clients, unless they have been trained by other therapies, usually accept the logic of meeting in a couple of weeks, or a month, or whatever time has been suggested.

2. Promotion of Confidence in the Solution

As the solution develops and the fact that the client is on track becomes apparent to her or him and to us, we want to space sessions to allow the client to have the experience of success with the solution and also in handling whatever setbacks that occur. Spacing out the sessions enables the client to have a longer perspective on solution construction and to put setbacks in perspective.

A longer time has the advantage of demonstrating change that a close-up look lacks. Metaphorically, the difference is like this: Parents who are with their children on a day-to-day basis may lose track of the extent their children are growing. A marker such as a birthday may help them notice that over a longer period of time their child has grown three inches.

3. Promotion of Independence from Therapy

As clients experience progress in their changing, the spacing of sessions over longer periods of time—from two weeks to three to six—can promote confidence in solving the problem.

We often have clients who mistakenly think that their changing is dependent on therapy and that we—the therapists—are responsible for the change. We want clients to see that *they* are responsible for the change and are capable of keeping the solution construction going.

We typically compliment clients on changing and suggest that we space the sessions so they can check out success in staying on track. Sometimes we spell out that part of our job as therapists is to make sure that clients recognize their own resourcefulness and their abilities to continue solutions. We might also explain how we believe it would be unethical for us to continue to see clients in a way that leads them to dependence on therapy or makes them feel we are needed when the goal is to be independent. In brief therapy, we want to promote the belief that clients are resourceful and that they are responsible for the changing.

Kral and Kowalski have described a procedure called "positive blaming," a tongue-in-cheek name for crediting the client for all the changing (Kral, 1986; Kral & Kowalski, 1989). In "positive-blaming," the therapist can preempt the client's crediting the therapist for the changes by saying something similar to this message: "You may falsely blame us for all your recent work and change. We believe, however, that all these positives are your 'fault.'" This is said in a joking or teasing manner. In a more serious and straightforward style, the therapist might say, "You may be too modest to think that all these recent changes are because of your own actions, but we believe you are accomplishing a great deal and deserve all the recognition and credit. After all, no one made you do any of these changes."

4. The Client's Responsibility for Therapy

This criterion is actually part of all the previous three. We think of clients as being responsible for their therapy and we determine with them the amount of time they should be spending on a task or what seems to be a suitable length of time between the current and following session, based on the confidence they have in their solutions.

NORMALIZING SETBACKS

Many clients regard problems and solutions in "all or none" terms. The first time they fall back to problem behavior, they can easily think that the change does not count or that the changing is not real. In the midst of changing, clients are often vulnerable to thoughts of failure.

We attempt to foster a more positive approach by introducing the notion that change usually involves "setbacks." We tell clients that for every three steps forward there are two steps back. While we tell clients that the two steps backward are normal, we also tell them that we are concerned that they will mistakenly see the normal two steps back as failure and possibly give up on what is working. Often, after this type of normalizing, we give clients the assignment to notice how they get themselves back on track when the setback occurs.

INQUIRING ABOUT DIFFICULTIES

As change occurs, we may ask what things are going on that may make it more difficult for clients to continue to do what they are doing or ask what things could make it tempting to go back to the old ways.

This technique, described by Kral and Kowalski (1989) as "flagging the minefield," is a way of fast forwarding into the future and facilitating how the client will handle difficulties and temptations that may come along. This questioning normalizes that there may be difficulties and focuses the solution process on how the client will handle these situations. The presupposition remains that clients will move beyond these times, that they will not be stopped by them in the longer perspective. For example:

Therapist: Are there times when you can imagine it will be tempting to go back to the old ways rather than thinking of yourself?

Client: I guess when my kids complain about my not staying home, I will probably feel guilty.

Therapist: So how will you be getting through those times despite the guilty feeling? (*Hypothetical solution frame*)

Client: I will remind myself that what is best for me in the long run is best for them and go out anyway. I just have to give myself a break and take care of myself.

Therapist: So, if you let your guilt stop you from going out, how will you be getting yourself back on track?

Client: I do not think the guilt could put me back for very long before I will realize that I need to be taking care of me.

CONCLUDING THERAPY

Concluding therapy is usually accomplished when we and our clients think they are on track in reaching a solution or getting what they want. When we ask how confident they are in continuing the changing, their response usually matches their criteria for what they believe would be reasonable for concluding therapy.

We sometimes offer clients some final feedback that may include several options for concluding therapy. One option would be to meet again in four, five, or six weeks as a check on how they are doing or what additional changes they have seen. Another option is to schedule an appointment with the same time arrangement, but with the option of their calling to cancel if they feel the appointment is not needed. The third option is just to leave the appointment open, with no specific date and with the option that the client can call and schedule one if wanted.

Because of the steps taken to promote independence and a sense of responsibility by clients about their changing, there is no need for a formal processing of concluding therapy. Therapy can be concluded with the option to return or to call at any time in the future.

CASE EXAMPLE

Session One

A man in his 20s came to see us because he was unemployed. When asked what he wanted, he said he wanted more "direction and flexibility." We asked, "What would you be doing differently if you had these things?" (hypothetical solution frame). He said he would "be thinking more"—that is, thinking through his decisions about jobs right now rather than just bouncing around from one idea to another or taking the first job that came along. He said he questioned if he wanted to stay in social work and he thought he would like to make more money. In the past, when he was out of a job, he would just take the first offer without much thought about whether he would like the work. He had thought only about the fact that he needed money.

We asked if he thought that his recent questioning about jobs and career might already be the beginnings of this "thinking more" about what he wanted. This was our attempt to bridge his recent questioning as part of being on track to getting what he wanted. He said, "Perhaps." This was our first invitation to him that maybe some of the questioning and thinking he was already doing was part of being on track toward solution. We took this questioning as an exception to his previous panic and taking of the first job that came along. We then bridged the exception to what he said he wanted, to be "thinking more."

He allowed that perhaps his questioning and thinking more was part of being on track. We asked what else he would be doing if he were handling this job transition in the way he wanted (*hypothetical solution frame*). He said he would be "taking a more reasonable approach." We asked how he will know when he is doing that. He said that if he were taking a more reasonable approach now, he would be contacting several agencies so he could create options for choice. He would also be arranging for information interviews. These would be interviews where he would talk to people in other professions so that he could check out his interest in switching from social work.

Since the client thought that he *always* acted impulsively in the past rather than thinking things through, we asked how he would predict he would do these other steps this time. (In our question we did not ask *if* he would do these other steps. Rather we presupposed that he *would do* them, and asked him *how* he would predict that he would do them.) He accepted our presupposition and predicted he would do these steps "carefully."

After returning from our consultation break, we complimented him on taking his situation more one step at a time, the start of doing things differently this time. We also told him that we thought his creating options for himself was part of the more thoughtful approach he was looking for. Since we thought—and he had partially agreed—that he was already doing some things in the direction he wanted, we suggested he observe during the next week anything *else* he was doing that he thought might be somewhat on track.

Our thinking was that we had some exceptions of the goal already happening in (1) his questioning what he wanted beyond a paycheck and (2) his creating options and steps that he would take as part of his more thoughtful approach. Since he perceived these things as being under his control, our idea was to have him do more of the exceptions and observe what else then happens.

Session Two

He returned the next week and reported that he was feeling calmer. He had taken intermediary steps by taking "grunt" work just to earn money while he explored his other options. He had set an appointment to talk with someone about business consulting and he had rewritten his resume. He had decided to be more "active and selective." He had decided that by working to earn money for awhile doing grunt work, he could explore other possibilities. At the same time, he wanted to be active about seeking out other careers and opportunities. He thought this was different on his part because he felt that in the past he either procrastinated or took the first job out of fear.

We spent the remainder of the session talking about this more "active, selective" approach and how he was going to keep acting in this style (*pursuing the exceptions as the goal of therapy*).

We asked how confident he was that he would continue to act in this "active selective" approach. He said 85 percent, which was close to the

95 percent he thought he would be at when he would be finished with therapy. To emphasize his resolution, he said, "There is no point in sitting back."

This answer told us that the meaning was different for him. He was convinced that he was "thinking more" and that his "active, selective" style was better for him than impulsively acting out of fear of no income. He appeared to just want more practice and time. After our break, we complimented him on the changing he was doing and on his realization that an "active, selective" approach was in the right direction. We scheduled the next appointment for two weeks ahead and that seemed about right to him.

Session Three

He reported that he was continuing to do the "grunt" work, that he had checked out two jobs, and that he had been turned down on one of them. However, he did not feel this was a setback and we asked if that was different for him. He said it was very different. He was more convinced that he wanted a job that was more than a paycheck and he had created some backups for himself like the part-time job. He said he was thinking differently and was much calmer.

He was not panicking and was even giving himself "think" time to reflect on each new step or bit of information. This was much different, he said, because in the past he would have told himself that he could not afford time to just think.

We asked what could make a return more likely to his old panicky thinking and more passive ways. He said a return would be more likely only if he had a real financial setback, but he thought he would want to take it slow even then.

This answer was a sign to us that he was not only on track but was growing in his conviction that he was on track as he learned through his new experiences.

On the break, we decided to find out if an appointment in a month would suit him. Our feedback message again complimented him on his continued changing and cautioned him about setbacks. We warned him that he could confuse normal setbacks with failure and that he should notice how he put himself back on track when the normal setbacks came along.

Session Four

He reported a setback in terms of having been turned down for a job that he thought would have been very good for him. However, he reminded himself that he needed to take it slow and to continue to take care of himself. He asked for an additional session in a month as a check on his progress.

DISCUSSION

QUESTION:
Do you contract for the number of sessions you will meet?

No. We do not want to set any expectations, one way or the other. Some clients seem to respond to a set session contract by waiting until the session or two next to last to make the changes they want. They seem to respond as if the set-session contract is a deadline, and thus they wait.

Others react with surprise or concern as if fewer than, say, 10 sessions would be such a short time for such a serious problem.

If asked about the length of therapy, we usually say that we will take as long or as short as required.

QUESTION:
Do you have many clients returning with the same problem or for some other problem?

Many clients will return to see us for some other problem. We take the return as feedback that they were satisfied with what they did in therapy with us and now have something else they want to take care of.

If your question is related to the notion of symptom substitution, we do not subscribe to that assumption and we have not seen any evidence that would make us think that symptom language would be useful.

EXERCISE

Ask your clients, "How will you know you do not have to come here anymore?" Then, as a follow-up, ask, "How confident are you that you are on track now to getting what you want?"

The responses to these questions will give you some hints about your next step. Are the clients saying they are on track? Are they saying they need further practice or something else?

10

Enhancing "Agency"

Facilitating What Seems Out of Control as Within Control

■ People have all they need to solve their problems.

Another way of stating "enhancing agency" is "co-creating with clients what seems out of control to them as in their control." For many of our clients, solving a problem seems nearly impossible because everything about the problem seems out of their control. The problem seems to continue almost on its own and the solution seems out of reach because it is contingent on things that appear to clients as out of their control.

Anderson and Goolishian (1989) define "agency" as:

. . . a sense of competent action, the ability to think and feel that we have a way of doing. As far as we are concerned any therapy that would be thought of as successful, regardless of the outcome criteria or theory, results in what might be thought of as a sense of agency, a sense of being able to take action. It is not that the problem is solved but that it is now described in a way that does not stifle capacity to take action. Things may still be problematic, but we can act.

If we stay true to our assumption that clients have all they need to solve problems, we believe they have the freedom and responsibility to bring about the changes they want to make. Part of our goal, then, is to enhance their sense of responsibility and agency.

Our job as therapists is to remain curious and supportive about how

159

clients will solve their own situation. Through our interaction with clients, we assume there will be change in the meaning ascribed to the situation which will allow them to do something different. By co-creating with clients a meaning of the problem or solution as being within their control, we acknowledge their resourcefulness and responsibility. The clients gain a sense of mastery and agency.

PRESUPPOSING AGENCY AND RESPONSIBILITY

As we noted earlier, our questions contain presuppositions which form invitations to our clients to enter a different way of thinking. We as therapists are "curious" (cf. Cecchin, 1987) about how clients go about doing what they are doing or how they will create solutions. In our curiosity, we ask questions that reflect our assumption that clients are capable, that they are already solving the problem, that they are responsible for solving the problem, that they have the freedom to do what they want, and that they are the experts on what they want and will do.

The following examples are different ways of using presuppositions in our questions to facilitate the client becoming more aware of a sense of agency:

1. Facilitating a reversal or expansion of their belief.
2. Focusing on the expectations of the future.
3. Asking directly.

1. Facilitating a Reversal or Expansion of Their Belief

In the following example, the specific words in bold type in the questions highlight the presuppositions into which the counselor is inviting the client. The presuppositions are that the client has control and responsibility for her success.

School counselor: What is your goal in coming here, Marie? (*Eliciting goal*)
Marie: I would like to be doing my homework. But I just cannot seem to get it done.

Counselor: So are there times when you get some of the homework done now? (*Exceptions frame*)

Marie: Yes, but usually it is when I am interested in the work, or I am in a good mood. (*She presents the situation as if her mood determines her actions or as if she cannot do her homework without some preceding interest in it.*)

Counselor: How do **you get yourself to be interested?** I am sure there are other things you could be interested in, at that time. (*The assumption is that she does something to get herself interested or cooperates with her interest.*)

Marie: Well, I don't know. I just get into it, and then it is okay.

Counselor: How do you **decide to get into it?** (*The assumption is that she decides to do it.*)

Marie: Well, I want to pass and I know I have to do something.

Counselor: (*Sympathetically*) Oh, you want to pass. That is important to you, to pass? (*Supporting the ultimate goal for getting her homework done*)

Marie: Yes, I do not want to repeat freshman year and I am tired of wasting time in class.

Counselor: So, you want to **do more things** like getting into the work so you can pass. Are there other things **you are doing** to help yourself pass? (*Expanding the context*)

Marie: Sometimes, when I am in a good mood. But I just wish I was as smart as my sister. Everything is easy for her.

Counselor: Yeah, I guess that might be easier. (*Sympathetically*) So how **do you do it** given that it does not come as easy for you? (*Acknowledging her wish and again asking her the same exceptions-oriented question*)

Marie: I just tell myself "I want to pass" and then I do it.

Counselor: But it does not sound easy at all and it sounds like you are not always in a mood where you feel like doing it. So, how do **you decide to do it** even though it is not always easy or you are not always interested at first? (*Asking for the exception to when she is not "in the mood"*)

Marie: Well, I just tell myself, I have other things that my sister does not have—and so I just do it and sometimes it gets easier.

Counselor: (*With curious tone*) Really? How do **you do it** and **make** it get easier?

Marie: Oh, I just stop thinking about the fact that I do not want to do it and then I get into it. (*A description that implies more control and initiation on her part. This is in contrast to her previous statements that her doing homework was due to her being in the mood or interested first.*)

Counselor: So, **you shift your thinking** and **make it more interesting for yourself** or at least **get some done.** That is great! I am impressed how you do that even when you are not in the mood or crazy about doing the work.

If you continued to do more of that—**deciding to get into it because you want to pass**—would you think you were more on track to getting more homework done and getting what you want from coming here? (*Bridging the exceptions as the goal of therapy*)

Marie: Yeah, I do feel better when I make myself do it and think I am going to pass.

Counselor: I can see that and you have been doing some more of that lately as you decided you wanted to pass and do something with your class time. How do you think **you will keep doing** this?

The counselor is patient and accepting of her responses and yet invites the client to new meanings by asking questions which presuppose her having control of the "exceptions." By focusing on the exceptions when she was already doing homework, the counselor concentrated on her ability and responsibility for the changing.

This focusing on the exceptions with "responsibility" and "capability" presuppositions is a subtle deconstruction of the limits of her beliefs and an opening up of new meaning. The old belief may have been that she could work on her homework only if she was interested in it first. Later, she reversed that belief as she saw that as she moved herself to work on her homework, she developed interest. The belief that she had to feel something first before she could do what she wanted was reversed to a new belief—that she could gain a new feeling by taking action first.

Another belief the client held may have been that she had to be as smart as her sister in order to do what she wanted. At the same time that this was accepted, we asked how she *does* the exception, given that it is not as easy for her as it is for her sister. With a raised tone, the question means that we are that much more impressed that *she* does her work given that it is not as easy as it may be for her sister.

2. Focusing on the Expectations of the Future

In the following example, the therapist focuses on the hypothetical solution and on the presupposition within that view.

Therapist: What is your goal in coming here? (*Goal frame*)

Anita: I want more confidence on job interviews.

Therapist: You want to be acting more confidently when you interview? (*Changing the noun "confidence" to more of a process description*)

Anita: Yes, right now I am always scared, and convinced that I am going to mess up the interview and not get the job. I think that deep down I do not like myself. Some people have told me that I have a fear of failure. Some others say I am afraid of success.

Therapist: So, when you are acting more confidently and handling the job interviews more the way you want to (*hypothetical solution*), are you thinking you will **never** be afraid and that you will always admire yourself? (*Slightly challenging the notion that she has to feel something different first*)

Anita: No, I think I will still feel scared and still have doubts about myself, but somehow I will get myself to go to the interview and think differently of myself.

Therapist: So, you will naturally (*normalizing*) still feel scared as you anticipate the interview, but you will be saying different things to yourself. Is that right? (*Specifying the goal in more behavioral terms and different meaning. The meaning of feeling scared will be different.*)

Anita: Yes, I will say things like, "I can get this job," and then I will go after it.

Therapist: So, even though you are sometimes feeling scared and perhaps even excited (*normalizing*), you will be saying to yourself that you can get this job. How will you be doing that even though it will be normal to have doubts and fears? (*Success is no longer conditional, it is presupposed. We are not asking if she will do it. We are assuming success and asking her to describe how she will be doing it, how she will put the words, the feelings, and movie together.*)

Anita: I will just be telling myself that the fear and doubts are just temporary and I have gotten through other fears.

Therapist: That sounds like that has been more workable, but how will you do that? It sounds like it could be easy or tempting to tell yourself that feeling scared means that you are no good or not capable of handling the interview the way you want to.

Anita: Well, I know, but I just need to remind myself of the bigger view, that I have had other jobs and other interviews and that this is just one of the tough times. It will pass and I will get a job.

Therapist: So, if you were saying these things to yourself, maybe even when the interviews do not seem to lead immediately to a job, you would think you were on track to getting what you want from coming here? (*Bridging the exceptions as the goal of therapy*)

Anita: Yes, I just have to keep those thoughts in mind.

Therapist: So, how will you continue saying these more useful things to yourself? (*Pursuing the exceptions as the goal of therapy*)

In this example, Anita may be expecting that in the future she will never have doubts or fears or discouragements. To her, this expectation probably seems out of her control. By the therapist presenting an exaggerated future of both *absolutely* no fears and of admiration versus doubts for herself, the client can present times or examples that counter this exaggerated future solution and focus in more on her expectations. She can say that she will still feel afraid, but that she will say something different to herself. The client can make a new meaning for herself in the scared feeling. Toward the end of the interview, she thinks of the fear as more normal and sees that she just needs to keep the bigger picture in mind. She cannot directly do much about the scared feeling, but what she says to herself and what actions she takes she can directly change.

She has, in effect, created new meaning of her present as she adjusts her thinking about a hypothetical solution. With the new meaning, her feeling scared is not a problem and (her goal) she perceives as more within her control, what she will do in the interviews.

Other clients see their solutions as out of their control because they see them as involving someone else changing or changing first. Since they have no direct control over the behavior of someone else, their solution is out of their control.

How to facilitate these clients' redefining their goals in a way that gives them control and responsibility will be discussed in Chapter Twelve.

3. Asking Directly

Sometimes, the easiest and quickest route is to just ask directly how the client is going to keep change going. By asking directly how clients *will do the changing*, you invite them to accept the presupposition of their *solving the problem or taking actions within their control*. For example:

Therapist: So, it sounds like it has been frustrating for the two of you trying to get your son to stay in school. You have tried talking to him and it seems that he just ignores your arguments of why school is the best thing for him. What are **you going to do?** (*Said with empathy for their frustration and at the same time presupposing that the responsibility for the solution is theirs and that they will do something*)

Parents: We have tried talking to him until we are both blue in the face and none of that seems to work.

Therapist: I guess talking is not the way. What are **you going to do?** (*Hypothetical solution frame, again with empathy and curiosity*)

Parents: I guess we will just have to make him go. We were hoping that he would like school or at least be serious about his future.

Therapist: That would be nice, but I guess he is not there yet. How will **you make him** go?

Father: I hate to be so autocratic, but we will just have to take the car away for awhile.

Therapist: What do you think he will make of that?

Father: He will probably get pissed off and make life miserable, but I think it will make him go.

Therapist: This does not sound like an easy thing to do and it sounds like it goes against your more democratic ideals. How will you do this, even when he gets pissed off? (*Hypothetical solution frame*)

In this example, the parents had been hoping that the boy would *want* to go to school or do it on his own without consequences. They are now faced with his failure. The therapist facilitates their constructing solutions by presupposing that *they will do it*. These questions are expressed by the therapist with a great deal of empathy for how much these parents are frustrated and how much they do not like using consequences. For the father, consequences seem like an autocratic means that is distasteful. For him to use consequences, he may need to expand his beliefs to understand consequences as more positive rather than dictatorial.

In facilitating a reversal or expansion of a belief by focusing on the expectation of the future, and by asking directly, the therapists assume that the clients can or will solve their situation. The skill comes in phrasing the questions so as to bring out what the clients do during their successes or exceptions. The other skill is in being empathic to clients in their situation and joining with them in how *they will solve the situation*. The therapist never accepts the responsibility for solving the problem!

DISCUSSION

QUESTION:
Some clients come to my office wanting me to make them feel better, make their kids better, or, in so many words, solve the problem for them. What do you do with that?

First, we usually explore with the clients their exceptions to the problem and what they did at those times. Sometimes, by exploring as we did in the above examples, what clients did during the exceptions, we can facilitate their recognizing their own potential for solving the problem. They then can give up their initial hope that you, the therapist, will do the solving and they can explore what more they will do.

For those clients who still want us as the therapists to take the responsibility, we usually take a one-down approach and explain that we cannot do that. Sometimes, we explain that we cannot change someone else or that we doubt that we could do anything more than the client has done. Sometimes, we explain that we would be misleading them by saying that we could solve the problem when, in fact, we cannot.

EXERCISE

With a partner playing a client presenting her or himself as one of the examples above, practice using questions that presuppose responsibility and resourcefulness. Tape the session and then go over your questions to identify which questions worked better. It is better to review the tape with someone else. Someone outside of your own personal beliefs can recognize the differences more quickly.

11

The Interactional Matrix

■ Actions and descriptions are circular.

This chapter describes how we utilize an interactional view to understand client interactions of solution descriptions and attempted solutions. We then describe how questions can introduce difference and how to choose questions that fit an interactional understanding.

THE INTERACTIONAL VIEW

As we described briefly in Chapter Two, we subscribe to an interactional view. We assume that the interaction of descriptions and actions is circular and that the interaction of meaning and action is circular. Together, descriptions and actions form experience. More pragmatically, we mean that there will usually be a fit or consistency of interaction between the way people describe a problem or goal and what they do about the problem or goal. If parents think that the situation with their child is one where the child is acting badly, they will take the action of punishment. If a husband thinks that the reason for conflict in a marriage is his spouse's stubbornness, he may try to fix the stubbornness by trying to change his spouse's attitude.

People usually use the same meaning to determine the outcome of the attempted solution or course of action. If parents punish their child for bad behavior, they will look at the outcome of that action for confirmation about the original decision about the behavior being bad. If a husband tries to convince his spouse to be less stubborn so that they have fewer fights, he will probably look at his spouse's response and actions for feedback about his original decision about the stubbornness.

With a solution-focus, we carry this interactional view into the con-

168

versation with our clients. We assume that there is a circular relationship between how they describe their situation and what they do about
it. So when we converse with them about their goal, their "exceptional
times," and their hypothetical solutions, we assume that a change in
the meaning or description may lead to more of what they want. Our
intent in conversation with them is to facilitate their opening up new
or different meaning so that they can do something different and get
more of what they want outside of the therapy time. The criteria for
the success of our conversing with clients is when the clients say that
they are getting more of what they want or that there is no more reason
for meeting with us.

This interactional view of meaning and action (meaning of the
stated goal and the resulting action) is exemplified by a young man
who is having trouble writing a dissertation for school. He complains that he cannot get started. When we ask how we can help
him with this, he states that he would like to be making more progress. Right now, he feels as if he is not getting much done, that he
is just procrastinating and worrying. He states, however, that this
past week he did get some of it done.

We ask about these times when he is getting something written. He
states that he recently decided to adopt a "first draft" mode. "How is
this different?" we ask. He says that normally he starts writing and then
thinks about all the mistakes or imagines that his advisor will think this
is not good enough. Then he stops writing. With this new "first draft"
mode, he does not stop to correct things as much and he just keeps
going. Despite the tendency to correct his mistakes or question the
thinking about the paper, he continues to write.

These thoughts and actions of the exception can be described as an
interaction of meaning and action taken. There are several differences
within the exception from the problem time. The client makes the initial distinction of "first draft" being different from finished copy with
which he would be more critical. He decides to continue writing
despite temptation to critically evaluate his writing as he writes. He
decides he is making progress because he has written several more
pages in less time than if he tried to judge the work as he went along.
All these differences act as feedback about his initial distinction of "first
draft." The differences serve as feedback also for his deciding to continue to adopt this new rule.

Given that he makes the distinction about first drafts being different from other writing, he goes on to write even more despite his urge to evaluate and rewrite. The fact that he has continued to write, seen through the lens of the "first draft" distinction, is feedback for him. If he gets stuck by a temptation to go back immediately and correct an error, he may see this as further evidence that he needs to stick with his initial decision to make this only a first draft. If he sees himself as making progress overall in getting something written despite the temptations to correct, he may see this as further evidence of the validity of his initial decision.

This "first draft" mode appears to have a more open meaning for him and one that appears to allow him to act in ways that enable more of what he wants. The circular quality of the new meanings could be described in this way:

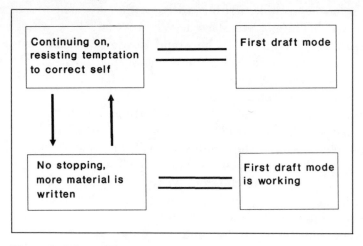

Figure 8. Solution Interaction

An interactional view can also be used to understand exceptions and solutions between people rather than only between meaning and action. In conversing with more than one person, we invite descriptions from each. We can put both descriptions together in terms of interaction. We can think interactionally about how each thinks of the situation and what he or she does. We can also consider the interaction between the two of them.

For example, in conversing with a couple about the exceptions to conflict, we would want to know the views of each and what each thinks she or he does differently. In a couple who had been married for several years, the wife complained that they had had so many fights in the past year that they were talking seriously about divorce. We asked about exceptions—that is, times when they did not fight or when the fights were okay. She said that there were some fights that were good or at least not destructive.

"What was different about those times?" we asked. She said that during those fights he did not walk away from her and leave her upset. Instead, he stayed until they were finished. "What did she like about that?" we asked. She stated that it gave her a chance to air her feelings and that it seemed to her that at least he cared enough to listen and hear her out. "What was different about that?" we asked. She said that other times when he would leave her she would then wonder whether he was blaming her for the fight and thinking she was just crazy.

We asked if this was true for him, too, that sometimes things went a little better when they did not fight or when the fights were okay. He said that was true. Sometimes she insisted that he "hear her out" and he would stay. "What was different about that for him?" we asked. He stated that when he did stay and listen sometimes she would eventually say what she wanted. He said that was different because she usually complained after the fact when it was too late for him to do anything. "Oh, so she has better luck getting what she wants from you if she tells you beforehand," we summarized.

He said, "Yes, but she is still resentful that I do not know what she wants." We asked if this was also true for him telling her. He replied that he did not think so because she seemed to know what he wanted, sometimes even before he knew.

We asked, "How did you decide to stay and listen?" He said that he knew she was serious when she told him directly that she wanted him to stay.

In this example, we can list the meanings and actions that provided for an exception interaction. For him, when she tells him what she wants, either by insisting that he stay and listen or on something else, he is more than likely to stay. He does not tell his wife what he wants, however, because he sees her as intuitively knowing what he wants and anticipating it.

For her, she sees his staying, rather than leaving her upset, as a sign of his caring. She likes the opportunity to air her feelings and for him to hear her out.

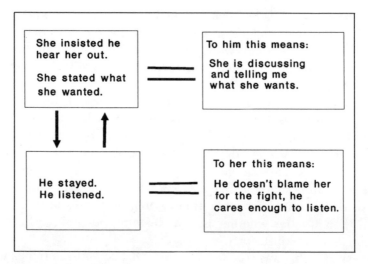

Figure 9. Exceptions Interaction

The client's descriptions of the exceptions can be put together as the more she tells him what to do the more likely he is to do some of it and listen—the more he listens, the more she thinks he cares and the more likely she is to continue to tell him what she wants.

In describing goals, exceptions, or hypothetical solutions, interactionally, we want to know the meaning that the individuals ascribed around their own as well as the other's behavior, and the course of action they take. Our knowing the meaning of each enables us to see how the two points of view and the corresponding actions fit together either as exceptions or solutions. A diagram of the exceptions might look like Figure 9.

As this couple further constructed their solution by describing the hypothetical solution, she discovered that his way of going about things was different from hers. Previously, she had thought that his not anticipating what she wanted was a sign that he did not care. Now, she thought of him as different, that rather than being intuitive about another's needs, he was someone who responded only to direct requests. This was neither good nor bad, just a different way of acting.

He continued to listen to her, and found out that she would very much like him too be more direct about what he wanted. We would describe their new meanings and actions as presented in Figure 10. This interactional view of the recursiveness of meaning and action

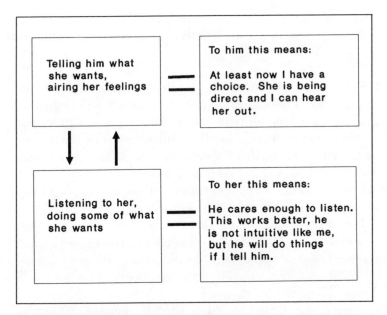

Figure 10. Hypothetical Solution Interaction

forms the basis of our understandings. As we mentioned before, we apply this interactional perspective to the client's actions with regard to solutions, the client's actions with others, and the interaction between the clients and ourselves.

INTRODUCING DIFFERENCE

When clients initially come in for therapy they usually bring with them their view of the situation and of the solutions they have attempted. Given how they view the situation and what they have been doing, they are looking for a change. We help them introduce difference to their situations by asking questions that invite them to a different view.

So far we have focused on introducing difference by using the major frames, namely:

1. "What is your goal in coming here?" (*goal frame*);
2. "How is it happening now?" or "When doesn't the problem happen?" (*exceptions frame*); and
3. "How will you be doing your goal in the future?" or "If a miracle

happened and you were on track to solving the problem, what would you be doing differently?" (*hypothetical solution frame*).

These frames invite difference for clients because most clients have not thought about what they *do want* or what life will be like without the problem. Looking for potential in the exceptional times also provides difference for them. Inviting difference with these questions allows the client to construct a more open meaning for a solution for themselves and, therefore, take new actions.

With many clients, these questions in these forms are all that may be needed to construct solutions. For others, these questions in the above form may be difficult for them to enter into. The questions just may not make sense to them. For other clients, these questions in these forms do not offer an opportunity for difference. We need to adjust the questions in some way as needed so that clients can enter the frames and find a difference for themselves.

For some clients whose troubling situation involves other people, a meaningful difference can come about through entering the other person's frame of reference. Questions which require them to enter the other's frame of reference can be difficult for some people but often provide a significant difference. For example, in the marital case cited above, the husband did not think that he was doing anything different during the exception times. He thought that all the change was done by his wife. To him, the change was his wife being nicer and so he was nicer in response. In order for him to recognize his part in the exception times, it was helpful to have him look at himself through his wife's eyes during the exceptions. By doing so, he could see that his actions were extraordinary and different from the problem times. Through her eyes he could recognize his actions of "listening," rather than of walking away in disgust, as useful.

Other clients can find a difference by taking a more detached position with regard to their situation. They are too close to the trees to see the forest, too much into their feelings of the situation to find a difference. By having them look at themselves from a detached position of some distance, we can facilitate their seeing the forest. By their gaining some distance from their immediate feelings, they can recognize what they may be thinking or doing differently during the exception times.

THE INTERACTIONAL MATRIX

The interactional matrix (Figure 11) is a tool for selecting questions to facilitate the solution-construction conversation from an interactional view and to invite clients into areas of difference.

Across the top of the matrix are the frames we use in various parts of solution construction. We introduce the conversational frame of goal, exceptions, or hypothetical solutions at different parts of the conversation, depending on where we are or where we want to go on the solution construction map of Chapter Five.

Along the left side of the matrix are the different reporting positions of the question and response. The first is the "for self" position. Questions of this position invite respondents to answer from their own position, that is from their own shoes, eyes, ears, thinking, and so on. The next position is "for the other." Questions from this position invite answers from respondents as if they were listening and reporting for someone else who is involved in the solution context.

For example, with a husband and wife, a "for the other" directed question to the husband would ask him to answer from his wife's point of view. He is requested to say what he thinks his wife would say from her way of thinking and in her words. Questions in this row usually begin with, "What would your spouse (or other family member or other persons involved) say . . .?"

In order to answer this question, the man has to suspend his way of thinking for the moment and imagine his wife answering the question. He has to either put himself in her shoes briefly or at least think of what she might say if she were responding to the question.

This change of reporting position for the client usually induces a search for (or the creation of) new and perhaps different information. Clients often stop for a moment as they experience this difference and they either recreate their experience from a different perspective or create a new experience.

For example, a husband states that his goal in coming to therapy is for his wife to change her attitude and for her to be more involved in the relationship. He states that he does not think that his wife loves him anymore.

When asked if his wife would say that she does not love him anymore, he hesitates and then reports that she would probably say that

CONVERSATIONAL FRAMES

REPORTING POSITION

	GOAL	EXCEPTION	HYPOTHETICAL
SELF	What is your goal in coming here?	What are you doing differently? What is your spouse doing differently?	What will you be doing differently? What will your spouse be doing differently?
OTHER	What would your spouse say is your goal in coming here? What would your spouse say is his/her goal in coming here?	What would your spouse say you are doing differently? What would your spouse say she/he is doing differently?	What would your spouse say you will be doing differently? What would your spouse say she/he will be doing differently?
DETACHED	What would I say is your goal in coming here? What would I say is your spouse's goal in coming here?	If I were a fly on the wall, what would I see you (your spouse, both of you) doing differently?	As a fly on the wall, what will I see you (your spouse, both of you) doing differently?

Figure 11. Interactional Matrix

she does love him. "Would she say there are times when she is more aware of how she loves you?" This exception-oriented question also invites him to enter her reality and search for what makes for the "loving" times for her. This slight change often leads to more solution-focused realities as the husband enters a different way of thinking. He may also begin to think in terms of the relationships of actions.

The third row on the matrix is reporting "for the detached position." This position is of someone who is detached from the problems and solutions and merely observing all the parties of the interaction impartially. We frequently ask a question like this: "If I were a fly on the wall observing you and your wife, what would I see you doing differently?" This question invites the respondent to answer the question from outside of himself or herself and from a neutral position.

Crossing these categories with the different conversational frames of goal, exception, and hypothetical solution provides us with a matrix of questions we can choose from for our interactional solution construction.

Each question or box of the matrix invites respondents into an area of experience different from their usual way of thinking.

How Difference in a Question Can Make a Difference

These difference-oriented questions of this matrix are invitations to clients to loosen old restrictive beliefs or rules they have about themselves or their experience and to create more useful beliefs. By accepting the invitation of the question, clients can suspend their restrictive problem frames and enter a reality of exceptions, hypothetical solutions, or someone else's position.

All of these alternative realities enable the client to move to a more expansive view. The exceptions frame can facilitate recognizing the potential of what they are already doing. The hypothetical solution frame can pop them out of an attempted solution and into a more positive and future reality. The "for the other" and "for the detached" reporting positions can facilitate a view of the impact of their own behavior on someone else or on themselves.

Using the Matrix

The matrix is a conceptual schema for organizing frames, reporting positions, and creating the questions that result from crossing these concepts. The matrix does not provide a decision tree for when to use each question. In general, the solution process and the client will tell you which question or questions to use.

However, there are some questions or areas of the matrix you will find more useful depending on how the client presents their situation or depending on the circumstances of the therapy.

Here are six contexts that lead to predominant use of certain areas of the matrix.

1. Client(s) present the solution as primarily their own responsibility: using the "self" row only

When clients speak of the solution in terms of what *they* will be doing differently based on their own responsibility or contribution to the future, there is no need to use questions other than the "for self" position.

For example, a family with three children came to see us because the children were all having different problems, but the chief problem was that the second child had recently been arrested for participating in a car theft. Problem-talk all centered on this girl.

When we asked the hypothetical solution question, however, of each family member from the self position, each person responded with what they individually would do as part of the future when there was greater "harmony," their stated goal.

The father had already recognized that he needed to be home more and not burden his wife with total responsibility for child rearing in the family. He had already stated at his job that he would not be taking on any more overtime.

The mother said she would be keeping the house clean so that everyone could see how the family needed to respect their home. The oldest boy said he already recognized how he needed to talk with his parents more. The girl said she would be taking care of the dog who was contributing to the mess of the house. The youngest boy said he would not be playing basketball in the house and would be listening to his mother.

Each person stated a solution within his or her responsibility and control. Asking each person how she or he felt or what they noticed about the other person's changing strengthened the solution.

For example, the mother was asked if she thought her husband's deciding to stay at home more could amplify the solution. Mother stated how much she liked his decision and how relieved she felt that the burden would not be all hers. She thought she might feel a little more like herself again.

The question was posed to her from the self position. There was no need to use the "for the other" questions.

Using questions from the other two reporting positions would probably get you more statements that are not necessary. We want to stay true to our rule of thumb: "Keep it simple." So we ask only for as much as we think is necessary.

2. *The client(s) present the solution as someone else's responsibility*

Very often one person, whether a husband, wife, parent, or in some other role with regard to someone else, thinks the problem is all the other's fault and, therefore, all the responsibility for change lies with the other.

The problem for clients is that the solution, as they see it, is outside of their control. They think it is not their responsibility. Framing the solution as someone else's responsibility leaves clients waiting for the other to change or frustrated in attempts to get the other to change. The goal needs to be framed as something they can do something about.

To help clients define a goal that is within their control, questions which require them to put themselves in the other's position are very useful. For example, a man came in with his wife about their conflicts. We had identified that there were exception times in which they were not fighting.

Therapist: So, Dick, there have been times in the past week and a half when there have not been the expected conflicts? (*Asking for exceptions*)

Client: That is right, it has been somewhat better.

Therapist: And what have you been doing different? (*Asking for specification and within the frame of "his doing something different," that is, within his control. The question is from the self row, exceptions frame.*)

Client: I really think that it is my wife that is different. She has just been more agreeable and less defensive. (*States the difference as being his wife's. So far this does not give him options for him to do anything different that is within his control.*)

Therapist: So you do not think you have been doing anything different?

Client: No, she has just been nicer.

Therapist: Would she say that you have been doing anything different? (*Exceptions frame, reporting for the other*)

Client: I don't think I have been doing anything different.

Therapist: I know. From your point of view, *she* has been different. From her point of view, would she say that you have been doing some things differently? (*Accepting his first response and asking the question again from the "for other" position*)

Client: Well, she might say that I have been less defensive, that I have been more likely to listen to what she has to say. (*Entering her view for the moment and reporting differences in his behavior.*)

Therapist: So, do you think that along with her changing you have been listening more? (*Inviting a different view of his behavior*)

Client: I guess I have, actually.

Therapist: How did *you* decide to do that? (*Asking for specification of the exception in "agency" language*)

With empathy and support, along with the "report for other" position questions, the husband is able to identify his part in creating the exceptions. He might see it initially only as his response to his wife's changes, but that is a start. We might suggest to him that he is more likely to continue to have more of the good times he seeks as he convinces her that he will continue to do what *she* thinks is different even if *he* does not think it is all that different from his own point of view.

The same can be done with the hypothetical solution frame. The client may initially think that it is his partner that will be different in the future.

Therapist: So, as you walk out of here today, Dick, and you and your wife are on track to solving these problems, what will you be doing differently? (*Hypothetical solution frame, reporting for self. Asking, "So, when you walk out of here today, what will I see you and your wife doing differently?" [Hypothetical solution frame, for the detached position could also be useful.]*)

Client: Well, I think it is Susan who will be different. She will be more agreeable and not so attacking.
Therapist: And when she is that way, how will she say that you are different with her? (*Hypothetical solution frame, reporting for the other*)
Client: Hmm. I guess she will say that I will be more engaging with her.
Therapist: More engaging? Does that happen a little now? (*Asking for exceptions*)
Client: I guess sometimes I engage a little.

In talking about a problem-solved future the client thinks that his wife will be different. This is probably consistent with his view that she is the cause of the problem. However, when you invite him into the future as he walks out of the therapy door and into his wife's point of view, he is able to identify how he might respond differently.

What he initially sees as only his response to her can be built as a step of solution for him. A task for him might be to see how his wife responds to him as he initiates by his "engaging."

3. Alignment of goals

Sometimes, clients are working under very different assumptions of what the other person wants. Questions from the "for the other" position can be used to align the goals of two or more people.

Therapist: So, Jim, what you want from coming here is to have more freedom to pursue your work and activities outside of the family.
Client: Yes. Right now, she is always on my back to be with her and her daughter more. She wants me home and taking more responsibility for the raising of her daughter. But she does not understand that I have to work these long hours and the weekends are the only time I have to get away and just relax. She wants me to be a slave to her idea of what a family should be. (*Appears to be reporting his wife's goal, but from his position and interpretation*)
Therapist: So, I can see why you are so anxious to ensure your freedom. So, if I asked your wife how the two of you will be acting differently when the problem is solved, she would say you will be acting like a salve? (*Hypothetical solution, for the other position*)
Client: Well, no, not a slave. She would probably say I will be coming

home more and showing as much interest in home as I do in my job.

Therapist: Is this something you are interested in, too, having more home life? (*Checking for compatibility of goals*)

Client: Well, yes, just not to the total detriment of my career. (*As we talk about more of the specifics, he aligns his goals more with what he thinks are his wife's goals.*)

Therapist: From your wife's point of view, what will you be doing differently when she thinks you are more interested in home life? (*Hypothetical solution, for the other position*)

Client: She probably would say she wants me home every night at dinner and taking her daughter to her swim meets on the weekends.

Therapist: Is this true, Margaret, you want these things? (*Goal frame, for the self*)

Margaret: No, I would be happy if he called to let me know when he is going to be late and if he went to a swim meet maybe once a month.

Having the husband speak from his wife's point of view in front of his wife enables him to acknowledge what he thinks are his wife's expectations. It also enables him to acknowledge how he might agree with her and for the two of them to mutually focus on what they want or will be doing differently in the future.

His speaking in front of her also enables his wife to agree or not agree about what she wants and to participate in the mutual construction of solutions.

4. Clients who think they will only be feeling different

Many clients respond to goal-oriented questions with the response that they will not be *doing* anything different, they will just be *feeling* different. This response is consistent with how they view their situation and themselves. They probably do not see action as the vehicle to change or as the means to new feelings.

These clients very often see any exceptions as rather spontaneous and change as outside of their control. They may think they have to feel different to do other things.

However, we want them to identify something more in their control to use toward their goals. To do this, we ask the client to answer from a detached position.

Therapist: So, you will be going about your day the same way, but you will be feeling more confident, is that right? (*Summarizing the goal as initially stated by the client*)

Client: Yes, it is terrible to go through the day doubting myself all the time.

Therapist: So, if I were watching you go through your day in this more confident way, how would I know you were feeling this way as opposed to something else? What would I see or hear different? (*Hypothetical solution frame, for the detached position*)

Client: I guess you would see me talk more directly with people. (*Client steps out of herself, observes herself as confident, and reports the difference.*)

Therapist: What would I see you doing that would tell me that you were being more direct?

Client: I would be saying what I want rather than waiting so long to figure out whether people would be offended by my request.

Therapist: And when you are doing that, will you be saying anything different to yourself? (*Asking for a possible meaning difference that will correspond to her actions*)

Client: I guess I will say to myself that what I want can be important. (*Contextual difference*)

Therapist: So, you will be saying different things to other people and to yourself. How does that happen now when it happens? (*Now that the hypothetical solution has been described, we try to bring the solution into the present with exceptions.*)

In this situation, the client initially thinks that only her feelings will be different. Through having to report for a detached observer in the hypothetical, she is invited to step outside of herself and view the differences in her behavior with this different feeling. These external differences are joined to differences in meaning in the things she says to herself, "that what she wants is important too."

Again, with these identified differences, we as therapists invite her to look for exception times when that is happening a little now. The exception times can then be built on to form solutions.

5. *When two or more people seem to be stuck in exclusive positions and seem to have difficulty reporting from the "for the other" position.*

Sometimes, taking the detached position can be useful as it enables the therapist to maintain a neutral position and the clients to step out of themselves to a more neutral position.

Therapist: So, in the coming weeks when the problem is solved, Dennis, what will your wife see you doing differently? (*Hypothetical solution, for the other position*)
Client: I don't know. I am not going to do anything as long as I cannot trust her.
Therapist: Yes, I suppose you do not want to let yourself be wide open to hurt again. And when the two of you are past this, what will I see the two of you doing differently? (*Accepting his expression and position and changing to hypothetical solution, for the detached position. He may be too angry at her at this time to want to step into her position.*)
Client: If I could trust her, you might see us spending time together again.
Therapist: What will I see each of you doing differently during your time together that will tell me there is trust? (*Asking for more specifics*)

This position of detached and hypothetical enables you, as therapist, to be neutral and the clients to see you that way. As the clients hear you stating the question as "What will I see each of you doing differently?" the implication is that you are not viewing this as a one-sided situation and that each of them is responsible for changing or creating something different.

Asking the question from the position of "for the detached" may also enable clients to step out of the emotions of their distress long enough to consider a more positive future that they can build on. With their description of a hypothetical solution, you can then ask about times in the present (exceptions) when the hypothetical solution is happening "a little bit now." (Cf. using the hypothetical solution of Chapter Six.)

6. Involuntary clients

Involuntary clients often state that they have no problem and have no use for therapy. We will discuss in more detail in Chapter Sixteen how you, as therapist, can facilitate creating goals for therapy with an involuntary client. At this point, we merely want to identify how questions from the matrix may be helpful for you and the client.

Involuntary clients often are in a situation where they have to fulfill some conditions set by someone else. By using questions from the "for the other position," with the "other" being the person ordering therapy, you can help clients identify options. For example, a client comes in to see a therapist after having been ordered to do so by the dean of discipline.

Client: I should not have to be here. The dean just has it in for me, and thinks that I am always making trouble.

Therapist: So, you think the dean has the wrong idea about you and, given this idea he has, he is requiring you to see me for counseling. (*Summarizing client's perception of the situation*) So, I guess one way to get out of having to come here is for you to convince him that *your* view of yourself is the more accurate one. From the dean's point of view, what will he see you doing when he agrees with you that you are something other than a troublemaker?

This question from the "for other" position invites this client to enter temporarily the perceptual position of the dean. The question also assumes by the verb "will" that a time is coming when the client will be convincing the dean and solving her or his situation. In answering the client will search for more positive behaviors or signs, from the dean's point of view. The client will then have a choice as to whether he wants to do those things.

Sometimes you may be in the roles of both therapist and evaluator. Perhaps you are a child protection worker and you are both a case manager and the therapist. You are responsible for making a recommendation as to if or when children may be returned to a parent. You are also responsible for monitoring the progress of the parent and for helping the parent make the needed changes. Posing questions from the "for other" position and the hypothetical can be helpful. In this situation, since you are the one setting the conditions, the "other" is you. For example:

Therapist: So, when *I* am more convinced that you are moving beyond your problems with drugs, what will I see you doing differently. (*Hypothetical solution, for the other position*)

Client: I guess you will see positive urine tests.

Therapist: Well, that might convince me you are clean. Is there anything else that would convince me, or even yourself?

Client: Maybe, you will hear me talking about things I want to do instead of getting high. (*Client attempts to enter therapist's position.*)

The client is invited to enter your position and view her or himself convincing you as the therapist that she or he is solving the problem.

DISCUSSION

QUESTION:
I have tried using some of these questions and the clients get confused. What do I do?

Clients very often will get confused in attempting to answer these questions. For some clients, putting themselves in someone else's shoes may be very different or awkward. To help them, you need to ask the question slowly, and maybe more concretely to ease them into position. For example, you might say, "Let's say the dean of discipline was here in the office right now and I were to ask him what he wants you to be doing differently, what might he say?" Or you might have the client actually pretend to be the other person for awhile. For example, you might say, "Let's say you are your wife right now, what do you want your husband to be doing differently?"

By gently leading the client into the situation by setting the stage a little, clients can begin to report from the "for the other" position or from the "for the detached" position.

QUESTION:
Sometimes clients object to my asking them to report for another when the other person is right there in the room. They say something like this: "She is right here. Why don't you ask her?" What do I do?

Clients frequently ask this. They appear to not understand why you are asking them to speak for someone else. To respond, merely say that you want to know what *they* (the person you are speaking to) think the other is expecting and that you will check out what the other person says in a minute.

EXERCISE*

In order to give yourself some experience with these different reporting positions of the matrix, try this. Pick a situation with you and someone else, a problem interaction. This may be a situation where you and someone else have had several conflicts.

Once you have identified a situation, either ask yourself or have someone else ask you each of the questions of the matrix. Go across the rows within the same reporting position—from goal, to exceptions, to hypothetical solution. Note the difference in your experience and then write down your responses. Take notice of changes in your internal movies or dialogue within or about the movie. Then, move to the next row of a different reporting position. Take note of how your experience changes and what differences are introduced. What differences do you notice in your movies and the dialogue? How do you experience things differently when reporting for someone else? How do the meanings of situations change as you report them for someone else or from a more detached position. Which questions give you greater difference or are more useful?

---

*We wish to thank Michael Banks who first suggested this exercise.

12

"But I Want Them to Be Different"

When Someone Else Is Defined as the Problem

■ Any change in how clients describe a goal (solution) and/or what they do affects future interactions with all others involved.

In Chapter Four on well-defined goals, we described the necessity to construct goals within the client's control. We have all experienced clients, however, who have said some variation on "I want the other person to be different" or even "I want you to change them."

These are both complaints that define the solution as a change in someone else. The problem for us as therapists is that we cannot change someone else, nor can clients although they probably have tried many, many times.

So, since we cannot join with clients in changing someone else, our task is to cooperate with them in ways which can lead to their creating goals within their control.

There are four ways we have found useful in taking these complaints about someone else and turning them into workable goals.

1. Direct: "I cannot change the other."
2. Exploring the future without a change in the other.
3. Exploring the hypothetical solution and exceptions.
4. Exploring the intent or goal beyond the attempted solution.

1. Direct: "I Cannot Change the Other"

The shortest route is often the direct and straightforward one. We simply explain how we cannot change anyone else. For example:

> You know, as much as I would like to help you out, your spouse is not here, and I know I cannot change her. None of us can really change anybody else. Is there some other way that I can help you?

Example:

Therapist: What is your goal in coming in? (*Goal frame*)
Client: My wife has this problem. I think she has low self-esteem and she just is not doing what is best for her or making the most of our marriage.
Therapist: I am not sure I understand.
Client: She is very overweight, and she knows it. She is depressed. She just sits around all day. She complains to me about what I am doing. She says I am not making enough money for the family, that I am not doing enough with the children, that I am always talking down to her and not being supportive. I do not think I am not supportive. I think she just has this terribly low idea of herself and cannot stand that I am doing better than she is.
I have tried to convince her to go to a therapist, but she says I am the one with the problems, not she. She thinks I have the low self-esteem, and that I put her down in order to feel superior.
I have tried to convince her to see a therapist. I have tried to support her in going on diets. I have tried doing her work for her. Nothing seems to get this woman to change.
I cannot deal with her anymore. Can you help me get her to change?
Therapist: Well, it sounds like things have been frustrating for you and that you have tried everything to get her to change. I wish I could help you with this, but I cannot change her. Actually, I do not think anybody can change anybody else. It sounds as if you already realize that yourself. Is there some other way I can help?
Client: Well, at the very least, I need some way to cope with her negative attitude. (*Goal statement*)

Therapist: If you were doing that, what might you be doing differently?
   (*Hypothetical solution frame*)

    This direct route corrects the frame of therapy away from his wish to have his wife be different to defining a path that he would like to take himself. The goal of "coping with her negative attitude" has more possibilities for him. Coping is within his control, while changing her self-esteem is not within his control.

2. Exploring the Future Without a Change in the Other

A way of redirecting the wish to change someone else is by asking questions such as "What if the other person does not change? What will you do?"
    This question explores the possibility of the other person not changing and the consequences of such an event. The question also explores what the client's fears are. "What if the other person does not change? What will you do?" contains the potential for the clients to define what they will do that is within their control even if the solution does not contain all that they want. For example:

School counselor: What brings you in, Jack? (*Goal frame*)
Jack: Mr. Simons kicked me out of algebra class, again. That jerk!
Counselor: Really! What happened?
Jack: He does this every time. The whole class can be talking and screwing around while he is out of the room. When he comes back, who does he yell at, and kick out? Nobody else but me. He says with my grades I can't afford to be screwing around. He just embarrasses me in front of the whole class. I wish I could embarrass him a few times. I wish I could get out of that class.
Counselor: Hmmm. What are you going to do? (*With curiosity*)
Jack: I don't know, he's such a jerk. He just decided the first day that he didn't like me and now he is after me every chance he gets. He should retire. He's too old to be teaching.
Counselor: Guess you figure he's too old to change, is that right? (*Clarification*)
Jack: Are you kidding? He is so crusty. He would crack at the joints if he tried changing. He shouldn't be teaching.

Counselor: Well, you might be right about his not changing. He might be set in his ways. So, if he is not likely to change what will you do? (*Accepting his frame, asking the hypothetical solution, and presupposing that he will do something*)

Jack: I am probably going to flunk algebra.

Counselor: Oh, and then you would have to repeat it?

Jack: Yes, and I can't do that. My parents would be all over me.

Counselor: Oh, no! What are *you going to do?* You don't want that. (*Presupposing that he will solve the problem*)

Jack: I guess I'll just have to bite the bullet and be mute in Simon's class.

Counselor: Will that do it?

Jack: No, he will still have it in for me.

Counselor: What would he say he wants you to do? (*Hypothetical solution, reporting for the other*)

Jack: Simons? He would probably say he wants me to "cooperate" in class.

Counselor: What do you think he would say would be signs, in his way of thinking, that you were cooperating? (*Hypothetical solution, reporting for the other*)

Jack: But I am a cooperative guy.

Counselor: So what do you have to do to be "cooperative" in Mr. Simon's eyes?

Jack: I guess he would say that I would not be screwing around when his back is turned.

Counselor: So, you would not be doing that. What would you be doing instead? (*Eliciting a positive representation for a well-defined goal instead of the negation*)

Jack: I guess I would be doing my work or at least keeping my mouth shut.

Counselor: This is what Mr. Simons would say? (*Clarification of reporting position*)

Jack: Yeah. He would probably say he would like me to volunteer more, too. (*Further description of the movie*)

Counselor: So, you think that might do it and help you pass. Are there times when you do some of this now? (*Bringing the hypothetical solution into the present*)

This interchange avoids the notion of changing the teacher and treats the teacher as just one of those unchangeable parts of Jack's circumstances. He is faced with the consequences of continuing to do what he is doing and flunking or *doing something different.* Cooperating with Jack's feeling of being victimized is a beginning. We do not, however, want to leave him there. We are sympathetic, yet asking him what he will do if the teacher does not change. He is now in a position to explore what *he will do to pass algebra* and how he will convince his teacher that he is cooperating. This is accomplished by using the "for the other" position questions.

3. Exploring the Hypothetical Solution and/or Exceptions

Many times, clients appear to see the solutions in a sort of linear fashion, with one event conditional upon another. They seem to think that change by the other person has to happen first in order for something else to happen that they want to happen. Married people often think their husband or wife has to change first in order for them to have the closeness or trust that they seek. As we have mentioned before, the clients appear to think as if the change by the other, "A," has to happen first before "B," the change in the relationship, can happen. They think "A" is necessary before "B" can happen. So they see themselves as waiting helplessly for the other person to change.

As mentioned in previous chapters, we believe that the reverse of the formula can also work. In other words, if one acts as if "B" were already happening, "A" often happens. By asking the hypothetical solution question, we can find out what clients think they will be doing differently when the solution is happening and the other person is different. After identifying what it is that clients will be doing differently, we can find a way of having them do their part of the hypothetical solution now. We could also have them look for "exceptions" and identify what they are doing during the exceptional times.

We can help clients reverse their presupposition, that getting what they want depends on someone else changing first. By identifying what clients think they will be doing when the other is doing the changes the clients want, we help them do their part, something within their control already. By acting as if "B," the hypothetical solution, were already happening, the client can bring about the solution. For example:

Therapist: Hello, Susan, what is your goal in coming in? (*Goal frame*)

Client: My marriage is not going well. I think Bill has fallen out of love with me and he won't talk about it. Whenever I try to talk about our problem or bring it up, he just puts me off with, "Not that again," and then he walks away. If I pursue him, we fight. He says there is nothing wrong, but I don't believe him. If he would just talk to me or show me that he loves me, I wouldn't be so upset. I tried to get him to come to therapy with me, but he said there was no way he was going to listen to more of my complaints in front of a stranger.

Therapist: (*After supporting her being upset*) I am sorry about all this. Can you tell me what the two of you will be doing differently when this is not a problem anymore? (*Hypothetical solution frame*)

Client: Well, if this changes, he will be talking with me. If he is unhappy with me, he will tell me instead of this silence. He will be more communicative and I think we will be spending more time together. (*Most of these responses describe changes in her husband. We want descriptions of what she will be doing as well.*)

Therapist: So he will be more communicative. What will you be doing differently?

Client: I guess I won't be so worried.

Therapist: That sounds better for you. When you are not so worried, what will you be doing differently or at least different in his eyes? (*Hypothetical solution, for the other position*)

Client: I guess he would say I would be more relaxed and secure, and I think I would. (*These descriptions are in feeling terms.*)

Therapist: What will he see or hear you doing differently that will tell him that you are a little more relaxed? (*Eliciting behavioral signs of "relaxed and secure" from the "for other" position*)

Client: I will be getting more into my own things, my own friends, my own chores and hobbies. He thinks I am too dependent on him right now. (*Meaning of the problem time*)

Therapist: So you think he thinks you are too dependent on him and that he does not like that. When he thinks that way, what would he say he does?

Client: He probably says that I disgust him and he wants to get away. Maybe he thinks he has to make me more independent.

Therapist: So you don't want him to pull away or make judgments about you. And when he thinks you are more relaxed or secure, what would he say he would do differently?

Client: He would probably say that he likes that more and . . . I don't know what he would do.

Therapist: If he were here, what would you guess he would say he would do? (*Hypothetical solution, for the other position*)

Client: I suppose he might say that he would feel like spending time with me or that he just likes to see me happy.

Therapist: Are there times now when you think you appear a little more relaxed to him, maybe when you are a little more into your own things or friends? (*Exceptions frame, for the other position*)

Client: Sometimes. Sometimes, I just give up on him and just do my own thing. Then he comes around. He probably thinks I am more independent then.

Therapist: You think he likes you acting independently. How do you do that?

Client: Oh, sometimes I just feel like it, or sometimes I just tell myself I can't look to him all the time. (*Difference of meaning and therefore contextual difference*)

Therapist: Is that different for you to tell yourself that? (*Exceptions frame*)

Client: Yes, I have been thinking that way more lately, more independently.

Therapist: So, how are you getting yourself to think and act more that way lately? (*Enhancing agency*)

Client: My friend has been suggesting it and I think she's right.

Therapist: Well, as you continue to think and act in this different way, what do you think the chances are of his thinking of you more favorably and you getting more of what you want? (*Bridging the exceptions as the goal*)

Client: I think it is probably the way to go. He does talk to me more when he thinks I'm happy as opposed to whining.

Therapist: So, if you continue to act more independently, would you be getting what you want from coming here, even if he is not always responsive? (*Bridging the exceptions as the goal of therapy*)

Client: Yes, I really need to be looking to myself first.

Therapist: So, how will you continue to do this?

By focusing on the hypothetical solution when she will be doing something different, she was able to recognize actions she could take to help her situation that would increase the chances for more favorable interactions with her husband. By identifying what she will be doing in the hypothetical solution, she was able to recognize times now when she is already doing things for herself and see how that activity is creating more of the things she wants—that is, doing and thinking for herself and creating more favorable interactions with her husband.

4. Exploring the Intent or Goal Beyond the Attempted Solution*

Another way of getting beyond the initial complaint about someone else is by asking:

"What are you hoping that will achieve?"
"What will that do for you when _____ changes?"
"How will things be different for you when _____ changes?"

All three of these questions can bring out the intent of clients' actions, the goal beyond the immediate actions or the belief behind their own actions. The goal beyond the immediate attempted solution is often more workable. For example:

Therapist: What is your goal in coming in, Mrs. Jansen? (*Goal frame*)
Client: It's my son. He was kicked out of another residence. This is the third one he has gone through and now he is back home with me again. I can't have him home with me again. I love him dearly and I won't have him on the streets, but he has to change. Every time I think I have him set straight and he is settled in a halfway house and staying straight, he screws up and is back home with me. I just can't have it. He is 28 and he should be on his own. I have tried everything, and yet he still blames me for his drug problems. He tells me that if his father and I hadn't been fighting and going through all the mess he wouldn't have these problems. He just has

---

*This procedure assumes that there may be a goal to the immediate attempted solution that has not been expressed yet. This notion is borrowed from Neuro-Linguistic Programming (Bandler & Grinder, 1979).

to get his life together. I can't keep going through this. You have to do something for him.

Therapist: Let me see if I have this right. You have worked very hard getting him into residences and helping him with his drug problems and it doesn't seem to be working. He goes back to drugs, or gets kicked out of the residences, and you have him back home with you. How will things be different for you when this situation is resolved? What will his changing achieve for him and for you? *(Asking for the goal beyond her trying to help and save her son)*

Client: I would be able to relax and know that he is on his way. Right now, I can never be sure and then I blame myself. I would like him to grow up and for us to have a good, adult relationship.

Therapist: So, his acting differently would enable you to relax, feel better about your parenting, and relate with him as adults. *(Clarification)* Tell me about times now when you relax some and do something different than blame yourself even when he is making mistakes? *(Exceptions frame, reporting for self)*

Client: Sometimes, I am more sure that it is not my fault and just tell myself that he has to work it out. Usually, that is when other people are supporting me about it. *(Difference of meaning, ". . . just tell myself that he has to work it out.")*

Therapist: How do you do that and still think you are helping, or that it is okay? You must still be worried some. *(Further specification and cheerleading)*

Client: Well, I do worry about him and I do feel guilty, but I know he has to do it himself.

Therapist: How do you know he has to do it himself? Sometimes, you must think you are responsible. *(Enhancing her agency by asking her how she decides he is responsible for himself)*

Client: I just know he has to grow up and he has to take care of himself. He will not have me all the time to bail him out.

Therapist: So you know that he needs to take care of himself because he won't always have you to look after him. So if you were letting him have the responsibility for his successes and mistakes more often and you were deciding that you were acting as a good parent, is that what you would like out of coming here? *(Bridging the exceptions as the goal of therapy)*

Client: Yes, I know that is what I have to do. It is just so hard to see him treating himself so badly sometimes.

Therapist: People who care the most such as yourself, sometimes find it the hardest. So, how do you let him have the responsibility for himself when you think you are acting more the way you want to? You obviously care a great deal about him and wish he could have guarantees. *(Further specification and cheerleading)*

Client: I just know that this is the only way we will cut the cord, so I do it. *(Difference of meaning)*

Therapist: I can see that, but still it must be very hard sometimes. How do you do that even when he is making serious mistakes and it is tearing you up to see him doing that? *(Eliciting exceptions within her frame of his making mistakes and her possibly feeling guilty)*

Client: *(Crying)* I just know that letting him go is the best thing for him in the long run.

This client initially states that she wants her son to be different so that she can let go, feel successful as a parent, and relate to him as an adult. However, changing her son is out of her control. As she continues to try to change him for the better according to her own criteria of what is better, she may ironically be fostering his dependence on her and defeating her own purposes.

As she outlines during the conversation, she wants assurance that her son will be all right and that she is not to blame for his mistakes. Beyond that, she wants to relax some even though the son makes mistakes and she wants to let him have responsibility for himself. She states she would like to have a good relationship with him as an adult.

This goal of letting her son have responsibility and her successfully letting go is beyond her immediate complaints about his being kicked out of the residence and her wish that the therapist would do something about him. The goal is certainly more workable than the initial complaints and wishes. Initially, she wants to change him, something beyond her control. By focusing on her intentions—that is, her goals beyond the immediate complaint—she is able to formulate a goal that is more workable and within her control. She can make changes in herself and, as she outlines, there are already exception times when she is letting him have responsibility now.

The goal or meta-solution beyond all the immediate attempted solutions can also be used to bridge what seem to be conflicting goals within a couple or family and where clients are saying the other person needs to change first. In a couples case, (Walter & Peller, 1988), the husband stated that he wanted his wife to be more responsible—that is, to take out the garbage, turn off lights, and do something about her weight. She thought that behind his complaints there must be underlying feelings that were not being expressed. So he kept trying to remind her to do all the things he complained of, while she kept trying to ask him what his underlying feelings were. They both saw these as conflicting goals in that each one disagreed with the other. The husband maintained that he had no other feelings underlying his complaints. At the same time the wife could not believe that if she fulfilled all his wishes he would then be happy and stop complaining.

When we asked about the intent of these immediate solutions, the couple replied that their ultimate goal was more "closeness." This was a more workable frame than all their attempts to change the other and the meta-solution of "closeness" could bridge the gap of the seemingly conflicting goals. With the new frame of "closeness," the couple could then begin to look at what each was doing within his or her control.

DISCUSSION

QUESTION:
Asking for the intent of someone's actions makes it seem as if you believe that there might be a secret agenda. Is that true?

No, we take people at their word in what they say they want. The notion of hidden agendas has sometimes been construed to mean that people have some hidden payoff for their problems, that there is some secret gain for holding onto the problem.

While we acknowledge that actions can be purposeful and that people can be ambivalent about change, we do not believe in a functional purpose for the problem.

For example, a therapist may believe that a person who acts shy and fearful enjoys the secondary gain of the nurturing and sympathy he receives from friends over his failures to get what he wants. A therapist who accepts that interpretation may then try to do something about the "payoff" of nurturing by trying to get the man to acknowledge the "payoff" and achieve the gain in some other way.

We look literally at what people say, the meanings or frames they report, and the actions they take. We stay away from interpreting someone's motivation and assume that what the clients say they want is indeed what they want.

EXERCISE

Using a partner to report a complaint about someone they want to change, use each one of the above procedures. By having your partner keep the same complaint for each procedure, you can identify how each procedure is slightly different and may fit better depending upon the client's initial presentation. Sometimes, a direct approach may fit better and sometimes not.

Be sure to switch roles. In the client role, you will learn immeasurably from the direction and invitation of the questions being put to you.

13

Cooperating

■ Clients are always cooperating. They are showing us how they think change takes place. As we understand their thinking and act accordingly, cooperation is inevitable.

In workshop after workshop, therapists have asked what to do with the "resistant" clients, those who do not want to change, who have some investment in the problem, who sabotage treatment, who "yes but" every suggestion you make, who are just plain stubborn, or who are defensive or resistant because of the pain or price of change.

We have difficulty answering these kinds of questions from therapists in the form the questions are usually asked because to reply to the questions as phrased would mean that we subscribe to the assumptions within them. Sometimes we say we do not have these types of clients. The answer is true, but not very satisfying to the therapist troubled by the clients who prompt these questions.

We have a different experience with our clients, not because we select out all the clients that others complain about, but because we work under assumptions that enable us to work with them in a different way that facilitates cooperative interaction.

This approach is a consumer model and a solution-or goal-oriented model. Jay Haley in *Problem-solving Therapy* (1976) made the very important distinction between problem-solving models and growth models. Problem-solving models, although not unique in this regard, tend to focus on what clients want and to see them as the experts on what they want. Growth models, whether they are based on norms of health, pathology, or self-actualization, tend to see the therapist as the expert about the problem and about what clients need to do.

A solution-focused approach is positioned on the problem-solving side of Haley's distinction. We assume that clients are the experts on what they want and that it is not up to us to tell them what is wanted.

Given the distinction between consumer model and therapist-as-expert-model, we can assume that clients coming in to see us want something. We do not have to take on the responsibility for talking clients into treatment, confronting them about what we see as the problem, or for solving the problem.

We do not claim expertise on mental health, normal development, normal family life, or normal marriages. Instead, our expertise and role are in asking questions that open up possibilities for clients to do something different or do what they want. We see this as similar to Goolishian and Anderson's "participant-managers of the therapeutic conversation" (Anderson & Goolishian, 1988). We prefer the words conversational facilitator. Our role is to facilitate conversation between clients and ourselves that enables them to get what they want. What the client wants may be the dissolution of a problem or getting on track to solving a problem or attaining a goal.

With this definition of a consumer model, we assume clients want what they say they want, that they are motivated toward the goal, and that our job is to cooperate with their endeavor.

Along with the assumption that clients come to see us because they want something, we assume people usually show us how they think change takes place with regard to their goal. It is up to us to cooperate with their view. Their beliefs about change, about the problem, and about the hypothetical solution fit recursively with their actions.

The onus is upon us to join the clients with their view and find ways to fit with their view, while facilitating a more open process that introduces difference. Whether constructing solutions and introducing differences takes place in conversation, in providing feedback, or in suggesting tasks, we need to communicate with clients in ways they experience as fitting.

The general principles of cooperating are pacing and inviting.

PACING THE CLIENT'S DESCRIPTION

The principle of pacing (Grinder & Bandler, 1976) involves reflecting back to the client or matching the client's tone, affect, and words. If the client talks in a low tone that might be described as sounding discouraged or depressed, we use the same tone. If the client talks in higher tones that sound more "upbeat," we use the same. If the client tends to talk in an intellectualized way, we do the same. If the client uses language loaded with action words, we respond with the same.

This is not just reflective listening. Although we are affectively empathic, we do not think of empathy as the only tool or as a primary treatment tool.

Someone doing reflective listening might say, "It sounds like you are very discouraged and angry with your children. How else does their behavior make you feel?" The intent of reflective listening is to facilitate the expression of feelings. Reflective listening follows the assumption that clients will change or grow in self-understanding by expressing their feelings and having the therapist understand and accept them.

The principle of pacing assumes that when clients feel supported by the same use of affect and the same language, they are more likely to accept our invitation to new and possibly more open directions or new language.

Pacing goes like this:

Therapist: What is your goal in coming here?

Client: I'm coming here because of my son (*said with low tones and sad affect*). He's been messing up terribly at school and I can't figure out what I'm doing wrong. I just can't see my way out of this mess. Friends at Alanon tell me I have to turn it over to my higher power.

Therapist: (*Also with low tones and sad affect*) So you are coming here because you want things to be different with your son with regard to school and it seems at this point like you can't see your way out of this. At the same time, your friends are advising you to turn it over. Is that right?

This response by the therapist reflects the same affect and voice tone while also referring to the areas of the parent's concern—her son's messing up at school and her search for what she is doing wrong. The response also reflects her use of visual terms and wanting to see her way out. Her language seems to be drawn from the 12-step program. Pacing is not only affective support, but also a joining in her worldview. In this example, sharing her concerns and using her language of the 12-step program paces her thinking, and joins her view.

With pacing, the client will give us indications of appropriate fit by both nonverbal and verbal responses. If the client responds with a head nod or additional statements consistent with our own, we know we have paced well.

If the client, however, frowns, shakes her or his head, or gives us some other cue, we guess that our response did not fit and we try something else.

If the client also gave us verbal feedback that indicated we were off track, then we would need to adjust. For example:

Client: No, actually, it is his father that I am most upset about. If he weren't drinking so much, I think we could see our way clear about what to do about our son. I need some help with what to do about his father's drinking.

Therapist: Oh, I'm sorry, I misunderstood. So, you are thinking that the way to make things better for your son and his school performance is by doing something about your husband's drinking.

This response would be feedback that her focus is more on her husband and that she sees a connection between her husband's behavior and a solution.

Responses by the client are feedback of what the next step is for us. If the client responds with acknowledging signs or language, we know we can proceed to possible invitations to new areas or ask for further clarification of what she has already said. If the responses are negative in some way, they are feedback for what we may need to do differently in order to cooperate with this client and her unique affect and thinking.

INVITING*

This principle refers to how we introduce "difference" and an opening-up process in the therapeutic conversation. While pacing is necessary for clients to initially respond as if they are understood both affectively and cognitively, inviting is necessary for further change. If

---

*This term was introduced to us in personal communication with Gene Combs and Jill Freedman. The term is used to describe how they use presuppositions within questions to open new experiences and storying with clients in *Symbol, Story and Ceremony* (1990).

we only did pacing, the risk is that we would just support the clients' view and solution may not be facilitated.

Inviting is the process whereby a therapist uses questions and the presuppositions within the questions to politely ask the client to search for or create a new meaning. Through the conversation centered around answering the questions (invitations), difference and new experience may be created by and for the client.

The introduction of "difference" on the part of the therapist and client comes about as a natural extension of the assumptions of the model. With the assumption that focusing on the positive, the future, and the solution facilitates change, we form our questions in line with the assumption. We ask about what the client wants, the times when change in the solution areas is already happening, and the hypothetical future.

Our questions which are positive, exception-oriented, future- or solution-oriented, are like invitations to new ways of thinking and act-ing. The questions are merely invitations and if the client does not respond or accept the first invitation, we try another.

MODES OF COOPERATING

Here are some ways of pacing and inviting the clients to advance the process of developing solutions.

1. Being Positive and Future-Oriented

When you are pursuing the pathways of the map and the clients seem to be talking in ways that open new possibilities, with more solution-focused talk taking place, then keep on doing what you are doing. The clients are then accepting your invitation to look at the positives in either the exceptions or the future. An example might go like this:

Therapist: What is your goal in coming here? (*goal frame*)
Client: I would like to have more harmony with my wife and her kid.
Therapist: How does that happen now, when it happens? (*exceptions frame*)
Client: I don't know how to explain it, but sometimes my wife and I

are right in "synch." You know what I mean, we both know how to handle her little girl and what the other is thinking.

Therapist: What are you doing when you know that the two of you are in "synch?" (*Specification*)

Client: We look at each other and I know that she agrees with what I am doing and she is supporting what I am doing.

Therapist: And what are you doing when she is doing that?

Client: I guess I have talked with her beforehand and so we are both on the same wavelength.

Therapist: Let me double check. So, you want to be doing more of the things like talking beforehand that make for more "in synch" times with your wife? (*clarification and bridging the exceptions as the goal of therapy*)

In this example, the therapist has used the client's language and invited him to talk about what he wants and some exceptions. The conversation seems to be positive and solution-focused. The tone is somewhat neutral, but the language is positive.

2. Supporting Clients Who Seem as If They Are Barely Coping (Berg, 1990)

Oftentimes, clients come in and describe situations that are horrendous or several situations that are overwhelming. An example might go like this:

Therapist: What is your goal in coming here? (*goal frame*)

Client: I just don't know what to do (*with low tones and looking down*). My son, here, never seems happy, my wife is on my back about him, my ex-wife is threatening to fight for custody of him again, and he is failing school. The school called me last week and called me over because they found marijuana on him. I try to stay on top of him, but I am changing jobs and my wife is working and taking care of the younger kids. I don't know what is going on anymore.

Therapist: My God (*with similar low and worried tones*), there is really a lot going on. All these things happening at one time. Even just one of these problems would be enough. How have you managed to stay on top of things as much as you have? (*In sympathy with the situation, but asking an exceptions-oriented question within the coping framework of "staying on top of things as much as you have")*

Client: Well, I don't feel very on top of the situation, but I just can't give up or let him go back to my ex.

Therapist: With that kind of pressure, how have you managed to stay on top even a little? *(Said with the expectancy that to not be on top would have been more likely)*

Client: Well *(with voice tone rising some)*, I keep reminding myself that he has gone through a lot and that it will take time.

Therapist: *(With similar rising tone)* How does it help to remind yourself of that? *(Specification)*

Client: Somehow, I can keep the longer perspective that way.

Therapist: Keeping the longer perspective seems to work better. How do you manage that perspective when there are so many things going on? *(Again with sympathetic tones, but oriented around the exception within his coping)*

Client: I just know that this is a crazy time and how much I care about him.

Therapist: Keeping this longer perspective works better even though from the short view it looks bad sometimes. So, I guess keeping this longer perspective would be more of what you want? *(Bridging the exception as the goal of therapy)*

Client: Yes. When I keep that perspective, things seem to go better.

In this example, the therapist acknowledges what the client says— that things are overwhelming. The therapist would be too abrupt to push for a goal immediately upon the client coming in. At the same time, positives can be brought out by scaling down the questions to a frame of "managing as much as you are." By asking him how he is able to manage or cope despite the overwhelming circumstances, the therapist acknowledges the situation, yet elicits positives and exceptions.

3. When the Client Seems to Be Supplying Every Reason Why Change Cannot Happen or Should Not Happen; When the Client Seems to Be Taking a Negative Approach About Change, in Contrast to Your Appearing Positive

Frequently, clients present situations with all the reasons why nothing will work. The clients may indeed feel frustrated because they may think they have tried everything, but nothing has worked. They may want to let you know how hard they have tried. Also, they may have been burned in their efforts so many times that they are very afraid of trying again. Whatever the reasons within their thinking, they seem to be saying "Yes, but" to any positive suggestion or to respond with more negative talk whenever you try to invite them to talk about exceptions. The "Yes, but" may go like this:

Therapist: What do the two of you want out of coming here? (*Goal frame*)

Husband: I don't want to get a divorce, but I cannot seem to please her.

Wife: That's not true, but he just doesn't act like he wants to be married. He is never home and when he is home he is so involved with his hobbies in the basement that he never acts as if he likes me.

Therapist: So, I guess you don't want things to continue this way. How do you want things to be different? (*An attempt to invite a positive statement of a goal*)

Wife: Well, I want him to pay attention and to like being with me. But he never will. He doesn't want a divorce because he can't afford one, but he will never be married. He is just so wrapped up in himself.

Husband: That is not true. You don't want me to be involved. Every time I suggest doing something, you say I don't really want to.

Therapist: So, are there times when things aren't so bad or that things go a little better? (*Searching for exceptions*)

Wife: Things have been like this for years, but I had the children to take care of before. But he has always been wrapped up either in the business or in his own things, never in me or the family.

Husband: She has never been satisfied.

Therapist: (*Adopting their view and cooperating with their seemingly more negative presentations*) It sounds like both of you are very unhappy. With things having been this way, what evidence do you have for hope that things can be any better?

Wife: When we were first married he was nice but not after the kids were born.

Therapist: (*With sympathy for her frustration*) I know and that was a long time ago. So is there anything happening lately between the two of you that gives you any reason to believe that it is worthwhile for you to try anything different? It sounds like you have tried a lot. (*Therapist cooperates with the clients' seemingly pessimistic view to find out if they will provide positives that can be built upon or if other options such as divorce are in fact what they want.*)

Wife: Not much.

Therapist: So, are all the recent things between you telling you that you should separate or divorce? (*Exploring the other options*)

Wife: Well no, I am not there yet. There has to be something that can be done.

Therapist: Perhaps, but it sounds like you each have been burned and you probably don't want that to happen again. Without any times recently when things have been at least tolerable, I would seriously wonder whether you might want to try again. (*Advocating for the part of them that has been hurt and disappointed in the past and at the same time indirectly asking if there are exceptions to the problems that would be a basis for hope*)

Wife: Well, he has been a good provider and he does come home.

Therapist: How does this make a difference to you? (*Exploring the meaning of his behavior to her*)

Wife: Well, because he used to just stay at work until late at night and I would never see him. Lately, he has been coming home a little earlier.

Therapist: How do you think he would explain that? Would he say that was anything different? (*Exceptions frame from the "for the other" reporting position*)

Wife: I don't know. I would like to think he was coming home earlier because he wants to make things different for us.

Therapist: I know, but you don't want to set yourself up for disappointment. How will you know if this is something for real? (*Still advo-*

cating for the part of her that does not want to be hurt again and asking about a hypothetical solution)

Wife: Well, if he keeps on doing it, or calls when he can't, or lets me know in some other ways.

Therapist: (To husband) This is true, you have been coming home earlier? *(Checking the husband's perception of the exception)*

Husband: Yes, I don't want to lose her, but I don't think she will ever be convinced that it is for real or that it is enough.

Therapist: How did you decide to make this change? You could have just thrown in the towel. *(Exploring the exception within the frame that he chose to make a change)*

Husband: Because I do love her, even if she doesn't think so. If I have to do a few things her way, then that's what I'll do.

Therapist: Well, I am impressed that you are persisting. But how will you know that she is becoming more convinced in your changing? If she is pleased, you don't want to miss her acknowledgments and then give up or be hurt. *(Cheerleading and exploring signs for him of her being pleased)*

Cooperating with this couple means pacing and joining with them in their skepticism about a positive future and supporting their disappointment and hurt. If you were to point out the positives in their relationship, the couple would more than likely shoot the positives down. For instance, if you said something like, "But there must be some reason that you are staying together, there must be some good things about him. He is a good provider after all, isn't he?" she might agree initially and then "Yes, but." She might say, "Yes, he has provided for us, but what good is that if he is never around!"

When the therapist advocates for the parts of them that do not want to be hurt again or are fearful of change, the couple can then offer the reasons for change and begin to bring out "exceptions to the problem" times as evidence for hope. These exceptions can then be used to build solutions. Even with the exceptions, however, the therapist must cooperate with their skepticism and caution.

The other possibility is that when you ask why not consider other options, the couple might actually choose other options and want your help in making the separation. That possibility is okay, also. Your work then lies in clarifying that as the goal.

The position you are taking as therapist is on their side—for them to get what they want. You are not necessarily advocating their staying together or separating, for change or no change. By supporting their fears as well as their desires for change, you free the couple to make their own choices.

4. Scaling the Vague Presentations*

Usually vague descriptions that clients present as goals are the broad meanings or contexts for specific behaviors or interactions that they want. We assume that a goal is more workable if the goal is defined as specifically as possible. We want the goal to be specific so that clients can more easily recognize their performance of it. Our concern with a vaguely stated goal is that clients may not have developed signs of the goal's occurrence and, therefore, miss occasions when the goal is already happening. For example, clients may state that they would like to have a "positive attitude." With the goal stated in this general form, we do not know and the clients may not know if "positive attitude" means: feeling good; feeling a certain level of positive; being positive *all* the time; being positive only in certain circumstances; being positive about certain things or situations; being positive in a way that is self-reinforcing; or something else. If clients meant a positive attitude was feeling positive *all* the time, they may think they are failing at any time they are less than positive. With such a vaguely defined goal, they would probably miss the potential of all the times they do something that leads to a positive attitude. Clients would also probably dismiss the times when they act with somewhat of a positive attitude because the attitude is not *all* the time.

Therefore, we want clients to go beyond the broad meanings and give us more detail of their goals so they can recognize how the goal may be happening now or how the goal will appear in the future.

Many clients report their situation only as they see it now—the problem situation and the end state when there will be no problem whatsoever. A behavioral technique of scaling enables clients to break down this "either/or," black/white, and vague way of thinking, and fill

---

*For other development and examples of this technique, see Lipchik, 1988a; de Shazer, 1988; Berg, 1990.

in the movie with some exceptions and some intermediary actions in a process and specific way. The scaling technique can be useful for clients to more specifically define goals, as well as exceptions or hypothetical solutions.

We use a scale from one to 10 as a behaviorally oriented therapist would do, but we add on our solution-focused presuppositions. For example:

Therapist: What is your goal in coming here? (*Goal frame*)

Client: I would like to get out of this depressed state. I'm being a total couch potato. I just keep on procrastinating and watching TV. I just keep getting more and more depressed.

Therapist: So, how would you like to be acting differently? (*Asking for a positive representation and in action terms*)

Client: I don't want to be depressed.

Therapist: What would you like to be doing instead? (*Redirecting to a positive statement*)

Client: I would like to be getting out of this depression and being more active about my day again.

Therapist: So, you would like to be more active about your day again. Tell me about times when that is happening now. (*Searching for exceptions*)

Client: I'm not active at all. All I do is sit around all day and feel sorry for myself.

Therapist: So, it seems to you like you have not been doing anything. Well, if we used a scale with one being total couch potato behavior, the worst you can imagine, and 10 being idealistically the most active you can imagine, how would you say you have been *averaging* this past week? (*Introducing the scale*)

Client: On an average, I guess about a two.

Therapist: About a two. So, I guess there have been some times when you have acted even less than two?

Client: Yeah, there were some totally bad days. I hardly made it out of bed.

Therapist: Hmm. You definitely do not want more of those, I guess. So, if two was the average and you had some one times, does that mean you also had some times where you were a little more active than a two? (*Exceptions frame within the scale*)

Client: Yeah, maybe a two and a half or three.

Therapist: What did you do differently at those times? (*Specification*)
Client: I just got so disgusted and bored with the TV that I decided that I had to talk to someone.
Therapist: How did you *decide* to do that? (*Using "agency" language*) You could have decided on something else less constructive, like drugs or a different TV channel. (*Cooperating with his anticipated disqualification and asking for more specification*)
Client: I know, but I am realizing that I have to do something.
Therapist: What do you mean? You could keep on doing what you are. No one is going to stop you, are they? (*Requesting that he convince you*)
Client: I know, but this is not a life. I want to do something more productive.
Therapist: (*After more discussion of the exception times of two and a half or three*) So this more active approach like you took the other day is what you want to be doing more. When you are no longer coming here, are you thinking you will be averaging a 10 or more? What will you be averaging then? (*Using the scale to create the signs for concluding therapy*)
Client: Well, a 10 average is not possible. But if I was averaging more like seven, that would do it.
Therapist: What will you be doing differently at seven? (*Specification*)
Client: I guess I will be making a plan for my day and sticking to most of it. You know, I will be going shopping and cleaning my apartment.
Therapist: So, are you thinking that as you continue to do more of what you are doing at this two and a half, this somewhat more active approach, that you will be eventually averaging seven? (*Bridging the exceptions as the goal of therapy*)
Client: Yeah, maybe. I just have to keep at it.

   This conversation uses scaling with a solution-focus. We facilitate the client breaking down his goal into an average between two extremes. As part of pacing, we then ask for examples of when he was below his average. He says there were some "one" times. We then follow the logic of "averages" and ask about times that must have been somewhat better than the average. This gives us the opportunity for exception talk. He describes an exception of being bored and his taking a little action. We then can use the exception to find more details of what his solution will be like. His solution becomes more specific—his taking a more active approach, making plans for the day, shopping, cleaning the apartment, and following through on more of such activities.

Using the scale along with the concept of averaging gives us a way to find or create exceptions and to get more specifics about his solution. We are interested in the "one" times only to pace him and as an invitation to find out about the times that were slightly above his average, the two and a half or three.

We could also have used the scale to break down his next step beyond two and a half or three. For example:

Therapist: So when you are acting more like two and a half or three, you are recognizing your boredom, deciding that you want something different in your life, and calling someone or doing something other than TV. What will you be doing when you are at three and one quarter?

Client: You mean the next step? I will be looking for a job and filling out job applications.

Therapist: That sounds like it could be higher than just three and a quarter. Can you tell me what three and a quarter might be like.

Client: I guess if I just unplugged the TV and cleaned up the kitchen.

All of these modes of cooperating with clients' initial presentation of their goal . . .

1. being positive and future-oriented,
2. supporting their barely coping,
3. supporting their pessimism and fears, and
4. scaling the vagueness . . .

involve accepting the initial statement by clients and then using questions that balance their presentation and invite them into more expansive "realities."

DISCUSSION

QUESTION:
Many of these modes of cooperating seem to be paradoxical and strategic. Isn't that what they are?

These modes of conversing with clients may seem paradoxical because the modes seem initially to defy common sense. However, our intent is not to be paradoxical or strategic. We think that it makes more sense to accept the meaning clients ascribe to their situation than to try to talk them out of it. To accept their fears or what seems like pessimism as honorable, given how they are constructing their situation at the time, seems both respectful and reasonable. If clients think we understand and respect what they are saying, they are more likely to accept our invitation to try a new question.

We also do not think of cooperating modes as strategic. As Lynn Hoffman has said (1990), the strategic metaphor is fairly militaristic. With the strategic metaphor, we can begin to think of tactics and outflanking our clients or outpositioning them. As a strategic therapist, we might act pessimistic in order to get clients to be optimistic. We prefer to think we are cooperating with them as they are with us. If clients are presenting their situation as they experience it, we do not have the right to say they are pessimistic or that we are more optimistic. The clients are only presenting the situation as they experience it and evaluate it with their standards. We cooperate with them by adopting their language, even if by our own personal standards their language seems pessimistic. If clients present their situation in what seems a fairly negative way compared to our own standards, who is to say the clients are not responding to what they think is our unrealistic optimism? There are no negative clients.

QUESTION:
How do you handle suicidal clients?

We usually accept clients who are talking about hurting or killing themselves at face value—that is, they are thinking about it seriously or want to do something like that. We imagine that they must feel extremely hopeless and desperate for that to be a possible alternative at that time. Therefore, we are extremely supportive in the mode described above as if someone is barely coping. With that kind of empathy, the client eventually initiates a slight optimism and, surprisingly, we can even begin to explore goals and solutions.

EXERCISES

1. Identify four clients or imaginary people who present their situations in a way that seems:

positive and future-oriented,
barely coping with life,
pessimistic and negative or scared, and
very vague in their descriptions.

With a partner, take on the role of the client with the orientations listed above and talk about a problem for possibly three minutes. Take note of how you think of yourself and the problem, as well as how you think and feel about the future and solutions.

Adopting the client's role should give you some sense of how some clients feel and the process of their experience.

2. Next, have your partner ask questions from this chapter and you, as the client, take note of your experience.

With you acting as someone with a positive and upbeat presentation, your partner is to say, "Tell me more about the problem." After you have described your problem for five minutes, take note of your experience. How did the question fit for you? How did you feel talking about the problem? Then have your partner say, "Tell me about times when the problem does not happen or how things will be when the problem is solved." Take note of your experience.

With you acting with a "barely coping" presentation, have your partner try to point out the positives or convince you that your situation is not so bad. After taking note of your experience and how the therapist's questions fit for you, have your partner say something like: "Given the circumstances, I am frankly impressed that you are managing as well as you are. How are you managing?" Take note of how your experience changes.

With you acting as having been burned and disappointed many times in the past and afraid of taking a similar risk again, have your partner try to point out the positives or to insist upon examples of good times. After you have taken note of how the therapist's responses feel for you, your partner is to advocate for a more cautious or a more no-change approach. Take note of the difference in your own feelings and responses in the two modes of cooperating by your partner.

Finally, with you as the client presenting a vague description of a goal, have your partner ask you these scaling questions and write down your answers.

(a) On a scale from one to 10, with one being the worst of the problem situation and 10 being unrealistically the best that can be imagined, what are you averaging in the past week?

(b) What are the times like when you are lower than the average?

(c) What are you doing differently when you are acting slightly above the average? How do you think differently or what do you say differently to yourself?

3. After going through the above exercise in the client's role, take the therapist's role and use the questions out of the cooperating modes with your partner.

14

Putting It All Together

Case Examples

■ Change is occurring all the time.

In the preceding chapters, we have detailed how to use the conversational frames, criteria for a well-defined goal, pathways of constructing solutions, use of feedback and tasks, the interactional matrix, and cooperating modes. We will now present case examples to help you pull all of the preceding chapters together.

The five cases will demonstrate constructing solutions with different circumstances, namely:

1. when the exceptions are perceived as within the client's control,
2. when the exceptions are initially perceived by the client as spontaneous or out of her or his control,
3. when members of a marital couple see the solution as a change in the other,
4. when a parent has a concern about her child but the child does not come in, and
5. when a spouse has a marital problem but the other will not come in.

CASE 1: EXCEPTIONS PERCEIVED AS WITHIN THE CLIENT'S CONTROL

Session One:

A woman came to me, Jane, because she habitually used cocaine. She reported that she would do $400 worth of cocaine almost every night. She wanted to stop. Through solution-focused questioning, it became clear that there were several periods during the week when she did not do cocaine.

Therapist: So, tell me about the times where you do not do coke? (*Exceptions frame*)

Client: Oh, there are lots of times that I don't do it. I never ever do coke when I am going to work or when I am at work.

Therapist: Really, how is it that you decide not to coke then? (*Specification of the process, implying an active decision*)

Client: Jane, I would never do that; I am a responsible person. My mother did not bring me up to be a coke head.

Therapist: Yes, but how do you decide not to do it?

Client: I just tell myself that my mother did not bring me up to be a coke head and I don't do it. (*Contextual difference*)

Therapist: Are there other times where you do not do coke? (*Exceptions frame*)

Client: (*Thinking for a while*) Yes, I never do coke when I am going to see my lover. She would kill me if she saw me high and she always knows. (*Another context*)

Clearly these were exceptions where she consciously decided not to do coke. They were exceptions that she perceived to be in her control and could continue to do.

Therapist: When was the last time you did coke? (*Attempting to set up the amount of time since she did coke as a further exception*)

Client: Well, actually four days ago. I decided that this had to stop and everyone told me that I had to go into a drug rehab center. I do not want to do that. I have seen too many people go in, clean up, only to come out and get high again.

Therapist: Four days ago! Four days without coke! That's great! How have you done that? (*Specification of the process of this most recent exception*)

Client: Well, I decided it was time, so I decided several weeks ago to stop buying large amounts of cocaine at one time and I also changed my home phone number so that only one dealer could get in touch with me. As a matter of fact, the last time I did coke, I did only $150 worth.

Therapist: Only $150 worth! How did you resist doing the usual $400? (*Presupposing that this is exceptional that she did not do the usual amount*)

Client: Well, as part of all this, I decided that I would buy only small amounts of coke at a time, instead of all at once. This way, even if I want more, I have to go get it. You know, I have to call the dealer, get in my car, drive wherever, bring it back. It's harder that way.

The client not only had exceptions to doing coke but had already changed some important parts of the way she normally did coke. Both the exceptions and the changes in her habits were very important first signs of her "on track" solution behavior. She did not perceive them, however, as exceptional or something that was substantially different yet.

Given her statements, I asked:

Therapist: So, at what point will you be convinced that the problem is solved? (*Eliciting signs for concluding therapy*)

Client: If I don't do coke for 10 days straight, I will be over the hump.

My first session feedback was designed to support the client in the changes she was already making and to help her to continue these changes while beginning to perceive them as more within her control:

(Compliments)

I am very *impressed* with your sense of integrity about when to say "no" to the coke. You never do it with your lover, at work, or when you think of what your mother wants for you. I am also impressed that you want to stop doing coke despite the fact that you still like it. However, you know that is a much harder job. If you did not like it, the job would be easier.

I am impressed with the steps you have already taken to get on track, not taking from savings, cutting the coke dealers except for one, changing the phone number, and buying only small amounts at a time.

(Message)

But especially, I am impressed that there are lots of times where you do not do it and where you say, "I have had enough."

(Task)

Between now and the next time we meet, I want you to watch for what is different when you do not do coke.

Session Two:

The second session was two and a half weeks later because the client had gone on vacation.

Therapist: So, what is different or better since I saw you? *(Presupposing change)*

Client: (With great excitement) I have not done any coke. Can you believe that!!!

Therapist: That's really great!!! How did you do that? *(Enhancing agency)*

Client: I just don't want to feel bad anymore.

Therapist: Of course you don't. But how did you do that? *(Specification)*

Client: Well, some of the time I was on vacation with my lover, so that helped a lot, but I could have gotten some coke. Mostly, I just put it out of my mind.

Therapist: Really, what were you thinking instead? *(Asking for the positive)*

Client: Well, I was thinking of myself more and I was sleeping better. Just generally calmer. *(Difference of meaning, "thinking of myself more")*

I thought this change was really significant and definitely on the right track, especially when she stated that she was 50 percent confident that she would continue in this manner. During this session, we explored what other things she would be doing instead of coke. She talked a lot about her dreams of changing professions and opening a store.

However, today had been a difficult day for her to say "No" to the coke. She really wanted to do coke and was therefore glad that she was coming to see me today. She could not explain how she had not done some coke today.

Fifty percent confidence is a good start, but neither the client nor I were sure that this change would continue without problems. I wanted to reflect that concern to the client and so I gave the following feedback . . .

(Compliments)

I am really excited and impressed that you have not done coke in over three weeks now. It is really great and you should be very proud of yourself. I am also very impressed that you have decided to be thinking of yourself more. How that will play out I do not know yet, but I am sure it will be helpful to you.

(Message)

I am absolutely convinced that you have a good running start with saying "No" to coke, but I do not think that you are over the hump—yet. Today was an example of the hump where you really wanted to do some coke and you did not.

(Task)

Therefore, I want you between now and the next time to watch closely for how you overcome the temptation to do coke—in other words, the ways you say "No" to coke.

Again, as in the first session, this feedback was specifically designed to help her perceive the saying "No" to coke as within her control.

The next session was scheduled for a week and a half hence because she thought she was shaky about these changes. Given that the time between session one and session two was two and a half weeks, I was concerned that an appointment sooner than a week and a half would be taken by the client as a sign of "no confidence" on my part in the changes she was making despite the shakiness.

Session Three

By the third session the client could be clearer on how she said "No" to coke. She stated that what happens is that she pictures herself going to buy coke, cooking the coke, getting high, and then realizing that she just cannot start again because it is never enough. She also talked about how she had started being around non-drug people, had given all her money to her lover to hold, and had worked out a way to get an allowance. "Otherwise, the money just burns in my pockets," she said.

These were all very positive signs of her continued efforts at saying "No" to the coke. However, she described one time where she had decided to do coke. In very clear detail, she described her decision, calling the dealer, making the arrangements, getting into her car, driving to the bank to get money, and going to meet the dealer.

Client: I had the stuff and I was ready. But then, I pictured myself doing it . . . (*described in detail*) and I realized that it would never be enough. Plus, it just did not fit with the other things I am doing for myself. I gave the coke away.

Even though she had not done the coke, she clearly was having a hard time continuing her efforts of saying "No." Clearly, there were times that were easier for her and times that were harder. I used scaling to help her measure her progress and confidence in continuing in her solution.

Therapist: On a scale of one to 10, one being easy for you to say "No" to coke and 10 being difficult, where would you say you are averaging this week?
Client: About a three to five, I guess.
Therapist: Okay. What number are you when you start having trouble with saying "No?"
Client: I would say a six and up.
Therapist: And what are you doing, saying differently when you are below a six?

The client described that when she is in the "lower numbers" she is doing various things that I classified as ritual behaviors, things that helped her to reinforce her doing something other than thinking about or doing coke. In the feedback, I wanted to build on those behaviors. Therefore, I offered her this feedback:

(*Compliments*)

I think you are doing really great!!!

Again, you are not over the hump ("Oh no, she said in agreement"), but I guess this episode let you know what the hump consists of now. Before, you did not know, so you did not know what to expect or how to get over it like you are doing.

I am really impressed and think that the things you are doing are clearly signs for being on the right track.

- turning the money over to your lover,
- remembering all the negative aspects of the coke,
- being around drug-free people,
- having goals for the store you are opening,
- doing something else other than coke, like your hobbies.

(*Message*)

I think that it is normal for there to be a psychological withdrawal. So a lot of what you are feeling is part of the territory. It is the nature of the beast to have it come up when you least expect it.

(*Task*)

I really like these ideas that you have when you are "below a number six" like (I listed what she had told me) . . . and I want you to do these things purposefully each day, kind of like a preventive medicine.

The next session was scheduled for one week later because the client thought that she was even more shaky than before about continuing these changes.

Session Four

When the client returned one week later, she reported that she had decided to do coke and she did the coke. The day after she left the session, she decided she would do $50.00 worth of coke.

Therapist: Really, how did you decide that?

Client: I really, really wanted some coke and decided I was just not going to avoid it. So I called the dealer, went down, and got it. I came home, cooked it up, and did it.

In solution-focused therapy, we think of change occurring with two steps forward and one step back. Therefore, what might seem like a failure, a negative, or a sign that therapy is not on track is really only part of the process of change occurring. Therefore, I asked further about the "step back," but with an exceptions frame.

Therapist: How is it that you stopped at $50.00 worth? (*Exceptions frame*)

Client: Well, once I got high, I freaked out. I got paranoid. I was looking in the bathroom mirror and my eyes were jumping out of my head, sweat was pouring down my face, and I freaked. And I thought, "Something is wrong here;" what would my mother say if I died of coke.

At that point, she made the commitment to the decision to say "No" to coke. The rest of the session focused on the other six days since she had the last session when she was continuing all of the changes she had made previously. She was beginning to think of the other changes as "all the positives to not doing coke." The feedback to her was:

(Compliments)

I am sorry to hear how painful this episode was for you, yet I am very impressed that you stopped at 50 dollars worth. Other people would have just continued.

(Message)

One half of me thinks this episode of doing coke was necessary, maybe even required or good that it happened, for you to learn that you can *choose* to do it. Therefore, it was a rational choice and not out of being a "drug addict." It is good that you know when is enough, and see the positives of not doing coke.

It is also amazing how you could truly look at yourself in the mirror.

The other half of me thinks that it is like Russian roulette, that you never know which of those times you would not stop.

(*Task*)

Continue to do and practice the positives and notice what happens.

Next session was scheduled for three weeks off because I was going on vacation. The client was given the name of another therapist to call, if she needed to be seen. She never called that therapist; she did not have to.

Session Five

When the client came into the session, she reported that she had not done coke and even gave a little laugh at my question of whether she had done coke. Her coke days were over, but she reported that she was feeling depressed and had cried a lot since we last talked. She was deciding and making some important decisions in her life about her relationship and her profession. All of these she thought were good, but very hard. My feedback to her was:

I do not think you fully realize the extent of the effort, energy, and force that you have put forth the last six months. I agree with you that, as you say, you are emotionally tired. Change is hard, it is a metamorphosis.

The client was confident that the changes would continue and therefore set the next appointment for four weeks. At six weeks, she was continuing her thinking of herself and a follow-up session was scheduled for three months away. At the follow-up, she was continuing to be coke-free and she and I decided that she could call if she needed another session. She came in again six months later about another matter in the process of her other personal and professional changes. She told me at that time that she had tried to do coke one time and, ironically, had failed. She went to buy the coke and started cooking it, slipped, and spilled it all over the floor. She went to get more coke and as she was cooking it, she spilled that amount too and it fell down the sink. At that point, she realized that it was just not worth it and has not looked for coke since.

CASE 2: EXCEPTIONS PERCEIVED AS SPONTANEOUS

A young man came to see us for fear of being fired from his job. He described an intense fear he had that people at his job thought he was stealing from work. He said he knew this because of the things being said to him and the way people looked at him. He had no idea why they thought he stole because he was a 100 percent honest person and would never do that. He felt hurt that they thought he stole and, therefore, he withdrew from interacting with them and kept to himself at work. His goal in coming to see us was initially stated as, "I am helpless in my job and I do not want to get fired from work." (Not yet well-defined)

Therapist: So, how will you be acting differently when you are not acting scared of losing your job? (*Hypothetical solution frame*)
Client: I will be more powerful at my job and continuing in my efforts in my outside life.
Therapist: When you are more powerful at your job, what will you be doing differently? (*Accepting the feeling statement of "powerful" and asking the hypothetical solution question again*)
Client: I won't care what people think of me. (*Negatively stated*)
Therapist: And what will you be thinking or doing *instead* when you don't care what people think of you.
Client: I will be taking care of myself. (*Positively stated and more behavioral*)

The conversation continued to clarify his goal of taking care of himself and acting in a more powerful manner with others at work. There were a few exceptions when he had acted in a powerful manner at work in the past, but not in the recent present. The exceptions were prior to his thinking that co-workers thought he was stealing. During the times when he had acted in a powerful manner, he thought that it was because he just felt powerful rather than something he consciously did. These exception times were perceived as feeling states that were something that just happened to him and not something he created. We wanted to help him construct a solution that he would perceive as within his control. Therefore, we gave him the following feedback:

(*Compliments*)

We are very impressed that with all this pain over being confused that you have not let it interfere with your performance at work or in class. We are also struck with your desire to be clear about what you want for yourself.

(*Message*)

We do not know if you are going to be fired at work or not. But we do know that you need to protect yourself. The way to do that is to take care of yourself at home so that you feel powerful with yourself and know what is true about you. We also know that if you act "as if" they are going to accuse you, you will start a cycle where you act guilty when you are not, but which will give them proof for their point of view that you are guilty! We know you do not want that!!

(*Task*)

Therefore, this might sound crazy but, between now and the next time, we want you to pretend to be powerful and act in a powerful manner with others even if you do not feel like it. When you do that, take note of what happens.

He came back two weeks later and reported with much surprise:

Client: Well, I did what you said and pretended in a powerful way and you know what? It worked! When I acted powerful, I could change their impression and then it became a reality! I knew what was the truth and told them. I even told them outright that I did not steal the desk cleaners.

This case is a clear example of what happens when clients pretend their own reality and therefore create the interchange they want to happen.

CASE 3: WHEN THE SOLUTION IS PERCEIVED AS A CHANGE
IN THE OTHER

Session One

A couple came to see us about some marital difficulties. They reported
a brief affair the wife had had about a year previously as having made
their relationship steadily worse. She stated that she felt guilty about
the affair and ever since that time had been trying to make up for it
and regain her husband's trust. The husband said he felt that he could
not trust her and that he was staying married to her because of the kids.
She said, however, that she would like him to trust her again and he,
too, after some time in the session, said that he would like that trust
again. We asked the hypothetical solution question and they responded:

Husband: I would like not to be mad. (*Negatively stated*)
Therapist: What would you like *instead*? (*Redirecting the negative state-
ment to a positive one*)
Husband: I would be getting over the affair and maybe feel for her
again. I don't know. I don't hate her, but I would just like to know
I am as important as the other guy was.
Therapist: How would you know that you were that important? (*Asking
for signs of trust*)
Husband: She had her chance and blew it. I asked her to tell this guy
off and not to call anymore. She did not do it. I was so mad. And
she still won't tell the guy not to call.
Wife: But I did tell him.
(*A brief argument ensues and therapist redirects the conversation.*)
Therapist: So when the problem is solved for you, Karen, what will you
be doing differently? (*Hypothetical solution frame, self position*)
Wife: I think when he is trusting again that we would do some things
together again, we would go out without the kids, and I would not
feel so guilty.
Therapist: So there are times now when he seems somewhat trusting
or the two of you do things together? (*Exceptions frame*)
Wife: Yes, there are some times when he will joke a little.

The remainder of the session was spent in discussion of the "joking times" and how they each brought it about. The husband could not explain how he sometimes forgot about the past and just joked around. The wife could not explain how she joked rather than letting her guilt stop her. They both agreed, however, that they liked the joking times and thought that those types of times were more of what they wanted.

The goal for her was his trusting her again. The hypothetical solution involved his getting over the past and feeling for his wife again. For her, she would be acting relaxed rather than guilty and the two of them would be doing things together again.

The exception was the "joking times" when both of them were thinking about something other than the past or how they felt about the past. We offered them this feedback:

(Compliments)

We are very impressed with both of your efforts to do things differently, your coming here and talking about things that are not easy to talk about. You both mentioned doing something that you think the other wants. It is obvious how much you care and how important it is to you that the other care.

(Message)

It would be normal to be scared at this point, scared that it might work and scared that it might not, scared of the changes you might make.

We are impressed with the "joking times," how each of you put your feelings and thoughts about the past aside or did something different so that you can enjoy yourselves for awhile. We are struck that you have the courage to relax like that.

(Task)

If you decide to come back, we would like to suggest that between now and the next time each of you notice what you do and what the other does differently during the joking times.

According to the solution construction map, we have exceptions, the "joking times." However, both husband and wife are looking for the other to change first and neither can explain what he or she does individually during the "joking times" that makes that a better time. To them, the exceptions seemed spontaneous and out of the individual control of each. We wanted them to find out more about those times and, more specifically, about what they individually did that contributed to those times being better. By identifying what they did, they could then have more control and the choice of making the good times happen more often.

We scheduled the next session one week later. A week allowed them time enough to do the task and would maintain continuity in the therapy process.

Session Two

When we asked what was different or better, they both said that things were better. She said that he did not seem so grim and unhappy and as a result she was more relieved. Since she was more relieved, she was looser with him and had more fun. She said that during this "relaxed" time he was more relaxed and that on her own she had decided to relax more even when he was not in a good mood. We asked how this was different and she said normally she would try to cheer him up or try to be as good as she could so that he would have no reason to mistrust her.

Her husband stated that he did not like how in the past she had tried to be perfect all the time. When she did that, she was defensive and she was always there underfoot. During those times, she stayed physically with her husband all the time so that there would be no way he could think she was doing something wrong. He liked much more the fact that, rather than being physically with him all the time, she had decided to do some of her own things.

He did not like her trying to be perfect for him. We asked how he will be different when she is not being perfect. He did not know. He just did not want to be hurt again. We asked if they were looking for guarantees. Both were looking for guarantees. He did not want to be hurt again and she wanted a guarantee that if she gave up trying to be perfect he would not leave.

Even though they described the above concerns about guarantees, most of the session was focused on the relaxed times when guarantees were not even a question.

They also stated an exception context. With regard to their parenting his daughter from a previous marriage, they did not let the event of the affair interfere. He was allowing his wife to assert herself as a parent rather than his trying to protect and stick up for his daughter. She was realizing that they had to work together. Parenting a teenager was getting too difficult to leave to just one of them.

In this session, we had more examples of the joking time and what each did differently. Both explained that they decided to joke around and not wait for the other to be in a good mood. Our feedback was:

(Compliments)

We agree with the two of you that you are on track by concentrating on what is important in the present and the future. You have been focusing on being a good parenting team with your oldest becoming a teen. You, Tom, have been deciding to let go of the notion of being a single parent. You, Karen, have decided to pick up on being a parent. You both have been realizing that there are no guarantees about the future or what the other might do.

Before, you, Tom, said, "If I am certain she won't do it again, then I can go forward."

And you, Karen, said, "If I am certain, that I have convinced him that I won't do it again, then I can relax and be myself again."

Now, you both are beginning to realize that those ways of thinking do not work and to look beyond the notion of a guarantee to create good times now that will be more the basis of your trust.

You, Karen, are saying, "I am just going to relax regardless of whether he is in a good mood or not."

You, Tom, are deciding to be yourself and not care so much about her feelings.

(Message)

We have one further thought. We know that you, Karen, have been working very hard to be perfect for Tom. But we are afraid that your being perfect and being always around may be too much of a good thing. It is a little like having a perfect chocolate cake every day. After awhile, you do not think much of it anymore. So we think you may want to think about how you can show Tom the not-so-perfect side once in awhile so that he can trust that side too. Tom, we suggest that since neither of you can change the past, you might consider how you will know when to trust and how you will let her know.

(*Task*)

In conclusion, we think you should continue to do what you are doing and keep notes of what you are doing so we can talk about it next time.

The next session was scheduled two weeks later to give them time to do the task and notice differences.

Session Three

Therapist: So what has been different or better? (*Presupposing change*)
Both: It has been better.
Karen: It has been better and harder.
Therapist: How do you mean?
Karen: Well, it has been difficult to go do my thing when he is in a bad mood or mad. I wonder what he is mad about and if he is mad at me. But I went and cleaned out my office, something I have put off for some time, and reacquainted myself with my weaving. It was hard because I was really tempted to hang around him and see what was wrong. (*Exception*)
Therapist: So, what happened? (*Specification*)
Karen: I do not know. I guess it was just a mood for him because later he was joking around. He has been back into his things too. I noticed he was back to his projects in the garage.
Therapist: (*to Tom*) This is true. Things were different for you? (*Exceptions frame*)
Tom: Yes, somewhat. Before I was so caught up in that stuff about the past. Now I am using more energy to get back into other things. (*Exception and new meaning, "using more energy to get back into other things*)
Therapist: How are you doing that? (*Specification*)
Tom: I cannot stay mad forever. I have to move on. (*Difference of meaning*)
Therapist: (*Cheerleading*) This must be a really big step for each of you. (*With raised voice tone and curiosity*) How are each of you doing this? (*Further specification with agency presuppositions*)

The remainder of the session brought out more details of how things were going with these emerging decisions to relax and get into her own things again on her part and to "move on" on his part. Each was identifying things that they were doing individually and within their control.

When asked how confident they were of continuing with these decisions, they both said about 90 percent. We asked what may have been some of the good things that came out of this event in the past. She said that it reminded her that she is not so strong. She used to think that she could do anything and that she was always honest. Now she knows she is not so invincible. Tom liked that they were even more together in sharing the responsibility of parenting.

We scheduled another appointment in two weeks as follow up on the changing they were doing. They called and canceled this appointment. They reported that things were going fine and they thought they were on track.

CASE 4: WHEN A PARENT COMES IN ABOUT HER CHILD BUT THE CHILD DOES NOT ATTEND

A mother had called and wanted to talk about getting her daughter into therapy.

Therapist: What would you like out of coming here? (*Goal frame*)
Client: Well, I would like to get some advice from you about getting my daughter into therapy. (*Complaint statement*)
Therapist: You think your daughter needs therapy?
Client: Yes, she is living at home, she is not working, she is not talking either to me or my husband, and she blames me for being unhappy. (*Complaint statement*)
Therapist: Uh-huh. Would she say these are problems or that she wants to be in therapy? (*Clarifying who is the client—that is, who wants what from therapy; the question uses the "for the other" reporting position.*)
Client: No, and that is the problem. She thinks I am her problem and she will not even consider therapy. She thinks that it is my fault that she feels bad about herself because I did not give her enough attention when she was a child. She is 22 now.
Therapist: I see. So if your daughter were doing more of what you want

her to, what would you be doing differently? (*Hypothetical solution*)

Client: Well, if she were showing some initiative and were a little happier, I would not feel so guilty. I could relax and get back into my own things. Sometimes, I think what she says may be true. I did favor my son over her. (*Appears to think changes in her daughter have to happen first before she will be relaxing and feeling some relief*)

Therapist: What would you be doing as you are relaxing and getting back into your own things? (*Specification of the hypothetical solution*)

She responded further to the hypothetical solution questioning by saying that she would be letting go of her daughter rather than worrying so much now. Now she was afraid to say anything—either to confront her or to remind her—for fear that what she might say would jeopardize their already deteriorating relationship. When she would be letting go, she would know that she had accomplished her job as a parent and she would be seeing friends again and thinking about what she would do for herself now that she was done with raising children. She thought that if she let go now her daughter might fail and be angry with her, while she herself would feel guilty.

In response to queries about times when she was letting go some now, she said that she was going off on a religious retreat by herself this coming weekend and was planning a Fourth-of-July picnic for her friends. She responded that this was different for her because she had been so worried about her daughter. When asked how she was doing this, she said that she was responding to advice from her minister that she had to let go.

We asked if, since she was not able to change her daughter or make her daughter's life happy, or even force her to make use of therapy, she would think she was on track for herself if she were continuing to "let go" and think of her future without childrearing. She said, "Yes," although she felt sad that there was not more that she could do for her daughter. We offered her this feedback:

(*Compliments*)

We cannot tell you how impressed we are with how much you care about all your children. You obviously have gone above and beyond the call of duty over the years in taking care of them and providing for them.

With your daughter, too, it is obvious how much you care about her. You may now at times think mistakenly that your only motivation is guilt, but we think your motivation is a deep love for her.

We also think that it is because you love her so much that you are finding it difficult to go through the transition that all families have to go through where kids go off to make their own successes and mistakes and parents let go and focus on the next phase of their life.

(*Message*)

We are very impressed with how you are already showing signs of letting go and thinking of yourself, namely, your going on this retreat and planning the picnic with your friends and not the kids.

(*Task*)

We think this is great for you and your daughter and we would like to ask that you keep your eyes open for other, maybe more subtle ways, that you are letting go and thinking of yourself.

Session Two (This was scheduled one week later to give her time to notice differences.)

Therapist: What has been different or better? (*Presupposing change*)
Client: Well, I have been getting back to reading and I have gone ahead with my plans for the picnic.
Therapist: Really, (*with curiosity*) how have you been doing that? (*Specification of the exception*)
Client: Well, my spiritual adviser gave me the same advice as you. So, I decided to get back to my reading and take the chance that if I have the party my daughter will not make a scene.
Therapist: So you are taking some risks. (*Cheerleading*) How are you doing this? I imagine you must have doubts and maybe feel guilty. (*Specification in a process form and within the frame of difficulty*)
Client: That is true and I am still very worried about my daughter, but I guess I am becoming more convinced that I am not helping by worrying so much.

Therapist: How do you think your daughter has noticed your changing? (*Exceptions frame and from the "for other" reporting position*)

Client: She has not said anything, but she did ask me about my spiritual retreat that I went to.

Therapist: Was that different?

Client: It is different for my daughter lately because she was not talking to me at all.

Therapist: What do you think she would say about your thinking of your future if she were here? (*Exceptions frame from the "for other" reporting position*)

Client: I am not sure. She might say it is good for me to do.

The client went on to say how difficult it was to plan this party for fear that her daughter would make a scene because the client's son was invited and sister and brother were not talking to each other. The daughter was terribly jealous of her brother.

Despite the client's concerns, the client was describing backing off and not trying to change the daughter like before. We thought she was on track in focusing on herself and her own changing. We offered her these compliments and feedback:

(Compliments)

We are so impressed with your deciding to focus on yourself and your own personal goals. We do not know if that is coming from an increasing self-respect or from an emerging knowledge that what is good for you is good for your children. We agree with you that contrary to sacrificing all the time it is better for you and for your daughter in the long run for you to be taking care of yourself. As you say, when you do not take care of yourself, you are irritable with her and with everyone.

We are just so impressed with your planning the party. We agree with you that your daughter will have to learn to adjust to her brother being around.

(Message)

It seems to us that your daughter loves you a great deal and that she is noticing these changes in you. We suspect that she may let go in her own way as she becomes more convinced of your letting go. Along the way, she may test your commitment, though.

(Task)
   Keep doing what you are doing and take note so you can tell us next time.

Given that she was now working on a goal that was within her control—focusing on herself and her own future rather than trying to change her daughter—and given that she was now entertaining the idea that it was also good for her daughter in the long run that the client focus on herself and let go of the daughter, we began to space the sessions and allow her to practice her new thinking. The next session was in 10 days, followed by sessions at two weeks, three weeks, and a month.

CASE 5: WHEN ONE SPOUSE HAS A MARITAL PROBLEM BUT THE OTHER WILL NOT COME IN

A young married man called for therapy about problems in his four-year-old marriage, stating that he wanted to come in alone. His wife had insisted that he had the problem and that it was not up to her to make changes. He at least partially agreed with her that the problems were mostly his, and also he wanted to talk with someone alone, without her.

Therapist: What is your goal in coming here? *(Goal frame)*
Client: I wanted to talk with you alone, because I want you to understand what the situation is like for me. My wife is totally fed up with my angry outbursts and she will not have anything to do with counseling. We have been in marital therapy before and she felt very hurt and discouraged. I have to agree with her that my anger is a problem, but she is so provocative. I do get violent, but it is not just that. She cuts me off at the knees. She just will not have any sympathy for me either about us or about my working. She is just so critical about everything and she argues over everything. *(Complaint statements)*
Therapist: So you want me to understand what it is like for you and that she won't come in. And it sounds like you agree with her that your getting angry gets out of hand, but you also think she is part of it. Is that right? *(Clarification)*

238   *Becoming Solution-Focused in Brief Therapy*

Client: Yeah. She sees everything I do as an opportunity to remind me of everything I have done wrong.
Therapist: So, what about this would you like to change? (*Asking for a goal statement*)
Client: Well, as much as I think she is wrong, I think I will never have a leg to stand on in arguing with her as long as my anger snaps. I will always be on the defensive or feel guilty about that unless I make a change. She is scared of me and I think my daughter is too. I need to be in control and acting proper in order for me to show her she is in the wrong.
Therapist: So you are hoping that by controlling your anger you can show her that she is in the wrong? (*Clarification*)
Client: Well, I need to know who is right so I can decide whether I have given it my best shot and it is okay to leave her.
Therapist: So, you want to be handling your anger differently so that when you do make a decision whether to stay or leave, it will be for the right reasons.
Client: Yes, I just have to be in control of myself so that I know it is not my fault if things do not work out. We have been married only four years, but I would not want a divorce to be my fault.

The statement "handling his anger differently" was accepted as a goal and we explored the hypothetical solution. He imagined that if he was able to handle the situation the way he wanted, he would be able to talk to her calmly, even if he was mad. He thought if he had more self-esteem, he would be able to act more calmly with her.

We complimented him on his sense of responsibility and honesty— that even though he thought he had many legitimate gripes about his wife, he was seeking to change his actions. We also complimented him on his sensitivity to his wife and child, that he was well aware of how he scared them with his angry outbursts. We were impressed that he wanted to do something about that.

The limited time of the session did not allow for any discussion of exceptions, so we based our suggested task on the hypothetical solution he had developed. We mentioned that we wanted to know more about the times when he believed he acted somewhat calmly with his family, or times when he could let go of control but did not.

In the second session he reported that he had decided to follow a little motto, that every day was a new day and he would try to make it a good day. This would be different than carrying over his resentments and feelings from the previous day. Several times he decided to join his family and do some things with them rather than retreating to the solitude of his study. He participated and tried to listen to his wife's side in a decision over the purchase of a new computer. He said both of these things were quite different on his part. He said that he found it very difficult to listen to her arguments about the computer and to compromise with her. However, he was pleased that he did not yell or lose control.

When asked how he decided to do these things, he said that he was determined to do his part to save the marriage. This was different in that he now seemed to be wanting the marriage to work out. Again, we shared with him how impressed we were with his determination to do his part to make things work and how that meant his doing some very difficult things such as making compromises and trying to resist viewing compromise as giving in.

The third session was several weeks later because of his schedule and ours. He initially reported that things were very bad but that one time when he was about to get into an argument, he said to her, "I don't want to fight. I just want to be friends." This stopped the argument and later she was friendly with him again. We asked if this was different and he said this was very different for him to say. Her talking with him again so soon after the argument was also different. We asked if this were true that he wanted to be friends. He said he was not sure it was possible but, yes, he would like to be treating her nicely and be friends again. He thought that friends cooperated rather than trying to win or make the other lose. This is what he wanted.

We again complimented him on his perseverance and on how he discovered that trying to be friends was somewhat helpful. When he thought of his wife as a friend, he was less likely to think she was trying to put him down and more likely to give her the benefit of the doubt. We asked him to notice what else was different when he thought of her as a friend.

In the next two sessions, which were several weeks apart, he reported several things he had done differently when he thought of her as a friend and not just a wife. He decided he had been selfish by withdrawing into his solitude and that he needed to participate more in family matters. One time he listened to her complaints about him and did not respond defensively. He merely stated that he was sorry that things were difficult.

We asked how he did that. He said he realized that there was nothing he could do about her complaints, so he just said he was sorry. He said she was just quiet after that.

By this time he was feeling quite good about his changes, that he was not flying off the handle. He was being calm and acting like a friend rather than being defensive or assuming the worst. He was pleased that she was changing, that she was being friendlier. He still wished she would give him more acknowledgment, but he was pleased that she was now willing to come to the next session.

When she came in she maintained that there was nothing she wanted to change. She was still waiting to see if these changes on his part were going to last or if she was going to be hurt and disappointed again. At the same time they both reported things the other was doing differently, as well as things *they* were doing differently. The remaining sessions continued to focus on what they were doing that was working and on how they would know and convince each other that these changes were for real.

Although this case began with a marital complaint, we did not insist that the wife come in. Instead we helped the husband focus on a goal that was within his control, "handling his anger differently," and assumed that with changes on his part, changes in the relationship would develop. As he made his changes, they both decided that she would join the sessions. She had no stated goal but participated in reporting changes and in identifying what good things she noticed.

Although in this case the spouse joined the therapy later, spouses do not always participate nor is their attendance necessary. The marital relationship can change as one person makes changes in their interactions. Marital therapy can work with only one person as long as the client defines the change as within her or his control and not exclusively a change in the other.

DISCUSSION

QUESTION:
Do you ever have cases like the above where the other spouse does not change and they divorce?

Yes. Just because one makes changes in the interaction with the spouse does not mean that the couple always stay together. Sometimes, as could have happened in the above case, one spouse makes several changes and then decides that she or he has given the marriage the best shot, but the marriage is still not working or the change is not worth it. Sometimes, the changes are too late for the other spouse.

However, some cases with a marital complaint can be more hopeful when we assume that a change by one of the spouses can make a difference and that both spouses do not have to be part of the therapy in order for the relationship to improve.

QUESTION:
What if members of a family or spouses have different goals?

We assume that very often family members or spouses will define their goals differently. Having different goals is fine, and we help them develop their own solutions while meeting together. Oftentimes the goals overlap. Sometimes a teenager may be trying to get more freedom while her or his parents may want to see more responsible behavior. These goals are very complementary even if the clients initially see them as contradictory. Usually, a teen gains more freedom by doing actions that her or his parents see as more responsible. A parent needs to reward the teenager with increased freedom in order to foster the responsible behavior.

When the stated goals are mutually exclusive, for example, when one spouse wants divorce and the other wants to pursue the relationship, we see the clients separately. We work with each spouse toward his or her stated goal. Eventually one or both goals change.

15

Voluntary or Involuntary

A Basic Distinction

■ The members of a treatment group are those who share a goal and state their desire to do something about making it happen.

A solution-focused approach is a consumer model—that is, clients are the experts in stating what they are coming to see us about, and in deciding what they want to work towards. With this as a given, an important initial distinction is to determine if those coming to see us do so because *they* want to or because *someone else* wants them to. If we assume that the clients are the experts, what do we do about those who seem to be saying they are not customers for what we have to offer? What do we do with someone who says, "I do not need to be here, I do not want to be here, and I do not have a problem"?

We all have experienced the difference between working with those who come in with something they own and want to work on and those who do not want to be there and may even think the problem lies with those who sent them.

We have all, probably, at some point in our careers been grateful for having a self-motivated client or felt the dread that goes with anticipation of working with someone who does not want to be there.

We have all probably tried similar efforts with varied success with clients who are ordered to come to see us. These clients may be students ordered by the principal or the dean of discipline to talk to a counselor; probationers who have to be in treatment as a condition of their probation; couples who have been told to see a marriage counselor before the court will proceed with the request for a divorce; drivers who were convicted of driving while under the influence and ordered for substance abuse counseling; parents who have been ordered into therapy because of abuse and as a condition for the return of the children; supervisees who do not think they need supervision; or children dropped off for treatment by parents who say it is the children's problem.

The distinction between voluntary and involuntary is basic to a consumer-oriented model and critical in the above situations. It is critical because we do not want to assume that clients are voluntary if, in fact, they are not. When this distinction is not made, the result is usually muddles of thinking, attempted solutions, and roles.

As de Shazer has stated, "Useful distinctions in conceptual schemes lead to explanatory or descriptive metaphors that have a clear form. Muddles, on the other hand, are created when useful distinctions that could be drawn are not . . ." (de Shazer, 1982, p. 71).

CONFUSING THE DISTINCTION AND RESULTING ACTIONS

Some examples of the muddles and role confusion where the voluntary/involuntary distinction is not drawn follow:

1. Confusing the Involuntary Client With a Voluntary Treatment Model

Therapist: What is your goal in coming here? (*Goal frame*)
Mr. Smith: Nothing. The judge ordered this treatment, but he does not understand that I do not need this.
Therapist: Mr. Smith, it seems to me that anyone with their second DUI conviction might think they have a drinking problem and should do something about it. (*Attempting to convince the client of a need of a change*)
Mr. Smith: Well, these convictions were a rigged deal from the git-go. I didn't have that much to drink and I was driving fine. The police in this town have decided they are going to get me.
Therapist: But, Mr. Smith, with both of these convictions and your previous auto accidents, do you really believe all these professionals are wrong and just out to get you? Don't you think you should take a look at this?

Mr. Smith: Whatever problems with drinking I have had, I have taken care of and I don't need any help.

In the client's view in this situation, the therapist has aligned with the decision of the court that he has a drinking problem he needs to work on. The therapist with an involuntary client has taken on the role of social control agent as an extension of the court. The therapist is attempting to make the involuntary client into a voluntary one through confrontation.

2. Who Is the Client?

A colleague recently told us of her new position as a social worker. She was working within a state contract designed to keep the chronically mentally ill out of state hospitals and off the streets. She had a sizable caseload of individuals who had recently been discharged from the hospital. She complained that none of these clients seemed to be motivated for treatment or to want to make any changes.

When we asked what her clients would say they wanted from her (goal frame, for the other position), she said that most of her clients would probably say they wanted nothing or wanted her to secure their government assistance for them.

She had been doing considerable work for her clients in arranging housing and government assistance, but she was feeling burned out and discouraged that her clients seemed to want to do nothing for themselves around issues she saw as problematic.

In this situation, the client seems to be the State; it is the State that is the party with a goal. The State has decided that the cost of maintaining people in the hospital is prohibitive and has designed a program whereby someone—the social worker—is to maintain these people. The individuals in her caseload have seldom stated any goal that they would like to work on with her.

In this situation, she seemed to confuse who was the real client for her work—and that was the State.

Optimal Settings With Involuntary Clients

There seem to be several roles for helpers and workers faced with involuntary clients. There is, for example, the reporter, the investigator, the monitor, and the therapist.

The reporter reports to someone in authority about some wrongdoing. The report often involves child abuse or neglect. The reporter is often a nonprofessional. Sometimes, the reporter may be you as the helping professional who hears the client talk about abuse or neglect that you are required to report by law. The reporter might be a neighbor or relative who witnesses or hears about the abuse. The reporter may be some medical professional who sees the signs of abuse or neglect.

The investigator is part of the state system that is required to investigate the situation and make an assessment of the wrongdoing.

The monitor or manager receives the case from the court, usually sets the requirements for change (requirements for return of children, conditions for probation, etc.), and monitors progress toward these requirements.

The therapist is the person who is assigned the role of facilitating solution construction with the client.

Keeping these roles separate and identified by using different people seems to be the optimal way of working with involuntary clients. You and the involuntary client can keep the roles and functions clear, avoiding the muddles of confusing these roles.

When involuntary clients can identify someone else as the investigator and someone else as the case manager, they can more easily identify you in the role of therapist as advocating their achieving their own goal. You are more cleanly in the neutral position of being able to identify a problem/solution of their choice.

When you are both therapist and manager, involuntary clients can have a harder time separating your role as social control agent who may take away their children or put them in jail from your role as a solution-focused therapist.

Ideally, you, as the therapist, want to be in a neutral, detached position whereby you can help clients identify what they may want. The therapist is not encumbered by other roles or demands.

How to work in the role of therapist with the involuntary client, is the focus of the following chapter.

DISCUSSION

QUESTION:
Don't you think some of these clients are in denial and our responsibility is to break through the denial?

In our *role as therapist*, we take what people say at face value. If involuntary clients say they cannot think of anything they want to work on in therapy, we assume that from their point of view there is no problem or goal they want to use therapy for at this time. We do not interpret a client's motivation or lack of it and we do not interpret what is "really" going on. Therefore, we do not try to convince clients that they have a problem.

This position is true in the role of therapist and does not mean that in other roles we might not make assessments beyond what the involuntary client says. Judges and protective service workers who are in the position of having to make some decision about the custody of children will look at physical evidence and make a decision about what is true about a parent in a given situation. In those other roles, judges and protective service workers make decisions, independent of the client's view, of whether there is a problem or not. In the therapist's role, however, we do not take on that responsibility or expert position.

EXERCISE

Go through your list of involuntary clients, and ask yourself who among them is stating that she or he wants something from the therapy. Is the person who comes to your office stating she or he wants something out of coming in to see you? Are others involved in that case saying they want something from that person coming in to see you? If the answer to the first question is "no," your client has no goal. If she or he says someone else is coercing her/him to come to therapy, you have an involuntary client.

You may find the next chapter useful in helping the involuntary client to identify goals and become a voluntary client.

16

The Involuntary Client

The involuntary client is someone ordered to come in to see you, by someone else. The involuntary client may or may not agree with the order or the reasons for the order. These clients may become voluntary clients by identifying a goal they would like to work on, but at least initially they have been referred and ordered to come in by someone else. Much of the early articulation of this schema was worked out by Insoo Berg and by Eve Lipchik (Berg, 1990).

Our work with them follows this schema:

Whose idea is it that you come here?

What makes _____ think you should come here?

What does _____ want you to be doing differently?

Is this something you want? (*Goal frame*)

    If yes, proceed as with a voluntary client.

    If no, ask: Is there something you would like out of coming here? (*Goal frame*)

        If yes, proceed as with a voluntary client.

        If no, explore the consequences of not coming to sessions.

Once the consequences are clarified, ask again what the referring person expects out of the client coming in for therapy.

    If the client knows, ask if she or he is willing to do what the referring person wants.

    If the client does not know, send her or him to the referring person to find out what the referring person wants as a result of completing therapy. Have the referring person be specific.

If the client is willing to do what the referring person wants, proceed with what the referring person wants as the goal.

If the client does not want to adopt the referring person's goal, compliment the client and . . .
(1) say goodbye or
(2) state conditions for further sessions if continued sessions are required by the court or agency policy.

The thrust of this schema is to explore the idea that involuntary clients may turn into voluntary ones with a goal within which you can be helpful using a solution-focus. If you and the client cannot identify a goal that you can agree to, then you can support the client enough so that if she or he ever decides there is something around which help is needed, the client may return as a voluntary client.

Simultaneous work may be necessary with the referring person to help the referring person clarify her or his goals and expectations of the client, to clarify your role, and to clarify the referring person's role.

Now that we have an overview of procedures to follow in therapy when an involuntary client is involved, let us go back to the beginning with an example. The social control roles of the investigator and manager have all been identified and are being performed by people other than the therapist.

Therapist: What is your goal in coming here? (*Goal frame*)
Client: The judge and social worker have decided that I need to come here.
Therapist: So, this was their idea. What makes them think you need to come here? (*Goal frame, for the other position*)
Client: They recently took my two kids away from me because they said I was neglecting them. The kids are in a foster home and the court has taken custody. The school social worker made the report. The judge says that if I want to get my kids back, I have to come and see you.
Therapist: Oh, I'm sorry about your kids, you must miss them very much.
Client: Yes, a lot. They are the world to me. All I have are my children and I just don't know what to do with myself.
Therapist: So, they are saying you need to parent differently? Is this your goal too? (*Clarification*)
Client: Yes, I haven't been too good with the kids sometimes. They just

get to be too much and I get myself in trouble with my drinking. (*Problem statement*)

This client has agreed with the reason for the referral and has begun to identify ways in which she is having problems. The therapist will proceed with this now *voluntary* client by helping her formulate her goals.

If this client had said "No," the therapist would follow the next step of exploring what the involuntary client might want that may be different from the referring person's goal.

Client: No, I don't think I have been neglectful at all. These social workers just don't know what it means to be a single parent. They think that just because you leave your kids alone for a moment you are doing something wrong or you don't care about your kids.

Therapist: Well, it seems to me that you must love your kids very much and want the best for them. (*Supporting the client*)

Client: That's right, and I don't need someone telling me what to do. My lawyer and I are going to take care of the social worker.

Therapist: I can understand that. So is there something apart from what the judge and social worker said that you would like out of coming here? (*Goal frame*)

Client: Well my oldest one is failing school. I don't know what is going on with her. She just doesn't study anymore and is skipping school. (*Complaint statement*)

Therapist: So, you would like help in changing that situation. What about this would you like to change? (*Asking the client to redefine her complaint as a goal*)

The client, although stating she is not in agreement with the reason for the referral, is stating a complaint with which she would like help. Given her statement, we would proceed with the complaint she has stated and work with her as a voluntary client. She is the voluntary client about the complaint she chose—that is, the complaint about her oldest daughter failing school. It is not up to us to make her work on the complaint of the referring person. We would need to clarify with the client that we would inform the referring person of what goals she was working on. The goals the client decides she wants to work on may not be acceptable to the referring person and more negotiation may be needed.

If involuntary clients state that they do not agree with the reason for the referral and do not have any problem or goal of their own that they want to talk with us about, we move onto the next step of the schema: exploring the consequences of their not coming to therapy.

Therapist: So your sense at this point is that the judge and protective service worker have it all wrong. They think that you are neglectful as a parent and so they have taken your kids from you and required that you come to therapy if you want the children back. However, you see it differently. You think that they just don't know the difficulties of being a parent and what really happened. And I imagine you have tried to convince them that they are wrong about the situation, right?

Client: I tried to explain that I just left the house for a few minutes and that I never would leave my kids without attention. But they just had their minds made up. That judge would only believe the social worker.

Therapist: So what is going to happen if you don't come to therapy? (*Eliciting consequences of not coming to therapy*)

Client: They say I won't get my kids back.

Therapist: So what are you going to do? (*Hypothetical solution frame*). You want to get your kids back, and so far you haven't convinced *the judge and protective service worker* that you are a responsible parent.

Client: I don't know; I just have to get them back.

This discussion of the consequences clarifies for the involuntary client and therapist the parameters of the situation. The situation is that the client *has* to come to therapy for something she does not believe is a problem. She has to do this in order for her to have the children returned—and if she does not attend therapy, she will not have her children returned.

Many clients need further clarification of the situation and your role in it . . .

Client: Can't you just tell the judge and protective service worker that I don't have to be here?

Therapist: As much as I would like to help you, I'm afraid I couldn't write a report about what I don't know.

Client: But you could tell them that I am a good parent and they would believe you.

Therapist: Without any evidence, I am afraid they wouldn't believe me either. I'm afraid I couldn't write any report like that, at this time.

Through this discussion, the client realizes that you are not going to write a report that would put you in an evaluative role of their behavior.

Therapist: So your situation is that you have to come here in order to get your children back, and you have to convince the protective service worker that you have changed in the way the worker believes to be more responsible. Tell me again what the worker wants you to be doing differently as a result of your coming here. (*Goal frame, using the "for other" position, for the worker*)

Client: She wants me to be more responsible. But I am responsible.

Therapist: What will the worker say you are doing differently when she thinks you are acting responsibly in her eyes, and allows the children to return? (*Hypothetical solution frame, "for the other" reporting position*)

Client: I don't know, she never said.

At this point, you might explore what the client thinks the worker wants and then instruct the client at the end of the session to find out in between sessions what specifically the protective service worker wants. You could contact the worker, too, and help the worker, if necessary, identify what would be signs for the decision that *he or she* will make as to whether to allow the return of the children to the parent. This coaching can help the worker clarify the criteria for the decision that will be made. You want to be sure to stay out of the position of being the decision-maker.

Therapist talking to protective service worker: I talked to Ms. _____ today and she said she wants to do what she needs to do in order to have her children back. She was not clear what she needed to do beyond going to therapy. I suggested that she speak to you and find out more specifically what your goals might be.

Worker: You know she isn't a very responsible parent. She had these children so young. She just gets overwhelmed and takes off for hours on end. She just does not know that she cannot be leaving these kids like this or trusting her oldest with the responsibility.

Therapist: I see. So, assuming she is sincere about turning this around, what will be signs to you that she is beginning to act more responsibly?

Worker: I will start allowing for supervised visits. On these visits, she has to show up and be on time. She has to play with these kids without flying off the handle and show some patience. When the kids don't mind what she tells them to do, she needs to show some skills in discipline. If she handles these visits, then maybe we will talk about further steps.

Therapist: Okay. I hope she will be asking you this same question so that she knows what you expect. We will keep in touch.

If the client speaks to the protective service worker and finds out specifically what she has to do, she can then use you for help in deciding if and how to comply with the expectations and how she will go about fulfilling such expectations. By keeping the decision about the disposition of the children with the worker, you are free to be the therapist for the client without mixing roles.

Client to Therapist: I talked to the worker and she says I can have supervised visits and that I have to be on time and be patient with the kids.

Therapist: Are you willing to do that and convince the worker? (*Goal frame*)

Client: I don't think I have much choice and I think I can do it.

Therapist: How will you do that? (*Specification of the process*)

Client: I will just have to plan ahead so that I can be on time. She wants me to be patient though and I don't think she knows how bad these kids can be.

The remaining part of the session would be used to explore how she might be "patient" in the worker's eyes and what she can do differently with the kids that might enable her to not only appear more patient but even have a better time with her children. This is discussed in terms of the "worker's eyes" since the worker is the one who has to be convinced and who will make the decision about the return of the children.

If the client had said that she was not willing to do what the worker said she had to do, then you have a choice of either saying good-bye or making arrangements for sessions without a goal.

If you say good-bye, you compliment the client on coming in and possibly on other things you notice in the session. The purpose of the compliments is to maintain rapport and ensure as much as possible that if the client later changes her mind about therapy, she will think of you as a sympathetic person and come in for help in the future.

If you have no choice but to continue to see the person because of the requirements of your situation, (agency policy, for example) you spell this out to the client and continue appointments without a goal and without trying to solve a problem.

DISCUSSION

QUESTION:
What about situations in which you are both the case manager and the therapist?

While these situations are beyond the scope of this book, a useful question can be, "What will you be doing differently when *I* (the therapist) am more convinced that your children can be returned? (*Hypothetical solution frame, from the detached position*).

Some clients will never perceive you as a helper. As the case manager, all you can do is set the requirements and hope that the clients will choose to comply. They may or may not comply.

QUESTION:
What about situations where you are required to submit a report to the case manager or protective service worker?

Whenever possible, create the report with the client. Try to make it a joint report. This facilitates further client rapport and cooperation.

EXERCISES

With a partner, play out each option of the above schema. Pay particular attention to defining what reporting position you want the client to follow. If the client is required to comply with someone else's requirements, be sure to use the "for the other" reporting position, with the referring person as the "other."*

---

*For a more complete presentation of how to work with clients in involuntary circumstances, see Insoo Berg's *A Solution-Focused Approach to Family Based Services* (1990).

17

It Ends with a
Working Solution

As we stated in Chapter Nine, therapy concludes when clients are confident they are on a solution track. This does not mean that the problem is totally resolved or that there is nothing more to do. A solution track merely means that clients now feel they can act (where before they may have felt stuck or powerless) and that the actions they are taking are working. In some cases, there may no longer be a problem. In any case, there is no longer any reason to meet and therapy discontinues.

Occasionally, therapy seems to be not working and we do not know what to do. In this, our final chapter, we would like to offer you our advice of what to do in those situations.

IF YOU THINK THAT YOU AND THE CLIENT ARE NOT PROGRESSING

If therapy does not seem to be progressing, there are several procedures that we reconsider or check.

1. Who Is the Client?

We want to check to make sure that the person we are working with is the person who wants a change. Sometimes, we have found that we assumed incorrectly that the person in our office is the client. Later, as we recheck and ask again what the client wants or how she or he decided to come to therapy, we find that attendance is not really the client's idea. A husband, a wife, a parent, a boyfriend, or some referral source may have strongly suggested that the client make a change. However, the supposed client is not interested in a change. The client may have been interested in pleasing the relative or friend, but has no real goal for therapy.

2. What Is the Client's Goal?

If you are sure that the person in front of you is there because she or he wants to be there and wants something, then the next thing to check is what is *the client's* goal.

Many times, when either one of us senses that our therapy is not moving along as we like, we use the other for consultation. The first question the one who is the consultant usually asks is, "So, what does the client want as the goal?" We often respond with an answer such as, "I think the clients want better communication. They are complaining of too many power struggles." At this point, the consultant asks, "Is that what the *clients say* they want?" At that point, we may be embarrassed to find that *we* have inadvertently decided what the goal is for the clients. We do not know for sure that what we have assumed was the goal is what the clients would say is their goal. Make sure, then, that the goal is what the client wants and not what you want or someone else wants for the client.

Then, make sure the client wants the goal more than you do! Sometimes, we find that somehow we have slipped into wanting the goal for the client, maybe even more than the client does. In those situations, we have inadvertently slipped into pushing the client or working more than the client is on coming up with a solution.

The sign we look for to indicate that we may be pushing clients is when they seem to be on the defensive and saying "Yes, but," or becoming very quiet. They can appear to be giving us reasons why change cannot happen or may have become quiet because they concluded that we are pushing, and are afraid to say anything more. These cues are our feedback that perhaps we need to do something different. We may need to back off and examine how we can cooperate more with the clients. We want to change our language or position so the clients know and perceive us as being behind them in a supportive fashion rather than pushing or pulling.

One sign that we are working too hard is when we find ourselves switching pronouns. We find that we have inadvertently switched to how are *we* going to solve this situation rather than how are *you* (the client) going to solve this situation—a sure sign that we need to back off and switch the pronouns back to the client.

Another sign that we are working too hard is when we catch ourselves sitting on the front edge of our chairs. We are talking much more than the client. At that point, we literally need to sit back in our chairs and allow the client the time and space to work toward solutions.

3. Do You Have a Goal and Not a Wish? Is the Goal Well-Defined?

You may be working on a level involving only a complaint or wish and may not have moved to a goal that is within the client's control. Ask yourself what the client is saying about what he or she wants to change in this situation. If the answer is a change of feeling or a change in someone else, then you need to literally ask the client again what he or she wants to change about the situation. Then use the questions for developing a well-defined goal, as well as the questions from Chapters Ten, Eleven, and Twelve on how to define a goal that is within the client's control.

4. Are You and the Client Looking for Too Much Too Fast?

Try looking for smaller change. Use scaling on the goal or on the expectations for the pace of change. If clients appear to be cautious about change, you may want to advise them to take it slower.

5. Do Clients Not Do Tasks While You Have Been Expecting Them to Do Something?

You may need to only provide some feedback for them to think about, rather than an action-oriented task.

Becoming Solution-Focused in Brief Therapy

6. If You Have Gone Through All the Above Steps, Is There Anything You Need to Do Differently, Between You and the Client?

You may find in your zeal to be positive that you have slipped into trying to talk your client into recognizing progress while the client is saying, "Yes, but you do not understand."

Since we may sometimes be too close to the trees to see the forest, we may not recognize a nonproductive pattern between us and the client. Sometimes, we are so involved with the session that we do not recognize a "Yes, but" pattern or we may not recognize how we have adopted the client's worldview. At such times, a team or consultant can be helpful to provide a more detached frame of reference. Seek out a different frame of reference when you can. Two heads are better than one.

A Final Word

Initially we worried whether this book would say all that was needed. We also wondered whether the book was complete. As we wrote, we found there was always more to say. As our thinking and work evolved during the writing process, the manuscript always seemed in need of revision. With each new revision our thinking and work evolved and moved on. Eventually, we realized that the writing, new thinking, and rewriting could go on forever. We then remembered our basic assumptions—that all is change and becoming. We remembered how writing leads to thought development, which leads to a change in practice, which leads back to a difference in what we have written, and so on, and so on. We found that no book is ever complete, that no book will ever be perfect, and that this book like any book is just a narrative of where we are at this point in time. We hope that what we do and think will continue to evolve. We know that any narrative is part of a larger conversation. We know that our narrative provides the opportunity for further conversation with the readers and they with us. In light of this assumption, we hope that this is the beginning of many useful conversations with you.

References

Anderson, H., & Goolishian, H. (1988). Human systems as linguistic systems: Preliminary and evolving ideas about the implications of clinical theory. *Family Process.* (27) 371–394.

Anderson, H., & Goolishian, H. (1989). Generation of human meaning key to Galveston paradigm: an interview by Lee Winderman in, Talk About, *Family Therapy News,* November/December, 11–12.

Anderson, H., & Goolishian, H. (1984). Problem-determined systems: Towards a transformation in family therapy. *Journal of Strategic and Systematic Therapies.* 5(4) 1–13.

Bandler, R., & Grinder, J. (1975). *Patterns of the hypnotic techniques of Milton H. Erickson, M.D., Volume 1.* Cupertino, California: Meta Publications.

Bandler, R., & Grinder, J. (1979). *Frogs into princes.* Moab, Utah: Real People Press.

Berg, I. (1990). *Solution-focused approach to family based services.* Milwaukee: Brief Family Therapy Center.

Cecchin, G. (1987). Hypothesizing, circularity, and neutrality revisited: An invitation to curiosity. *Family Process,* (26) 405–413.

Combs, G., & Freedman, J. (1990). *Symbol, story, and ceremony.* New York: Norton.

de Shazer, S. (1982). Some conceptual distinctions are more useful than others. *Family Process,* (21) 71–84.

de Shazer, S. (1985). *Keys to solution in brief therapy.* New York: Norton.

de Shazer, S. (1988). *Clues: investigating solutions in brief therapy.* New York: Norton.

de Shazer, S., Berg, I., Lipchik, E., Nunnally, E., Molnar, A., Gingerich, W., & Weiner-Davis, M. (1986). Brief therapy: Focused solution-development. *Family Process,* (25) 207–222.

de Shazer, S., Gingerich, W.J., & Weiner-Davis, M. (1985). Coding family therapy interviews: What does the therapist do that is worth doing. Presentation at Institute for Research and Theory Development, AAMFT Annual Conference.

de Shazer, S. & Molnar, A. (1984). Four useful interventions in brief family therapy. *Journal of Marital and Family Therapy,* 10(3), 297–304.

Dilts, R., Grinder, J., Bandler, R., Bandler, L., & DeLozier, J. (1980). *Neuro-Linguistic programming: Volume I, The study of the structure of subjective experience.* Cupertino, California: Meta Publications.

Dolan, Y. (1985). *Pathway with a heart: Ericksonian utilization with resistant and chronic clients.* New York: Brunner/Mazel.

Erickson, M. (1954). Pseudo-orientation in time as a hypnotic procedure. *Journal of Clinical and Experimental Hypnosis, (2) 261–283.*

Erickson, M. (1980). The dynamics of visualization, levitation, and confusion in trance induction, unpublished fragment, circa 1940's. In E. Rossi (Ed.) *The nature of hypnosis and suggestion: The collected papers of Milton H. Erickson on hypnosis (Vol. 1).* New York: Irvington.

Fisch R., Weakland, J., & Segal, L. (1982). *Tactics of change: Doing therapy briefly.* San Francisco: Jossey-Bass.

Gallwey, W. (1974). *The inner game of tennis.* New York: Random House.

Garfield, C. (1984). *Peak performance.* Los Angeles: Jeremy Farcher, Publisher.

Gilligan, S. (1987). *Therapeutic trances: the cooperation principle in Ericksonian therapy.* New York: Brunner/Mazel.

Grinder, J., and Bandler, R. (1976). *The structure of magic, Volume II.* Palo Alto: Science and Behavior Books.

Haley, J. (1976). *Problem-solving therapy: New strategies for effective family therapy.* San Francisco: Jossey-Bass.

Haley, J. (1980). *Leaving home.* New York: McGraw-Hill.

Hoffman, L. (1990). Constructing realities: An art of lenses. *Family Process, (29)* 1–12.

Keeney, B. (1983). *Aesthetics of Change.* New York: Guilford.

Kral, R. (1986). Indirect therapy in the schools. In de Shazer, S., and Kral, R., eds., *Indirect approaches in therapy, The family therapy collections, vol. 19,* Rockville, Md.: Aspen Press.

Kral, R., and Kowalski, K. (1989). After the miracle: The second stage in solution-focused brief therapy. *Journal of Strategic and Systemic Therapies, (8)* 73–77.

Lankton, S., & Lankton, C. (1983). *The answer within: a clinical framework of Ericksonian Hypnotherapy.* New York: Brunner/Mazel.

Lipchik, E. (Ed.) (1988a). *Interviewing.* New York: Aspen.

Lipchik, E. (1988b). Interviewing with a constructive ear. *Dulwich Centre Newsletter,* Winter, 3–7.

Lipchick, E., & de Shazer, S. (1986). The purposeful interview. *Journal of Strategic and Systemic Therapies.* 5(1) 88–99.

Madanes, C. (1981). *Strategic family therapy.* San Francisco: Jossey-Bass.

Maturana, H. & Varela, F. (1987). *The tree of knowledge.* Boston: New Science Library.

Minuchin, S. (1978). *Families and family therapy.* Cambridge, Mass.: Harvard University Press.

Molnar, A. & de Shazer, S. (1987). Solution-focused therapy: Toward the identification of therapeutic tasks. *Journal of Marital and Family Therapy,* 13(4), 349–358.

O'Hanlon, W. (1987). *Taproots: Underlying principles of Milton Erickson's therapy and hypnosis.* New York: Norton.

O'Hanlon, W., & Weiner-Davis, M. (1989). *In search of solutions: A new direction in psychotherapy.* New York: Norton.

Peller, J., & Walter, J. (1989). When doesn't the problem happen? In M. Yapko (Ed.) *Brief therapy approaches to treating anxiety and depression.* New York: Brunner/Mazel.

Riverside Publishing Company. (1984) *Webster's New Riverside University Dictionary.* Boston.

Rogers, C. (1951). *Client-centered therapy.* Boston: Houghton Mifflin.

Selvini-Palazzoli, M. Boscolo, L.; Cecchin, G.; and Prata, G. (1978). *Paradox and counterparadox: A new model in the therapy of the family in schizophrenic transaction.* New York: Jason Aronson.

Speer, D.C. (1970). Family systems: morphostasis and morphogenisis, or, Is homeostasis enough? *Family Process* (9) 259–278.

Tomm, K., (1985). Positive connotation requires coherence and authenticity. A presentation at the 1985 American Association of Marriage and Family Therapy annual conference.

von Foerster, H. (1984). On constructing a reality. In P. Watzlawick (Ed.) *The invented reality: How do we know what we believe we know? Contributions to constructivism.* New York: Norton.

von Glaserfeld, E. (1984). An introduction to radical constructivism. In P. Watzlawick (Ed.) *The invented reality: How do we know what we believe we know? Contributions to constructivism.* New York: Norton.

Wall, M., Kleckner, T., Amendt, J., & Bryant, D. (1989). Therapeutic compliments: Setting the stage for successful therapy. *Journal of Marital and Family Therapy.* (15) 159–167.

Walter, J., (1989). Not individual, not family. *Journal of Strategic and Systemic Therapies.* 8(1) 70–77.

Walter, J., and Peller, J. (1988). Going beyond the attempted solution: A couple's metasolution. *Family Therapy Case Studies,* 3(1) 41–45.

Watzlawick, P., Beavin, J., & Jackson, D. (1967). *Pragmatics of human communication: A study of interactional patterns, pathologies, and paradoxes.* New York: Norton.

Watzlawick, P., Weakland, J., and Fisch, R. (1974). *Change: Principles of problem formation and problem resolution.* New York: Norton.

Watzlawick, P. (Ed.) (1984). *The invented reality: How do we know what we believe we know? Contributions to constructivism.* New York: Norton.

Weakland, J.; Fisch, R.; Watzlawick, P.; and Bodin, A. (1974). Brief therapy: Focused problem resolution. *Family Process,* (13), 41–168.

Weiner-Davis, M., de Shazer, S., & Gingerich, W. (1987). Building on pretreatment change to construct the therapeutic solution: An exploratory study. *Journal of Marital and Family Therapy,* 13(4), 359–363.

White, M. & Epston, D., (1990). *Narrative means to therapeutic ends.* New York: Norton.

Name Index

263

Subject Index

Action
  circularity with meaning, 26, 34, 168–170
  control of, 107
  maintenance, 57–59
  responses, 66
  solution, 55
  taking, 159
  thinking of, 78
Agency
  definition, 159
  enhancing, 159–166, 196, 220
  language, 180, 212
  presupposition, 232
Ambiguous figures, 17, 18*Fig*
Association, free, 49
Assumption. *See also* Presupposition
  in cheerleading, 108
  communication theory, 49
  diagnostic, 22
  of exceptions, 82
  identification, 9
  reversing, 58
  in solution-focused approach, 10–35
  in therapy models, xi, 1–8, 3

Behavior
  learned, 3
  normative standard, 29
  ritual, 222–223
Behavioral model, 3
Belief
  expanding, 160–162, 166

nonpathology, 23
  restrictive, 177
  reversal, 160–162, 166
  wellness, 23
Brainstorming, 111
Break in session, 111–114
Brief Family Therapy Center, 7, 73, 77, 111, 126
Brief Therapy Model, 4, 43

Case examples
  change in others, 228–233
  controlled exceptions, 218–225
  duration of therapy, 154–157
  hypothetical solutions, 83–85
  parent about child, 233–237
  spontaneous exceptions, 226–227
  spouse about other spouse, 237–240
Change
  action in, 182
  beliefs, 201
  client thoughts on, 21
  continuing, 142
  credit for, 114, 119–120
  desired, 76
  expectations, 7
  facilitating, 24, 37
  in goal description, 30–31
  goals, 60
  in interaction, 30–31, 35
  inviting in, 203
  lack of interest, 256
  methods, 10

265

Tasks, 220, 221, 225, 227, 229, 232,
    234–235, 236
  doing more positives, 128–129
  for exceptions, 129–131
  in feedback, 124–135
  first session, 7–8
  hypothetical solutions, 131–135
  non-compliance, 257–258
  observing positives, 126–128
  scaling down, 131
  of therapy, 68
  time needed, 150
Therapy. *See also* Case examples
  assumptions in, xi
  beginning, 41–42
  client responsibility, 152
  completed, 142–143
  concluding, xii, 153–157, 255
  continued, 143–145
  couples, 22–23, 237–240
  differing goals, 28
  duration, 140–157
  evolution of models, 1–8
  family, 16, 22–23, 32
  function, 29
  goal focus, 28–30
  independence from, 151–152
  interactional, 6

long-term, 28, 35
models, 4
non-progressing, 255–258
outcome-oriented, 61
simplicity in, 39–40, 179
solution focus, 28–30, 32
spacing sessions, 150–152
subsequent, 145–150
supportive, 3
team approach, 41, 112–113
Trance, 49, 77–78
Transference, 119
Treatment group membership,
  31–35
Trust, 42

Unity, 30–31

Verbs
  use in solutions, 17
Voice tone, 201–202
  in cheerleading, 109, 111
  in complimenting, 115

Wishes, 65, 257
  changing to goals, 66, 67
World view
  client, 43, 44, 78, 80